BEFRIEND
THE UNKNOWN

BEFRIEND THE UNKNOWN

KEN FOO

Trafford rev. 04/10/2012

 www.trafford.com

North America & international
toll-free: 1 888 232 4444 (USA & Canada)
phone: 250 383 6864 ♦ fax: 812 355 4082

Contents

This book is dedicated to my daughter *Jasmine* who gave me inspiration and spiritual strength to put my thoughts and beliefs in writing to share with everyone.

Introduction

We live in a world where Mother Nature does not disclose her *secrets* readily and man's drive to comprehend and control the unseen forces is one of the great themes of human history. *Where* did we come from? Is there an *agenda* for everyone walking the earth? We have witnessed the destructive force of the *tsunami* in South Asia on Boxing Day 2004, but were there *mega tsunamis* of such catastrophic and *unimaginable* force that they could change the landscape of planet earth and swallow up legendary cities like *Atlantis* in prehistoric times? Is there an earth cycle for past and present events similar to life and death for man?

The journey of life is a rocky road with many ups and downs because we are here mainly to experience pain and joy and learn from mistakes. Sages and great thinkers have chanted down through the ages that we are imperfect beings thrown into a materialistic arena for *lessons* so that we can progress and live harmoniously with everyone. Our parents may have given us a few pointers in righteous living but unfortunately, history has shown us that mankind has been misled for thousands of years by flawed leaders in sheep's clothing. World peace is not foreseeable in the near future as many are not honest and wise to shape a peaceful world.

On the positive side, human consciousness is evolving all the time and people have come to look beyond political and religious doctrines including traditional beliefs and existing science to search for answers on seemingly insoluble issues, especially in matters of health and personal philosophy of righteous living. How might the reader use this book in making such a search? Firstly, read with an inquiring mind, keeping an eye on *ideas and questions,* because they form the essence of the unknown. Secondly, take note of such words and phrases as '*perhaps,* '*probably,*' '*it is said*' and '*as the story goes.*' These terms are vital to a fair and balanced presentation of complex and controversial issues. When they appear, no matter how imposing the material they qualify, they mean that the stories and accounts have not been totally verified. Thirdly, whatever the evidence for and against, the reader must decide for himself because human perceptions and experiences vary. Those who wish to *Befriend the Unknown* should treat it as a *personal* journey.

But rest assured that no matter what route is chosen, you will be in good company. You will meet many strange and wonderful characters in the following pages—the many messengers of God, scholars of past and present, the good and the bad, the happy and the sad including stubborn people who do not believe that life is all about *change.* If that's not enough, take the '*s*' out of *cosmic* and enjoy what's left! But pay attention, you may meet yourself here.

'Truth' is veiled in the unknown and readers are requested to be tolerant in passing judgment. The *unknown* is a beguiling realm and this book is an attempt to piece together the beliefs of reputable sages and great thinkers from all ages. I have condensed some of the thoughts of the masters because their words have filled me with inspiring lessons and astonishing revelations of universal balance that I love to share with readers. I like to clarify to scholarly readers that certain quotations and phrases in this book are taken from the masters but I can't give credit to some because of an old habit. Since my working days, I used to scribble on a notebook or a slip of paper on anything that had an appeal on me whether from a book, magazine or newspaper. I have no idea that I would end up using some of my scribbling to write this book and it would be impossible to backtrack and provide references of some words.

In fact, one of the most reasonable approaches to the unknown may have been that suggested in Taoism which says: *'The line between confused human beings and sage is, in reality, a thin and tenuous one. All it takes is being open to learning, to growing, to making mistakes, to confronting our own fears and ambitions and a willingness to leap into the unknown.'* In this spirit the book is offered to you as you journey into the unknown.

Chapter 1

DESTINY

Palmistry

When I was just a little boy,
I asked my mother what will I be,
Will I be handsome?
Will I be rich?
Here's what she said to me:
Que sera, sera,
Whatever will be, will be.
The future's not ours to see,
Que sera, sera.
What will be, will be.

Lyrics from 'Que Sera Sera'

From the day we are born, our destiny is already imprinted on our palms. Of course this can only be true if you believe in palmistry. But the fact remains that one of the most basic human desires is to have foreknowledge of the future so that we can have control over personal destiny. There are so many different arts in predicting the future such as numerology, astrology, tarot card, crystal ball gazing, clairvoyance, and so forth. But palmistry is chosen for discussion not only because it is the oldest form of character reading based on the written lines and markings, but also because of its many links with astrology as each finger is connected with a planet that can influence our personalities and destiny. Another strong point in favour of palmistry is that there's no fakery about the imprinted lines and they serve as a constant source of easy reference with no confusion on details compared to other arts. In other words, the lines do not *conceal* but only *reveal.* I find palmistry simply amazing with all the tiny details and timing of events in our lives. Are our hands a divine coding of what we *should* be and a window to our souls?

Predestination

An expert explained that with a right-handed person, the left is the 'birth' hand and will show inherited predispositions of character and fate in past lives. This assertion concurs with philosopher/ healer Carl Jung when he said that humans were not of today but of immense age. The right hand reflects individuality, mental and emotional states, flexibility and potential. The palmist went further and mentioned that the lines on the left palm rarely change because everyone is born with special 'assigned' characteristics and with a certain level of success in life. This means that in every man and woman there are certain qualities already being developed or awaiting development based on past experiences and decisions. However, what have been shown on the left palm may not necessarily materialise because our own action or freedom to act in later life determines the future. The right palm shows the course of the future and how all is going to end. This is the reason why it is common to see changes on some lines on the right at the later stages of life because what is 'prescribed at birth' did not work out as planned because we are able to change the course of our lives through *free will* which can be a blessing or a curse!

It must be perfectly clear that life is what you make out of it based on your own choice of action or free will. Your birth hand may have all the signs that you could be a millionaire but things did not work out that way because you took it for granted that you would be rich but failed to work on it. There is no such thing as *predestination* when you are born or else words like progress, courage, foresight, patience and falling in love, would be quite meaningless when there is no struggle, pain, joy or challenge to reach a goal or attain a specific result. What is the point of going to school to improve our knowledge, taking up a professional course in a university, learning a trade or spending millions courting a beautiful princess when we know the outcome of our future? The ancient Greek astrologers were spot on when they said, *'The stars only impel, they don't compel'*.

Case study

Take the case of Alex for example. Alex may be destined to be a very wealthy man because he is born with a silver spoon and pampered by his rich parents who own a chain of hotels. After the passing of the parents, it is only natural he inherits the family's fortune for being the only son. Alex is given a kick-start in life but he has to put in the necessary effort and dedication to sustain or strengthen his inheritance. He has to prove he can stack up the gold pieces on his own instead of resting on his family's laurels. Getting hired hands to run the show is rarely a good option compared to getting personally involved in the normal running of the business. If he squanders the wealth away by changing fast cars and women like he is changing shirts, it will be a matter of time when his 'castle comes tumbling down.' A comedian used to say, 'When money stops talking, *she* starts walking!' All successful people understand that they need to *'abstain to sustain.'*

'No money, no talk?'

There is a common philosophy among certain cultures that happiness comes from having lots of money or 'no money, no talk.' This may be so, but only up to a point. When you can afford to own a nice home, able to enjoy good food with friends, owns a Mercedes Benz car coupled with the occasional vacation, the extra dollar you earn may start to have less significance because it will be like diminishing utility. It's similar to quenching a man's thirst with a jug of water; the last few mouthfuls will not be life and death to him.

Certain people have higher expectations on how much they want to make and chances of success are not guaranteed in many undertakings. When you have a talent for building houses and landscaping, you might embark on a big project by buying a few acres of land to build fifty homes. You take high financial risk which can make or break you. But another similarly talented builder is more cautious and works differently; he specialises in buying and selling smaller property. He enjoys hunting for an old home, selects the best bargain and loves renovating it all by himself according to his plan and later sell it for a profit. Smaller investments are safer and with less stress and that is why many people with humble responsibilities find contentment in different ways. It's all about different lifestyle and expectations and the reason why it takes all sorts of people to make the world.

Sweating it out

Happiness is not entirely based on money alone though it takes away many problems. Harmony with self and those around you is crucial for everlasting bliss. If you have poor relationship with people or a rotten marriage, life can be miserable despite your millions. 'Riches to rags' stories are widespread in all societies and living examples are there for you to see almost daily in the media. A poker player sums up well when he said that *'Life consists not in holding good cards but in playing well those you hold.'* It is not hard to find out some key reasons for 'fallen angels;' they are greedy, unrealistic, rarely struggled to earn a living and hardship is just a word to them. The value of money is best appreciated when you *sweat* for it through making mistakes and *rectifying* them.

Moulding Character

Sometimes fame and fortune come too quickly to the young and they have difficulties adjusting to their new status. This is not unusual especially for some young executives who went through the promotion process in a short period and suddenly realised that there are so many perks and privileges that go with the higher rank. People start to notice them and their circle of friends gets wider especially when travelling and being away from home is part of the added responsibilities. In such a scenario, it will require a very strong-willed person to stay content and not prepared to experiment new things that arouse his interest. It could be a desire to frequent nightclubs, casinos and be entertained or the sudden love of fine brandy or whisky as nightcap instead of milk! Perhaps even the temptation to have a casual relationship creeps into the mind even though knowing fully well that it can backfire into *'fatal attraction'* and creating domestic turmoil.

The newspapers are regularly filled with gossips of marriage break-ups of the travelling executives, sportsmen, actors and politicians. Away from home is no good thing for some; it exposes their weaknesses. Being young and learning to focus is one of the biggest tests in life. It is perfectly okay to enjoy yourself and let your hair down sometimes, but the point here is mainly to emphasise that one must learn to cultivate self discipline in any new found status so that *character is moulded* at an early age.

Don't take life for granted

There are also those who are groomed to rule the nation but ascension can be put on hold when some do not live up to expectations. Royalties are given long titles, live in castles and mansions and enjoy all the luxuries in life at the expense of taxpayers. Their welfare is being taken care of from *'womb to tomb.'* They are required only to conduct themselves in a dignified manner to uphold tradition but some shameless royalties are fond of hogging the headlines with broken marriages, infidelity and excessive lifestyles that can do more damage than good for the country.

It was reported in the media that a prince spent more than twenty thousand dollars on drinks alone in a night with his mates in a pub at taxpayers' expense. In another example: a playboy prince abused his influence and power by snatching somebody's pretty wife to stay with him for the weekend. In another laughable case, a royal family went on a world tour but made it compulsory that all public servants have their salary deducted by 1% to fund the trip and shopping expenses! Do you want such people to be your future king? It's all about discipline; those who are in the spotlight should behave like role models for the young to learn and be respected at the same time. It is no longer shocking news but boring stuff when we hear about divorces or the many love affairs of irresponsible princesses and princes and the kind of money they throw away just for a good time. But who is brave enough to discipline them and risk facing the firing squad when stern action failed to win public sentiments?

The law of nature is such that no one should take life for granted. What is given to you can also be easily taken away. Those who are born rich but behave like spoilt brats and living without a conscience will eventually end up with a miserable life as pay-back for bad karma. Whoever you are, there are simple rules to lead a good life. So take heed and watch your actions; they become your habits. Watch your habits; they mould your character. Watch your character, for it will become your destiny.

The game of life

During the course of our lives, circumstances change all the time. When our star is shining, we capitalised on opportunities opened to us and our fortunes can change dramatically. Arnold Schwarzennegger was only a body builder in Austria hardly able to speak English. But he was determined to capitalise on his muscular physique and improve his communication skills in order to become a movie star. He shot to fame quickly and became top box office material in Hollywood and later to Governor of California. The African statesman, Nelson Mandella is another one. He was from very humble beginning but made the mark as the most popular freedom fighter for the Africans and was elected the first black president in South Africa in1994 despite being imprisoned for 27 years.

The reverse scenario is just as common when high fliers suddenly refused to put on the brakes by throwing all cautions to the wind and resort to dirty dealings or get hooked on drugs, womanising, and all the bad habits. This is self-destruction. So, in our society of equal opportunity, 'rags to riches' and 'riches to rags' situations are dependent on how well you play the 'game of life'.

The intent of this section is not to teach you to be a palmist so that you can go for plastic surgery and add or minus a line or two on your palm! But more for you to sit back and ponder why everyone has his fate or future inscribed on his palms like a *divine coding*. Is there a plan for us after birth? Is 'someone up there' trying to assign a role for us to play? Is there a job description prescribed for us? Is our world only a stage for lessons to learn?

Starting a Career

All life is change.
Don't become attached to the good times or
worry unduly about the bad times.
Change is inescapable;
we have no control over it.

Taoist Text

Early whims and fancies

'I want to be a pilot so that I can see the world.' 'I want to be a doctor so that I can cure the sick.' The next one may say, 'I want to be a golfer like Tiger Woods so that I don't have to work.' These are some of the answers we give to our parents and teachers who are fond of testing our intelligence and maturity when we were kids. But as we grow older, the *'que sera, sera'* situation will start to change when we develop preferences on certain subjects or trade taught in school or college—an early sign drawing us closer to destiny.

When I was an average student during high school, I used to struggle with most subjects. But during year 8, I showed strong interest in History and Literature. I surprised myself that I was able to do my homework with ease on these subjects. The best part, I was enjoying what I did. I scored good marks in my two favourite subjects in my School Certificate exam but the results of others were miserable. In my later working life I started to develop an interest in Chinese antique porcelain because I was fascinated by the history connected with the various dynasties like 'Ming' and 'Ching,' especially each period had its own distinctive production style and motifs. Unfortunately I have yet to own an imperial ware and has been tagged the 'junk collector' by the good wife! But lovely antiques and historical events always fascinate me.

Stepping stone

When you start your first job, there is no certainty that you would have a life-long career with the initial organisation. It is a common practice that after you have completed your secondary or tertiary education, there is a tendency to apply for jobs that are related to your qualifications. If you are a graduate with a Degree in Commerce, it is likely that you would be attracted to sales, marketing, finance, banking or management positions. If you specialise in Information Technology, communication companies or related field would be your target. But does it always work out that way?

Competition in job applications is stiff today as many employers rely on employment agencies to recruit the best candidate to fill in a position. It's not uncommon for job seekers to attend three rounds of interviews before a decision can be made whether they are in or out. It is not surprising to see a guy with an Engineering Degree starts his first job selling doughnuts in a cafe or a girl with a Degree in Fashion Designing ends up as a bar hostess. These are not only the realities of life but also the beginning of a struggle to see how your future takes shape.

Your first full-time job is usually only a stepping stone for your intended destiny to unfold. This stage is like an exploratory period for you to gain some experience and find out *what* and *where* you really fit in. Making job switch in the early part of working life is inevitable in many cases. But before proceeding any further on early working life, 'dharma' needs to be clearly understood first because it is a major element of destiny.

Dharma

To dream the impossible dream
To fight the unbeatable foe
To bear with unbearable sorrow . . .
This is my quest to follow the star.
No matter how hopeless
No matter how far,
To be willing to give
When there's no more to give . . .

Lyrics from 'The Impossible Dream'

During one of my 'karaoke' sessions with my mates after a birthday party, we had too much to drink and everyone was slurring with words and sang the above song screaming our heads away, probably trying to out-shout one another! Did the words of the song touch our hearts? Who cares, it was party time. Now that I am sober reading the words, it gives me goose pimples. They are so potent and meaningful as if God has just scribbled a message to mankind that survival is all about our fighting spirit 'to beat the unbeatable foe'. There is always a solution to all our woes when we think hard about it and do our best. I have no doubt that some song writers, including musicians, film makers, poets and even cartoonists, are gifted people with uncanny sensitive perception compared to many of us. They are the forerunners of the entertainment world and I humbly *bow* to them.

How it works

The word *'dharma'* is derived from Sanskrit; reputed to be the oldest language in the world and originated in ancient India. It means 'to provide support with positive action.' The word also has a spiritual connotation as dharma is frequently referred to be the life sustaining force with divine guidance.

Everyone has dharma. If you are a teacher, your dharma is to ensure that you make the effort to explain clearly on all the lessons so that the students understand well on what have been taught. It is also your duty not to show favouritism and provide special attention to weaker students where necessary. If you are a soldier, your dharma is to defend your country and stay alert at all time. When there is an outbreak of war, you are required to shoot and kill, not run or surrender! For a professional tennis player, his dharma is dedication to train hard, keep fit, find new technique to ensure he stays at the top of the game. He must also exercise discretion to abstain from alcohol and other distractions and play his best and not giving up easily in any match as some mad punters may have put their houses on him to win! The key words on the three professions mentioned are *'effort'* and *'dedication,'* the ingredients necessary for the manifestation of your destiny. Another way to define dharma is; 'follow and act according to your given responsibilities even though situations are not ideal.'

Shape up or ship out

Everywhere you go, it is so easy to identify good, loyal workers and bad ones. I came across a classic example that is worth mentioning. Funk was a Sales Supervisor in a tobacco company. He was a good field man well liked by his superiors and dealers. When a new position of 'Sales Manager' was advertised, Funk was confident he would be the ideal candidate to fill the position. However, an outsider with a Degree in Marketing was selected. Funk could not believe it that he was overlooked and his world suddenly came crashing down. The management later revealed that Funk had only Year 7 academic qualification and his communication skills; especially written, were limited and the position of Manager required strong communication skills with other departmental heads, advertising agencies including sensitive meetings with the Trade Ministry on health issues.

Funk became a changed person after that and began to slack in his work. For three successive years, not only did he fail to achieve sales targets, he boycotted the company's annual dinner like a vendetta! When it came to annual pay rise, he received a meagre 2 % increase compared to 6% jump from his fellow supervisors. He wallowed into deeper depression and resorted to heavy drinking and was nicknamed 'the unquenchable' and a man of high fidelity—*staggered* home to his wife every night! Words got into the ears of his boss who took quick action. The Manager told Funk to move on elsewhere if he was unhappy with what he was paid to do. He wanted a team player that would be an asset to the company not someone who is a liability. It was *'shape up or ship out.'* Funk started to whinge on the past again and was given the axe. It took Funk two years to find his next job and the salary he got was half of what he used to receive.

Funk's situation is not an isolated one and is fairly common in the business world. Many employees like to spend 'happy hour' in a pub with colleagues as pastime in running down their own employer and management team. Such people do not know their dharma when they broadcast their dissatisfaction publicly about their employer who provides them with a pay cheque to feed their families. If they throw caution to the wind, they may end up digging their own graves. In the case of Funk, he was too *sensitive* and did not do a reality check and *overestimated* his own ability. Sure, disappointment hurts, but is it realistic to brood over a single issue and ruin a once colourful career? There's always another chance for promotion if you learn to cultivate patience and *'cheer up and wise up.'*

Push and pull

One of the most comforting allies you can get in the workplace is not to win over your boss' secretary but the practice of the 'push and pull' principle. 'Push' means you push yourself by working diligently under all situations similar to doing dharma. 'Pull' is to rope in your superiors or management to your side. Show them the proper respect and make them your friends if possible. You don't have to suck up to them or be a 'yes man' of course, just hold your own ground and act sensibly when facing them. Your immediate superior especially, can be instrumental to your climb on the promotion ladder because a few good words about you can carry a lot of weight in management decision. When you are able to combine both push and pull in the workplace, you are well armoured and office 'injustice' such as being overlooked for a higher post or being treated poorly, are unlikely episodes in the story of your life.

Reward for good dharma

What happens to someone who does her dharma all the time? Take Jane for example. She worked as a Customer Relations Officer for a financial investment company where clients are paid high interest rate for short—term cash deposit. The company was running a booming business in the initial two years until an important client started to withdraw a big chunk of cash for personal reason. Rumours started to circulate among depositors that the company was going bankrupt and there was a run for withdrawals. The company was actually sound but the rumours began to spread like wild fire and depositors were banging on the door! Jane did not panic but continued to do her best to calm down disgruntled clients by explaining that the company was not going broke but needed more time to gather sufficient cash for withdrawals at short notice. Clients insisted on seeing the Managing Director but Jane was very loyal and gave excuses for her boss because she sensed danger regarding the safety of her boss when confronted by fiery clients. She did not shirk in her job and worked overtime to help and resolve the crisis. In the end, the company wound up and landed in receivership.

Jane lost her job but within two weeks, found a better one with more perks and a higher salary. Jane knew her dharma and did her best even in the face of crisis. The lesson here is clear; act responsibly at all times and the grace of the unseen hand will work in mysterious and wondrous way to push you ahead.

Change is inescapable

Failures, disappointments and setbacks are normal occurrences in our daily lives. It is part of life's journey to learn from past mistakes so that we can change and progress as we grow older. But it must be emphasised that the really serious and damaging thing is allowing these things to get you down over long period of time. It is imperative you don't indulge in self-pity that is likely to drain away your energy and making you look pathetic at the same time. Never dramatise your problems to friends and colleagues and allow your emotions to flow like a tap. Learn to endure and accept hardship with *dignity* by showing your inner strength. Give your mind a good workout and cultivate mental toughness. Friends can be sympathetic only to a certain extent; if you continue to bore them with your whingeing; they would prefer to be in the company of winners than losers. There's nothing to gain from losers other than sharing their sorrow and pain.

This is a wake-up call. Don't live in the past: learn to let go and get over it. The ancient Tao and Zen sages have taught us that all life is *change.* Don't become attached to the good times or worry unduly about the bad times. Change is inescapable; we have no control over it. For example: an organisation can close down or be bought up by another company leaving you without a job. In another situation: you look forward going to work everyday because you get along very well with your boss. But your boss got transferred suddenly and the new guy hates your guts. Survival is dependent on the present. Don't moan for the past or even worry about the future. Don't pay undue attention to your failures; but *honour* your successes, no matter how small.

The present moment holds the key to liberation and positive action should be taken in the 'Now'. Author Eckhart Tolle says, '*Nothing ever happened in the past; it happened in the Now. Nothing will ever happen in the future; it will happen in the Now.*' Losing a loved one, being jilted, collapsed in business or being made redundant unexpectedly is common realities of life. But it is not the end of the world as quick recovery means immediate adjustments to new environment or situation and start afresh. Learn to be mentally and spiritually strong by *going with the flow*—be more sensitive to the natural flow of each moment as it is born out of the previous and flows into the next. What is considered appropriate action in one instance may not be appropriate in the next.

Life is never dull if we cultivate mental toughness and take action in the Now. It is likely your financial, emotional or social status may have taken a dip on your new start, but work on them and remember that Rome wasn't built in a day. Start rebuilding your life now and traumatic events that took place in the past will fade and become only a faint memory if you learn how to persevere and follow the flow.

Career Switch

Do, or do not. There is no 'try.'

Yoda in 'The Empire Strikes Back'

Now that dharma is understood, it is easier to expand on the relationship between work and destiny. The journey of life is not meant to be smooth sailing or else our existence is quite meaningless. Imagine a world with everyone playing, getting into mischief, eating, sleeping and dreaming away without any responsibility or role to play. If our survival is all about *fiesta and siesta* where the mind is not put to the test to face challenges and experience joy and pain, life can be pretty boring doing the same old thing all the time.

Our Creator might as well bring in the 'big flood' and say '*ta ta*' to all of us!

Realising a dream

'What should I do?' is a common question. There must be something you enjoy doing, irrespective whether they are big or small tasks. Take the initiative to try out a few things and take it from there. Sooner or later you should be able to find your comfort zone in the workplace. If you are good in maths and accounting, perhaps taking up a course in 'Accountancy' may have more appeal to you than trying to be chef especially when you are a vegetarian. Why do you want to be a salesman when you are uncomfortable meeting people especially playing the violin is your passion? Why do you want to be a nurse when you can't stand the sight of blood? You may have a secret wish to become a model but instead of maintaining your girlish figure, you doubled it through excessive eating and ended up looking like a barrel. Another person may want to be a soccer star but regular hangovers and love affairs prevented him from training and the coach gave him the boot.

Learn to live your dreams by waking up now and take action quickly. Expecting success needs planning but it doesn't mean that you expect to be right five times out of five. It merely means that once you have carefully examined the facts and acted on them, you have a right to expect success. If you do not make the commitment to focus in achieving planned goals, destiny will always be only a dream as you did not give it a chance to materialise. There's a saying that true love never runs smooth, so is destiny. There is work to be done to achieve a happy ending. If you are not focused and 'I'll do it later,' becomes a regular habit, blame yourself and not the world for giving you a miserable life because time and tide wait for no man.

Self-discipline

One of the biggest obstacles for an aspiring young person to make good in life is self-discipline. This virtue is becoming out of fashion as the world today is cluttered with so many temptations turning it into an age of indulgence. The commercial world targets the young in most advertisements because they are vulnerable and are easy prey for the banks, fashion houses, entertainment centres, beauty parlours, restaurants, shady activities and so forth. *'Let's go,'* or *'let's do it,'* are some of the prevailing mottos today. There is this undisciplined pursuit of pleasure lurking in our society today and one has to be mentally strong to avoid the many pitfalls in life. Do not get attach to bad habits and ruin your life. Do things in moderation and you will not be clouded with distractions that could impair your vision to serve appropriately.

It will be a fine start when we take a new look at life and 'reinstate' self-discipline as top priority if we wish to find meaningful existence or to attain our intended destiny. We have to go through many obstacles and different experiences such as; learn to take some hard knocks in life and how to overcome them, observe the many 'dos' and don'ts,' in a workplace. We are also required to experience different degree of pain and joy, consequences of attachments and obsessions, ego and hate, and many other lessons. Only then, wisdom can eventually become our strength and the path to destiny becomes clearer.

Stages of working life

After we have found our first job, making a switch later on is very common. It is a well known fact that a person has to go through a period of discovery during the early stages of her career because as the years pass regardless of her profession or skills, she is likely to find her work less interesting, stimulating or rewarding. Exposure in various work environments is necessary to equip a person with knowledge and prepare her to assume higher responsibilities. That's not all, complex work situations is an ideal vehicle to test your range—forte and weaknesses. You know your capabilities and limitations when thrust in various work environments.

By midlife, many may feel the need for greener occupational pastures. They yearn for opportunities to prove their worth and to express the needs and use the talents of a different stage of life. Some people feel they are no longer in the running for advancement; some think that their talents and skills are not fully utilised; while some feel they have outgrown their jobs or disciplines. Others, feeling blocked by being in the wrong industry or position, are bored. Some simply cannot cope and are looking for a way out!

If you strongly believe that your life on earth has a purpose, you can be assured that the road map to achieve your destiny is well drawn out without too many obstacles along the journey. Why? You are prepared to try new ideas and not ashamed of past mistakes but accept them as part of learning before the unfolding of your destiny. This is the basic truth of our training or lessons: to remain calm when under pressure and work out the best solution to resolve a problem at hand to minimise error in judgement. Remember those simple words of wisdom, 'practice makes perfect,' and 'a stitch in time saves nine,' for successful living? Every incident or event that happens in your life has a purpose irrespective whether it is positive or negative. How you handle each incident dictates how far away or how close you are from reaching your destiny. A guru once said that life is a series of near misses because we do not see what others see. What is ascribed as 'luck' is actually not luck but pursuing a vision.

During midlife, or between the ages of 30-40, are highly creative periods. This is the stage where destiny will take shape. The career pattern becomes clearer and tends to seek stability to gain a greater sense of personal security. If you have been doing your dharma, intuitively you know that 'this is it.' It is logical to assume why many people get stabilised in one job after 40 years. This is the time to consolidate their position or situation. Any switches from thereon are usually continuation along established line than breaking new ground. Of course dramatic changes can also occur, especially when you may have to start from scratch again after moving to another state or country. Sometimes redundancy or closure of companies can be heart breaking for many. But is starting afresh bad? I am sure you have seen many migrants making their mark everywhere. Grace of dharma?

Trust your Intuition

> *Following your heart's desire will lead you*
> *in the direction your spirit wants to go.*

Oprah Winfrey

Call of God?

Let us look at the case of Phoebe for more enlightenment on this section. Phoebe was a trained teacher. She loved kids and teaching in a private primary school appeared ideal for her. She was a dedicated teacher and her presence was a breath of fresh air to everyone because her cheerfulness and great sense of humour were infectious to all. The principal knew that Phoebe was an asset and had a soft spot for her because the school enrolment was getting better each year partly due to Phoebe's popularity.

But one night Phoebe had an uneasy dream. She felt as if a 'silent voice' was telling her to move on. The dream did not reveal what she was supposed to do next. Most dreams come and go, but this particular dream was a lingering one as she got flashes of it even when teaching. Trusting her heart, she decided to do the right thing and handed in her resignation that was met with resistance from the principal. The concerned and caring principal insisted that Phoebe took one month's leave with full pay to reconsider her decision.

On the first week of the 'vacation,' she took her mother to visit a sick aunt in the country. Her aunt had back problems and Phoebe accompanied the aunt to the local clinic when she experienced pain. The clinic was packed with patients. While waiting for her aunt to be called, Phoebe took a casual glance at some patients and was suddenly overcome by a strange feeling when her hands started to tremble! All the patients were in distress and in pain. Compassion came over her and she wanted to touch and console them but was not in the position to do so. She was just about to burst into tears and decided to walk out of the clinic. While strolling along the park pondering what was bothering her, flashes of her earlier dream suddenly came back. Like a *revelation,* the 'little voice' was telling her that helping sick people would be her next role. This was like *'a call from God'* and she knew immediately she had to make the switch from teacher to healer. Her adrenalins kept pumping because destiny unfolded right before her eyes and she had never been so sure that *'this is it!'* But a reality check told her what could she be, or what was she going to do?

Upon her return from the country trip, she checked her mailbox and saw a pamphlet which said, "Enrol for a course in Spinology and be financially independent for life." It was as if 'all has been arranged' for Phoebe by an unseen force. The rest is history. Phoebe has never been happier in her new career. Her clients love her and it was reported she has gifted hands. Her nimble fingers can provide very soothing sensation on sensitive spine and muscular discomforts as though they were *charged* with healing energy!

Life is full of dramas

I came across an article recently and decided to add it in for this section. It refers to movie star David Caruso's rocky road to stardom again. He was a big star on the former NYPD series but decided to switch to the big screen at the height of his success. He was unable to turn his small screen success into big screen profits for the next ten years and his once colourful acting career appeared all washed-up. He was tagged the unlikely hero to rise again partly because his looks are like an ordinary man in the street coupled with the fact that there are now more 'lines' on his face and the hair is thinning. But lady luck was on his side, he was offered the lead role on the small screen again in 'CSI Miami' and the series is an instant hit and Caruso is back in business again.

'Life is about exploration and taking chances, making mistakes as well as having successes. I wouldn't be here if I didn't go through what I went through 10 years ago,' Caruso says. 'There's also a cyclical nature to careers. Sometimes, no matter how right it feels or how effective you think you're being, it's just not working,' he added. Life is full of dramas, the key is to learn from them and move on. Experience doesn't really mean much if you keep on making the same mistakes.

Know your dharma, trust your intuition and listen to your heart when making tough decision. Please understand that dharma doesn't mean that you have to be a workaholic, sacrificing family time or other activities important to healthy living. Just do your best in a given situation: work smart and not overtime in most cases. Let's look at another element necessary for destiny to unfold.

Free Will

> *Bridled the mind, for it is like a wild horse.*
> *Try to catch it, ride it and lead it by the reins.*
> *With firmness, gentleness and patience, the horse will be tamed and*
> *the master known.*

Taoism

God is great but God is also strange. He bestowed upon us the divine intelligence of free will where we can either love or deny Him. We are given a mind that is hardly able to stay still and acts like a wild horse that is hard to tame. This freedom of action is our most testing lesson on earth as it can turn us into angels or make us look like idiots stumbling along all the time. We have to do battles with *ourselves* and *conquer* ourselves because our greatest enemy is also ourselves due to our cravings and attachments in a materialistic world. For a change, instead of expanding on this subject, the following poignant prose summarises the cause and effect of free will.

Your life is an expression of your mind.
What you think and see in your mind makes your world.
This is why you are the creator of your own happiness.
For as a human being, you are free to will.
But free will or choices are only earthly lessons.
They can turn you into an angel or make a devil of you.

It is said that love is blind, so is blind passion.
Be diligent, be passionate but don't live in a world of fantasy.
Humans are endowed with strong cravings and emotions.
Your worst enemy is yourself and reason is the greatest tool.
You are not required to change the world.
The only change needed is for you to conquer your weaknesses.

The journey of life is simply lessons to correct our imperfection.
'Truth' is veiled; like ravenous wolves in sheep's clothing.
Let reason and humility be your friend; discard arrogance and haste.
Peace of mind comes from harmony with self, work and home.
Happiness and harmony are inseparable like a rotating wheel.
When decisions are not supported by loved ones, it's a wake-up call.

Karma teaches us to correct past mistakes; not compounding them.
The quality of your life is measured by the quality of your work.
Realize that the one thing you have absolute control is your attitude.
See the effect it has on those close to you. Is it good or bad?
In reality, we need wisdom to exercise free will to balance our life.
It can be a blessing or a curse; it is entirely up to you.

F.S. Khean

Free fall

It is stale news to read about fallen angels or young adults ruining their lives because of lack of discipline or through irresponsible behaviour. Former world heavy weight boxing champion Mike Tyson comes to mind. He is well known as champion basher both in and out of the ring and prison is like a second home to him. 'Whacko Jacko' Michael Jackson is another unforgettable character who went under the knife to be 'white' and later fled America in the aftermath of his child molestation trial. What about those countless irresponsible celebrity actors and sportsmen who ruin their colourful career through drug abuses, over-drinking or sex scandals? Some make their own free fall from riches to rags and end up as welfare recipients. Take Australian actor Heath Ledger for example; he was a rising star just about to become box-office material in Hollywood after his stirring performance in *'Brokeback Mountain'* that won him an Oscar nomination. But he died suddenly all alone in his apartment at the age of 28 due to habitual drug and alcohol abuse. It is very sad to see the early demise of a young man who failed to reason with himself to kick away a bad habit despite growing fame and fortune. Righteous living requires discipline and this virtue is becoming to be rare in current changing time of *'permissiveness'* where law enforcers turn soft and prefer to close a blind eye on undesirable activities harmful to good health.

Some parents are having a handful controlling their grown up children who sprouted wings earlier than expected. They are real estate agents' best friends because it has become fashionable for young adults to have their own space and live away from home. Cash management or budgeting is normally not their forte and they prefer to live in elite suburb not realising that 'rent money is dead money'. Owning a few credit cards is the trend and many only pay the interests from monthly statement while the principal amount of owing keeps piling up and the bank has the last laugh. When there is freedom, temptations creep in such as staying out late, eating in posh places, desire to have a live-in partner, mixing with shady people, playing unbearable loud music or over-decorating a rented home. These may be all part of growing up but how many know when to draw the line to protect their spending, security and career?

There are also the unfaithful ones. These are the adventurous married men and women today who are fond of secretly keeping a lover but would be prepared to plot murder when the lover kisses them goodbye for a younger or richer person. Such people have lost touch with morality and abuse the gift of free will. There is little *reason* for some to go berserk and inflict harm on others simply because of possessiveness and the loss of face! Infidelity is bad karma as unnecessary pains are inflicted on innocent family members.

The ruin of reason leads many to self destruction. What about some of our current leaders whether political or religious including business people with insatiable hunger for power? How many really care about our needs other than exploiting us to fatten their personal piggy banks? Don't fall into the trap of being too trusting with those you hardly know, especially sweet talkers that are long on promises but short of memory with nothing to show. Free will can be a curse when we are like puppets on a string—always being led or controlled by others with impure intentions.

Nature's Gift

> *When I stand before God at the end of my life,*
> *I would hope that I would not have a single bit of talent left,*
> *And could say, 'I used everything you gave me.'*

> Erma Bombeck

Are you on a mission?

Do you know that despite of more than six billion people in the world, no two persons are exactly alike? If you agree, it is not hard to believe that everyone is born with a special talent no matter how insignificant it can be in many cases. Some are even multi-skilled. It is Nature's Law to make sure that each of us is equipped with a 'special gift' so that we can be of service to mankind. Our existence must be meaningful or else there should be no such word as 'destiny.' Sit back and think hard for a moment; are we here simply to make up the numbers or here on a *mission?*

In our daily conversation, we commonly refer to social insects with admiration and a touch of envy. If only we could always be 'as busy as bees' or tackle jobs 'like an army of ants,' most of our work problems would vanish, we believe, and civil strife would end. All kinds of ants and many types of bees, wasps and termites form communities in which individuals are divided physically into distinct classes. Each class performs a special task for the common good. Co-operation is essential. Only as a group are they biologically complete. Some members are only good for breeding while others are used as soldiers and workers to obtain food. No individual can do both. The understood maxim is, *'unite or perish*'! Is there a hidden message on human survival strategy?

You are the most intelligent creature walking the planet that can read and write, relax or work at your leisure, hop into a car or take a plane when feel like travelling. Do you think your creation is simply to occupy the wide space on earth without an agenda? Even the lowest level of creation; the insect kingdom, has a system and purpose in life. Work it out: very likely the most hardened cynics would blush and think twice that humans are created solely because of chemical reactions from our parents!

Talents are unlimited

A good sales person speaks with conviction because it is his business to persuade you to buy his product. A manager has organisational and delegation skills to run a company effectively. A priest is compassionate and understanding and makes himself accessible to the public for advice and comfort. A security guard is hired because of his physique and ability to stay awake at night. A mother may not have formal schooling but is a great mum and an excellent cook. A blind man may be handicapped but his ears are sharper than most! As for politicians, . . . eh, eh, honesty is their policy—when they are bought, they stay bought! You can count on them to lay down *your* life for the sake of their country! The list has no end, everyone is talented. But the only problem is that we tend to overlook certain skills or abilities that appear to be relatively unimportant. Do you know that it needs courage and skill to beg or sing on the street? Can you do it? When you see a retarded or a handicapped person, his presence could simply be a reminder to all that the world is not perfect and we have to show more love and compassion to the unfortunate. Do we make such connection?

Passion

It is by design that we uncover our talent only at a later age through trial and error in most cases. It's part of the learning process of self-discovery. What are these 'special gifts'? They are those things we love to get involve with and we do it passionately and get lots of satisfaction out of it. Learn to give yourself free rein in doing what you love best; it could be any job such as being an advertising manager, designer, journalist, counsellor, florist, cartoonist, tradesman, chef or even playing tennis. When you have firm footing on something that appeals to you, your confidence rises and you feel a sudden freedom of expression that not only lifts your spirit but also gives you pride in your work. Your creative nature will start to surface more and desires, needs and goals will slowly be fulfilled because you are now *living in harmony* with yourself.

When you are balanced or in control of self, nothing is beyond you because you are born with a creative mind to tap into the vast unknown that is forever vibrant. The key word is *'passion,'* you will never be bored with any work if you have it. When you see a beautiful garden in front of a home, it is likely the owner is house proud and prepared to 'sweat and toil' in the garden, all done with love and appreciation in the beauty of nature. If you have a passion for home renovating, your mind and hands are not only always working, but you may end up living in your dream home.

Share your gift

There is a purpose for nature to provide you with a special talent. Keeping it all to yourself is not the plan, but expressing it in services to your fellow mankind is the real intent. For example: if a person has an exceptionally good singing voice but sings only in the bathroom, he is doing an injustice to himself and will not make it to the 'Australian Idol Show,' or even as a club singer. If a gifted artist keeps all his painting in the attic, it is a long shot that he would be discovered. But if he promotes his paintings through an art gallery, there is a fair chance he may be discovered and 'strike gold' one day with the art industry. If inventors, doctors, scientists and entertainers keep all their discoveries strictly to themselves, the world would be very boring and backward and we would be lucky to be still hanging around by age 50!

Imagine a world without music, sports, television and exotic food to whet our appetite. Without them even dreams can be very dull then! Learn to utilise your talent as a benefit to humanity because it is not only your meal ticket but also your passport to future happiness. It is all about sharing. When you are in the habit of sharing your talents and gifts with others, you will not only get inner joy and satisfaction, but also reap the future reward of 'one good turn deserves another' due to good karma. Don't forget that your generous nature also attracts spiritual growth making you a wiser person all the time because it is all part of nature's law.

High expectations

It is quite amazing that some parents are fond of making decision for their budding children ranging from school subjects, courses or profession to take without any consideration or consultation with their children. Nature's gift can become parents' curse sometimes as the young adult may have wasted precious years trying to be a doctor for example just to please the parents instead of playing tennis or golf that he or she excels. Parents should be realistic with their children's ability and encourage them to speak their minds for greater understanding of their needs. Mum and dad should not force their authority on the young and shattered their dreams. This is one of the reasons why there are so many unhappy people in the various fields because they are not meant to be there.

It is also not unusual for some parents to have pre-conceived notions that when their son or daughter is a top student in high school, he or she is assured of a bright future in any chosen profession. This is a *myth* as many with a string of academic qualifications have turned out to be ordinary people struggling to pay their mortgages. Passing exams in a university and making good in the workplace are different ball game. What is taught in school or university is very *structured* and predictable. When a student is attentive in class, does the homework regularly and study hard, the chances of scoring good grades are only expected. Unfortunately working hard is only one of the *many components* required before a person is able to shine out in the workplace. He or she needs to have some basic survival qualities like leadership, diplomacy, loyalty and assertiveness in order to serve well. You are required to work like a team player and not a loner—that means co-operation, dialogue and respect for colleagues. On top of that, the person must not be sensitive to constructive criticism and be adaptable to new environment. 'I don't want to be transferred', or 'I don't want to work under a woman', are statements from those who are not prepared to meet challenges and changes. The workplace is a *'come what may',* situation and one has to be on the toes all the time to face the unexpected and weather the storm to show resilience.

The Big Picture

> *Little drops of water make the ocean.*
>
> Proverb

Tenacity of purpose

It should be clear by now that in order to remain in control of ourselves and our lives, we need to stand firm and stick it out especially in unpleasant or tough situations because the journey of life is all about learning from both the good and the bad. We must have a *definite* plan and decide how we set about achieving what we want to do. But that doesn't mean that we have to stick to *one* plan forever as destiny usually unfolds at the later stage of our lives. In this context, it makes good sense to review our progress each year and check out whether what we have done is *worth* the effort or not. Our goals should be treated like a *business plan* that is subject to *amendments*—adding a bit there, altering this and that a bit—until the business shows profit where everyone is happy. It's pointless trying to bulldoze onto something that is not working or practical giving ourselves unnecessary stress, heartache and lack of harmony with everyone.

Most of us have to spend the best part of our waking lives earning a living. If we show the minimum of interest in our daily work and give the minimum of effort to our duties, a large sector of our existence is going to be sterile and impoverishing. When we take greater interest in our work, the rewards or benefits can come in many ways such as transforming us from ordinary to respected people; book-keeper to accountant; nurse to matron, real estate sales person to part owner of agency, slaves to artists; kitchen hands to chefs and mechanics or factory workers to foremen. Visualising the finished product and the pleasure and satisfaction it gives to others is another way of keeping our interest alive. Learn to see yourself as playing a vital role in creating that satisfaction and rendering that service. Apply imagination to your work in other ways. Ask yourself whether it could be done differently, and whether time and materials could be saved. The secret of *tenacity of purpose* is to have something you want to do and really believe in. It is worth repeating that we must learn to be passionate in whatever we do because when you have done your best in a given situation, you breathe freely without any sense of guilt.

Don't be a defeatist

Success is all about focus and positive thinking. A loser is one who may easily think: 'I am never the one to get the lucky breaks' or 'I have never had much of an education,' 'I am not good-looking and attractive like others, that's why I am getting nowhere in life.' Almost certainly, a 'surrender attitude' or some sore memories will come to mind and cause strong negative feeling that would sap up your energy and turning you to a defeatist with no more heart to fight. You must erase the painful past and their influence in the present and soldier on. Another common problem that hinders progress is that we stop ourselves by being not *flexible* in our thinking. Instead of being like water flowing through a ravine we stop the flow by our own thoughts and attitude. The recipe for reaping the rewards of your effort is similar to weeding a garden. You must take out the weeds before the flowers can grow. And you must keep on weeding regularly.

Team player

If you look at the big picture, it is very logical to say that in reality, each one of us is a team player doing your part in servicing the needs of the world. 'Serving' comes in countless ways and the most common one is to be an employee where you are expected to work *diligently and faithfully.* It could also be running a business where you provide good service without exploiting your customers. It's all about acting responsibly similar to what have been mentioned earlier about the duties of a teacher, soldier and a tennis player. The list is endless as cheering up a friend or making someone laugh is also a way of serving. Does it make sense to say that only a life lived for *others* is worth living? No matter what role you play, the world needs your support irrespective how insignificant your contribution may be. Remember those everlasting words of wisdom such as; 'It takes all sorts of people to make the world,' and 'A little drop of water makes the ocean'? If you study the words with a spiritual perspective, they have a very powerful message. If we use our talents effectively, we become 'the little drop of water' that makes up the mighty ocean. If we learn to live in harmony with one another and look at the big picture, all living creatures become one. The *whole* must blend as *one,* and that, my friend, is what life is all about. But . . . how long do you think this will come about?

Management Skills

Success is the result of good judgement.
Good judgement is the result of experience.
Experience is often the result of bad judgement.

Management Journal

Missing the boat

There are those who have all the ingredients required of a top executive but can easily fall victim to greed and distractions that will turn them into mediocre people instead of managers or leaders. A person could be brilliant in some ways but hardly made it to the big time because he could be one of those who is not prepared to share his knowledge or prone to bribery. The promotion ladder is always there but are you ready to climb? I remember in my previous workplace where the chief accountant was groomed for the top post but missed the boat because he had no sense of humour, dressed sloppily, rarely socialised and hardly showed any interest on the progress or welfare of subordinates.

It is also impossible for any big organisation to have a perfect workforce as not all workers have the same level of productivity coupled with the fact that many are not passionate in their work to boost company's progress. There will be workers who are struggling to make ends meet and their work contribution for growth is negligible because they only look forward to payday to settle bills and feed the family; going through the process of finding out how far they can climb the promotional ladder can be the furthest thing on their mind.

Passing the baton

A 'Manager' is one who manages people: that means *training* and delegating the various tasks to subordinates to get quality results. Unfortunately not all are born leaders: the collapse of many companies is partly because of poor working relationship between management staff and workers. Many mediocre managers are fond of throwing their weight around with little interest on staff development. It is quite common in public service where young graduates are tired of putting up with some managers who adhere strictly to rules and regulations and hardly attentive to new suggestions to improve productivity or make an effort to create a happy working environment. What are the ingredients required of a good manager who can command respect and productivity in the workplace?

I came across numerous opinions in management books regarding the qualities required of a good manager but none impresses me more than the down to earth insights of Linda Goodman who is not a business person but an astrologer! She says that good managers are like teachers who have a remarkable knowledge into your feelings. They will understand everything you say with uncanny accuracy, and the unnerving part is that they're also perceptive enough to sense the meaning of the words you leave *unspoken.*

The ideal manager is prepared to roll up the sleeves to teach and train you because he or she believes in *leadership through example.* You'll learn more in one month from this person than you will in a year from others. The most important thing you'll learn is *consideration.* Linda also mentioned that a good manager is sometimes similar to an astute businessman who drives a hard bargain, but the *guru* is fair while being shrewd. Playing a game of win and lose with the big guys who hold the blue chips is one thing. Taking advantage of the innocent is another. Your guru or boss should essentially be a kind and decent person, who's moved to deep pity by both cruelty and misfortune. Courtesy and compassion aren't old-fashioned words to the seasoned manager; they are part of the guiding light that success and experience is the result of good judgement. If your intentions are sincere, your motives are sound and your heart is honest, this person will back you through mistaken opinions and personal troubles.

In a nutshell, a good manager is a caring person, like a mother to a son or daughter. He or she doesn't *hold back* in developing you to your full potential and passing down the baton to a well deserved candidate is looked upon like a succession plan; all part and parcel of the *unwritten* job description. Like any sporting coach, your progress is the pride and joy of the coach: your mentor is not threatened by your success other than a personal satisfaction that his time and judgement are not wasted. There are some who climb the ladder of success by kissing the feet of the one above him and kicking the head of the guy below him! These people may become your boss one-day, but likely to be tagged the 'cunning' or 'slimy' one; not the great one.

Is your jar full?

I have a simple philosophy:
Filled what's empty.
Empty what's full.
Scratch where it itches.

Alice Roosevelt Longworth

During a seminar, an expert in time management was speaking to a group of business students and, to bring home a point, used an illustration those students will never forget. As he stood in front of the group of high powered over-achievers he said, 'Okay time for a quiz.'

He pulled out a one-gallon, wide-mouthed jar and set it in the table in front of him. Then he produced about a dozen fist-sized rocks and carefully placed them, one at a time, into the jar. When the jar was filled to the top and no more rocks would fit in inside, he asked, 'Is the jar full?'

Everyone in the class said, 'Yes.' Then he said, 'Really?' He reached under the table and pulled out a bucket of gravel. He dumped some gravel in and shook the jar causing pieces of gravel to work themselves down into the space between the big rocks. Then he asked the question, 'Is this jar full?'

By this time the class was on to him 'Probably not,' one of them answered. 'Good!' he replied. He reached under the table and brought out a bucket of sand. He started dumping the sand in the jar and it went into all the spaces left between the rocks and the gravel Once more he asked the question, 'Is the this full?'

'No!' the class shouted. Once again he said, 'Good.' Then he grabbed a pitcher of water and began to pour it in until the jar was filled to the brim. He looked at the class and asked, 'What is the point of this illustration?'

One eager beaver raised his hand and said, 'The point is, no matter how full your schedule is, if you really try you can always fit some things in it.'
'No,' the speaker replied, 'that's not the point. The truth this illustration teaches us is: If you don't put the big rocks in first, you'll never get them in at all.'

What are the 'big rocks' in your life? Your partner; your children; your loved ones; your education; your dreams; a worthy cause; teaching or mentoring others; doing things that you love, time for yourself; your health and all those things significant to you.

Remember to put these BIG ROCKS in first or you'll never get them in at all.

If you sweat on the *little stuff* (the gravel, the sand) then you'll fill your life with little things you worry about that don't really matter, and you'll *never* have the real quality time you need to spend on the big, important stuff, the big rock.

Have you found your destiny? Yes, if you are always excited to get up early and greet the new day to complete some unfinished tasks that you are passionate about. The long and challenging journey of life is complete when you have successfully discovered your passion and prepared to share it with the world.

'Is Your Jar full' is extracted from the Newsletter of 'Earth Star Publishing Pty Ltd' featuring 'Success Magic.' Earth Star specialises in meditation techniques and can be contacted at info@earthstar.com.au

Humour

The best medicine

The scene was an up-market restaurant called 'Four Seasons' on a busy Saturday night. A stranger walked in and boastfully announced that, even with a blindfold on, he could identify any wine.

The challenge was immediately accepted. A dark cloth was placed over his eyes and wine after wine was handed to him. 'St Hugo, Shiraz 1998,' he would announce. Or, 'Wolf Blass, Cab Sav 2004,' and he was always correct.

Finally, someone handed him a glass he couldn't identify. He sipped and then sipped and sniffed again. Suddenly he spat it out and pulled off the blindfold.

'Hell man! This is urine! Plain fresh urine!'

'Yes,' said Alex the owner in the background,' but whose?'

Chapter 2

THE AWAKENING

Consciousness Shift

> *Be open to new opinions and viewpoints*
> *no matter what age you are.*
> *Closing your mind impedes*
> *your spiritual and emotional growth.*

Louise L. Hay

Kyron

We are now venturing into the realms of metaphysics and spirituality and the materials in this chapter may be entirely new to some and can be quite unsettling at times. It is understandable and normal to feel strange or uncomfortable when stepping into unfamiliar grounds. But like what was mentioned before, life is a constant education. Who knows, sometimes the best thing in life comes about in the most unsuspecting way. Learn to explore intriguing possibilities by maintaining an *open and inquiring mind* as an unexpected event may have immense relevance to your next phase in life.

One morning after a game of golf with my sister Irene, she handed me a book and said, "This may be what you want, it's 'C*ry On*'. For a fleeting moment, I became sensitive and took offence to what she said. She may have beaten me in a game of golf that morning, but it was unnecessary to add salt to my wound! But when I took a closer look at the book, it was actually titled '*Kryon*.' From thereon, 'Kryon' became my regular reference on the mystics because it is a refreshing change of new concepts when absurdity can become a possibility. One of my favourite phrases in the book is, '*The reality of today is the magic of yesterday*.' Even though there are sections that are still questionable, I left that as 'maybe' and 'perhaps' since metaphysics and some unknowns are still on-going researches.

Some of the materials in this chapter are partly condensed from the book 'Kryon,'[1] written by Lee Caroll who is also the channel for the non-physical entity Kryon. It is suffice to say Kryon is a highly evolved master spirit or *celestial entity* from a higher dimension that specialises in Magnetic Service and responsible for the new alignment of the magnetic grid of our planet.

Messengers of God

It is predicted by American Edgar Cayce—arguably the most respected clairvoyant in modern time—that the Great Pyramid of Egypt is also part of a hidden message where the new earth cycle will change effective 1989 and great masters will arrive and revive spiritual truths again. The prediction is right on target as a host of master spirits are with us since the late 1980s to fast-track our connection with the universal plan. The old method of sending prophets like Rama or Jesus in human form and plodding on foot where they were likely to suffer from blisters is obsolete and no longer the *modus operandi*.

These higher entities are invisible *'senior messengers'* of God where only their 'energy' can be felt. It is reported that that there are eight such messengers spread out in various continents to enlighten the many races. This also indicates the urgency of our time to change by having so many master spirits at one time to help mankind to progress to a higher level. They communicate with us through *channelling;* or making use of the voice of a normal person to communicate because spirits are invisible like radio waves. Channelling can be defined as a *modern* process of direct communication between spirit and human without the presence of a medium like in the old age. Spirit enters the body with its *cosmic current* or energy but only *'borrows'* the voice of the human who is conscious all the time and able to hear what is spoken. This new method of communication between the two dimensions is obviously less spooky when the channel is a normal person who speaks like a professor and not some screaming mediums with strange voices like we used to know!

Doubters

The mystic presence of master spirits in our midst may be a bit rich or too far-fetched for some readers and it is perfectly normal because we are now living in a new consciousness that may require time to adjust. The new age believes in open mindedness and freedom of choice; everyone is entitled to his own spiritual thoughts and beliefs. But to progress in life, we need to change our perception on certain ideas when they are no longer productive or real. For example; is idol worship a source of protection for our security or simply an unknown fear? We need to keep on facing new challenges to advance our knowledge and get rid of some undesirable traits at the same time. 'Challenge' should not be a frightening word and its not like a battle between David and Goliath; its only about getting rid of bad habits and learning new ways to resolve problems.

Nostradamus

The great *Nostradamus* predicted 500 years ago that men would soar like a bird and fly into the sky. He was ridiculed by his countrymen who thought he had gone '*cuckoo*' because no one at that time was able to visualise the modern aeroplane. Even if it were 200 years ago, you would probably chuckle to yourself if someone told you that it would be a matter of time where voices or messages from friends can be heard or read from Paris to Australia instantly, or you can watch *live* war and bombing of another country by sitting in the comforts of your lounge. Our atmosphere is surrounded with transmission waves all the time but it took ages for humans to invent radios, telephones, television and computers. The reality of today is truly the *magic* of yesterday. We know we cannot live without oxygen but we can feel it although we cannot see it. We communicate through sound; can we see sound or voices? Is invisible master spirit still *unthinkable?*

Some of the revelations can be very unsettling because the logic behind some information may be the opposite of what we used to believe. It seems that our current science and medicine are scandalously over-rated systems for misinterpreting ascertained facts. They have sent physicists and scientists tumbling over their chairs because some principles of science practiced today are considered incomplete, as they are 'human science' and *not universal science!* Real science can only be achieved by the marriage of the physical and spiritual that has long been regarded as non-scientific by present '*experts.*' Many are humbled by very persuasive evidence and decided to put on a new thinking cap as the unknown has opened up new possibilities between the connection of spirituality and physics. The following topics are food for thought to greater understanding of human existence.

Why are we here?

It was explained that humans are created and put into *lessons* for the purpose of raising the vibration of the whole, which is the universe. How we deal with our lessons or efforts put in during each lifetime create energy that determines the growth or progress of our planet. However, energy generated by each lifetime and future incarnation or rebirth, can be positive or negative energy. The positive must outweigh the negative or else our earthly existence is meaningless. This is called *planetary healing;* the main reasons why we are constantly in lesson to raise the vibration or frequency *not* only for earth, but also the grander scheme of the universe. Planetary healing is like adding fresh air into a stifling room.

How well did we play our part in the universal community?

It was disclosed that positive energy for our planet has been gathering momentum since the 1960s and our normal egoic mode of consciousness is slowing giving way to a new level of consciousness *never experienced by humans* since the beginning of time! The common people from all over the world are starting to have faith by *praying* for peace and unity. We are starting to show signs that we are able find our way back to our spiritual side again—our mission and survival on earth—by waking up that *greed and attachments* are the downfall of human survival. This is the most wonderful news for mankind because planet earth was nearing the end of its life cycle and the next phase was either termination (remember the Ice Age?) or be given a *new lease of life* to expedite our long cycle of incarnations and sufferings. The seal of approval for humans to progress further will be brought about by a *consciousness shift* where mankind will be able to work with fresh concepts and work more intelligently to preserve peace and unity like a new beginning. Do you realise that the fact you are reading this book is indicative that you are experiencing a new consciousness shift or spiritual evolution previously unknown to you?

Duality

> *He who dwells in the body is eternal*
> *and can never be slain.*
> *Therefore you need not grieve for any creature.*

Lord Khrisna, Bhagavad Gita

Spirituality

We have used the word *'spirituality'* very often but what does it actually mean? It is less a religion and more a philosophy. It is a belief that there is more to life than what is manifested as the material or outer world where we can see and touch. There is also the existence of the *invisible* inner world: the sacred human *soul* abiding within that is eternal and can never be slain. When a person is able to blend his outer nature with the inner, he is working towards wholeness and is regarded a spiritual person.

The timeless soul is God's creation and possesses the sacred faculty called creative imagination or *the divine spark of God.* The ancient Greek philosopher Aristotle defined the soul as our life-force and *'inner genius'* that can be called upon to provide us wisdom and happiness. If you agree that a drop of ocean water has all the properties of the ocean itself, then it is not difficult to understand that as a spark of the divine, you have the same energetic properties as God.

The Soul

The soul is put into a lower world of matter and coarse vibration and abides in the human body to experience the physical *five senses* that are always hungry after their objects. However, the soul is given plenty of time to learn and attain wholeness through the many incarnations of rebirths where the soul will eventually be purified and return to its original realm ready to serve God. The *core of every human is spiritual* coupled with the fact that there is a *heavenly mission* for everyone walking the earth. But are we aware of it and are we willing to make the bridge to connect with the *guiding light*, the creative power of the soul?

How many people can take it seriously when told that there are actually two entities in their bodies? Because we cannot perceive the soul by our blunt senses, we deny it. But bear in mind; can we see air or sound knowing very well they are there? Who is there to question that all humans have consciousness? A body without consciousness is a dead body and the mouth will not speak and the eyes will not see. It is a scientific fact that consciousness is absolutely necessary for the animation of the body. But what is this consciousness? Just as heat or smoke are symptoms of fire, so consciousness is the symptom of the spirit or soul. The energy of the soul is manifested as consciousness.

Who's the real you?

You are clothed in a material body mainly because your sojourn to earth is strictly a training ground for you to find enlightenment and realise your own identity as a divine soul. Many may find it difficult to understand that the '*real you*' is your soul, the invisible higher self that cannot be destroyed by fire nor water and is *eternal*. The *'phantom'* or other half is your physical self with the body, brain, heart, limbs, and wrinkles. Now you know why you are here *only* for a short visit because the life span of a person is rarely expected to surpass a hundred years.

Learn to come to grips that it is nature's law that your present stay here is only temporary but likely to return again as another person or else there will be no such words as 'soul,' 'karma' or 'reincarnation'. This is the basis of *duality*—the combination of the physical and spiritual self. The funny part is that we perceive the phantom as *'me'*, unaware that the real *'you'* is inside the body waiting to be awaken. I used to laugh until my eyes run dry at one time when told that the real 'me' is hidden within suffering silently while I was having a great time. This is a case of *mistaken identity* of the highest order in our materialistic world today because we are brought up that way! Take a break and regroup if you are dazed by this revelation.

A spark of God

Your higher self is represented as a microscopic liquid light in your body. This spark is the real you, 'the divine spark of God.' You are also enveloped with another special light surrounding the body; some call it the magnetic field but it is commonly referred to as the *aura*. This special light has various shades of colours and is really the light emitted from the seven different *charkas*. Each of the charka has its peculiar colour of awareness or consciousness and to a trained clairvoyant, the aura betrays the habits, attitudes or health of a person. It is fair to say that human beings live in two realms; the physical and spiritual consciousness. The old expression, 'Our heart is in heaven but our feet are on the ground,' makes sense.

Reincarnation

Oh my mind!
Once you made me a king
And then you made me an outcast,
And to beg for my food.
Sometime you make me live
In mansion of the gods
And dwell in luxury and ecstasy,
Then you plunge me
Into the flames of hell!

Buddhist Text

The scary truth

My, my—some of the old classical texts give you a chill in the spine because they do not believe in beating around the bush and come straight to the point. You can be a king one-day and the next time around, you may be begging for food. What a dramatic change from one life to another!

Reincarnation is a belief that when the physical body dies, the eternal soul may re-enter the known world as another person. Hinduism is pre-eminent among organised religions in its belief in reincarnation. Fundamental to the Hindu creed is *karma*, which suggests that each rebirth is either a punishment or a reward for deeds done in a previous life. The Hindu also believes that the soul may increase its purity during successive existences until it ultimately reaches a divine world or *'nivarna.'* If this is accurate, faith in reincarnation can be regarded as a gift; a reward for the soul advanced enough to search for the meaning of its existence in the universe and *consciously* work out its karmic obligations in the present life.

Wide acceptance of truth

Like the Hindus, the Egyptians, Chinese, Tibetans and even the Greeks share the same belief that different types of experiences help to perfect the soul. The Christian faith is vague on this subject and the belief is that when death occurs, the soul would ascend to *'Pearly Gate'* and stand for judgement. The soul would either meet up with God and his angels or be damned. According to the Bible, Jesus Christ was resurrected after the third day of his crucifixion but strangely, he came back as *himself* and not as another person and then disappeared again after a vaguely painted short period. This is the most controversial section in the Bible as most theologians don't buy it.

Most Western cultures are accustomed to think that no one knows what lies beyond the portal of death. Some assert that death lands the soul upon some mystic shore where it will be like the 'river of no return'. Others assume that death is final and the end of the person. It is time for people to cease to think of death in such gloomy moods because the physical body serves only as a shell for the eternal soul who will more than likely return with a new personality in another place.

Egyptian beliefs

An unusual practice by ancient Egyptians on '*Letters to the Dead,*' deserves a mention here. These were special messages often inscribed on the pottery vessels used to provide food for the departed. Some letters urged the dead to aid the living; others were defensive and fearful, worrying that the dead person might return for vengeance. One highly unusual inscription, dated 71 BC, supposedly bears a message from an Egyptian woman who had died, to her living husband. It is a remarkably poignant message that suggests the death fears of the living. The inscription reads:

> *"I no longer know where I am,*
> *now that I have arrived at the valley of the dead.*
> *Would that I had water to drink from a running stream . . .*
> *o that my face were turned by the north wind . . .*
> *that the coolness thereof might*
> *quiet the anguish of my heart."*

What will happen next? Of all the questions men and women have asked in their pursuit of the unknown, this is perhaps the most constant and compelling.

Dr. Ian Stevenson

There are countless reports on reincarnation and many are documented. 'Truth' is always difficult to conceal and it surfaces in mysterious ways. A strange case was documented in the early 40s when Dr. Ian Stevenson, a researcher, uncovered a case that is provocative in both Hindu and Western terms. During his studies on the Indians of Alaska, he stumbled into an instance of '*a prediction of rebirth prior to death*'. An Indian named William George Sr., a celebrated fisherman, once told his son George and his daughter-in-law, '*If there is anything to this rebirth business, I will come back and be your son*'. He also told them that they would be able to recognise him 'because I will have birthmarks like the ones I now have'.

As it happened, events seemed to bear out the words of Williams George Sr. In August 1949, he disappeared on a fishing trip and was presumed dead. Soon thereafter his daughter-in-law became pregnant and gave birth to a boy. The baby had pigmented birthmarks on his body that resembled those of his grandfather, not surprisingly he was given the name William George, Jr.

As the child grew, his parents felt that they observed in their son certain characteristics that, in Stevenson's words, '*strengthened their conviction that William George Sr. had returned.*' For instance, the child walked with a limp, much as his grandfather had moved as the result of a basketball injury. Like the elder William George, the boy tended to fret and to warn other people of various dangers, and he 'showed a remarkable knowledge of fishing and boats', and 'exhibited a knowledge of people and places that, in the opinion of his family, transcended what he could have learned through normal means.'

Another strange element in the case was before he died, William George Sr., had given his son, the boy's father, a gold watch. One day when his mother was sorting through her jewellery, the boy saw the watch and seized it, saying, 'That's my watch'. He clung desperately to the watch, and it took the boy's mother a long time to persuade him to release it. Even so, the boy remained emotionally attached to the watch into his teens, when, Stevenson observed, he had 'largely lost his previous identification with his grandfather.'

Linkage of past and present

Stevenson also conducted studies on children and discovered that they can recall past lives but such memories seem to fade when they grow older. The recall is usually lost by the age of six or seven and in adulthood, it is lost altogether. It was speculated that young children 'are much closer to the people they once were, in another place, another time.'

Stevenson's research was very detailed. He has found, for instance, fear of water among several people who reported that they have drowned in previous lives. He also chronicled compulsions of a harmful sort such as the existence of surprising appetites for alcohol among young children who claimed to remember their previous lives as heavy consumers of the hard stuff. Included in the lot was the discovery that many who died from violent deaths in previous personalities are likely to have a desire for vengeance in children born, as many are, 'within the same culture and near the community where the previous personality has lived and died.' This may be the reason why there are still some 'warring countries' today because revenge has created so much hatred in people's hearts!

In addition, Stevenson believes that genetics *cannot* always completely explain specifically located birthmarks found on the bodies of subjects where 'bullets or bladed weapons fatally wounded them in the previous lives which they seem to remember.' These, he said, are usually much larger than common freckles or flat moles; they often resemble the scars of acquired wounds.

Deja vu

Does reincarnation have anything to do with '*déjà vu*'? French for 'already seen,' the feeling that one has been in a certain place previously, perhaps, as believers in reincarnation suggests, during an earlier incarnation? Neurological explanations for such feelings are fascinating. Yet they seem inadequate in accounting for stories such as this one reported by the writer William Chapman White. It involved an American couple, Mr and Mrs Barone, who left their cruise ship in Bombay, India, and had an odd experience.

Mr Barone said, 'Never having been out of America before, obviously I'd never seen Bombay, but as soon as we landed I had a strange feeling. As my wife and I started to walk the streets, I said, 'When we round the corner we'll come to the Afghan church', and a little later, 'Two streets down and we'll find De Lisle Road'. My wife gave me a funny look and said, 'You certainly know your way around. Or maybe you feel that you've been here before'.

'I was astonished at that. It was precisely what I did feel. I cannot tell you how our bewilderment grew during the day. We went around the city as if we had known every street and every old building all our lives or in some other life.'

When the Barones took another walk in the city, they asked a policeman whether there was a big house at the foot of Malabar Hill, with a big banyan tree in front. The police officer told them that such a house had been on that very spot but had been torn down 90 years before. The policeman's father had been a servant in the house, which had belonged to the Bhan family. And yes, there used to be a large banyan tree in front of it. It was at this point that the Barones recalled that they had named their son Bhan Barone because 'at the time it seemed most fitting'.

Crossing Over

Wherever your life ends, it is there.
The advantage of living is not measured by length,
But by use; some men have lived long, and lived little;
Attend to it while you are in it.

Michel de Montaigne

Our greatest fear

Death is inevitable and probably our greatest fear. We don't think much of it when we are young because its nature's way that we focus and work out the road map to enable us to travel the unpredictable journey of life. Our life cycle is timed in such a way that we have to go through the stages of infancy, adolescent, adulthood, employment, marriage, achievement and retirement before 'going home' comes strongly to mind. As author Joan Baez says, '*You don't get to choose how you're going to die, or when. You can only decide how you're going to live, now.*'

Death usually crosses our mind when we are very ill, had a nasty accident or when growing very old. How we *react* towards it is actually the true measurement of the somewhat long and arduous journey. Are we able to say with a clear conscience that we have *served* well and, at the same time, have strong faith in the survival of karma? If yes, we have done well and able to meet death with a bow.

Life goes on

We are born with strong emotion and the demise of a loved one can be very painful. Let time do the healing. But if you understand reincarnation and the workings of the eternal soul, the blow can be softened because very likely, a positive universal energy is released and the 'loved one' has done his part or made his contribution during his time on earth. It is likely that he will return again as another person in another place, *if* he chooses to do so. Perhaps the next life will be better than the previous one. We must learn to accept the fact that death is a *natural cycle* of our existence.

Do not allow sorrow and pain to have such a strong impact on you when a loved one has departed. Learn to let go and regain your strength after a short while because *life goes on* not only for you but also the *departed.* It is very harsh to say that from the day we are born, our days are numbered; only the date is not disclosed. Isn't this a reality of life?

Burial

It is the common practice to bury the dead. In some cultures, particularly the East, great expense was involved in buying selected burial site, expensive coffin, erecting a beautiful grave, marble tombstone, and so forth within the wealthy group. These are all unnecessary because the dead body is not sacred but rotting away. Do you think the rich should be buried differently from the poor? Cremation is the way to go and retaining the urn in an expensive jar is not only spooky but also impractical. Come on, did the departed look like ash? A nicely framed picture of the loved one is a better way for remembrance.

'Bon Voyage' to Ed

Death is fearsome to most but there are some that take it as the 'next phase of life'. An ancient sage, Chuang Tzu, once said, *'How do I know that in clinging to this life I'm not merely clinging to a dream and delaying my entry into the real world?'*

A good friend, Ed, is currently suffering from cancer. He has been given less than two years to enjoy life. But he has surpassed that time frame mainly because he is a well-read person on spiritual matters and accepts his passing as part of life's journey. He is still maintaining a good attitude and has not allowed fear to have a grip on him. Even in his present frail condition, he still has a good sense of humour. He joked with his sisters and reminded them about his favourite clothes and the shoes that he would like to wear on his passing and his ashes to be thrown into the sea. *'No tears please, be happy as if I am going for a long trip and everyone is bidding me bon voyage,'* Ed said. If everyone is prepared to accept death as only a change of scene for another new life, it should be treated as an event for celebration and not a period for mourning. But are we *brave enough* to change the tradition? Our blessings are with you, Ed.

There are cases where the dying appear very blissful with a faint smile on their last breath as if looking forward to *'going home.'* I remember a close relative had cancer and was on his deathbed with his wife next to him. When he was just about to go, he turned to his wife and said, *'I am going now and it is so peaceful. Sai Baba is putting me on his lap.'* Although the demise of the husband brought early grief to the wife, she managed to overcome her sorrow quickly mainly because she found inner peace that her husband was 'well taken care of.'

The Producer

My life is a performance for which
I was never given any chance to rehearse.

Ashleigh Brilliant

What will happen next after the physical body has stopped functioning? This is probably the most scary part of human existence especially when you are sick and sense that your time is up. Is your demise going to be your final departure on this planet?

The Roaming Soul

Death of the human is a metamorphosis,
just as a pupa becomes a butterfly.
The inner core is the same;
only the outer shell is discarded.

Dr A.K. Tebecis

The rotating wheel of reincarnation and karma refers to an afterlife. However, the activities of the soul immediately *after* physical death gets a bit hazy, as research within many teachings does not touch on a common belief. Reports from clinical deaths—probably more reliable—are fond of mentioning the soul going through a dark tunnel, landing in paradise and meeting up with deceased relatives and so on. Many Eastern teachings are in agreement that the soul is allowed to go free and roam the physical and the astral worlds for *49 days* after death. This is the transition period which allows the soul to come to grips that the *phantom self* is gone and it's now a free spirit. The soul is not alone; *the guardian angels* are there to guide and accompany the soul in the spirit world. The soul is likely to be hovering over the dead body upon death and may be in initial shock to see mourning relatives and friends. The 49 days enable the soul to adjust and free itself from earthly attachments such as longings for loved ones, loss of material wealth, unfinished work and so forth.

Last good-bye

The soul that has abided in the human body for a lifetime needs a bit of time to undergo a short purification process and, at the same time, bid farewell to loved ones in mysterious ways. The deceased could appear in a dream, giving a gentle touch, making an unusual but familiar sound like coughing, scent of perfume, flowers and even lingering alcohol smell if the departed was a drinker!

It is beneficial to share an experience of the passing of a family member. Some years ago a brother-in-law died in a plane crash that exploded into the sea. He was a bachelor and left behind a house. His sister Queenie used to drop in once a while to clean up the place and the *brother* was fond of 'showing his presence' by some unexplained ways: his habitual jingling sound of car keys indicating that he was home; an unopened chiming card suddenly flapped up with happy music as if to say 'hello'; unexpected gust of wind;

whistles of his favourite tunes; the nauseating stench of someone nearby! But Queenie was always calm to all these phenomena and said, 'It's only my brother, I can feel he didn't come back to harm anyone.'

Here's another example of a memorable last good-bye. My ex-neighbour and buddy Les had a heart attack and passed away unexpectedly. The last time we spoke over the phone was about getting together soon. Two nights after his demise, I slept early and my wife heard a gentle scratching noise on the sliding door of our house. When she went to investigate, she found a *friendly* white rabbit staring at her as if trying to say 'hello.' After a few seconds, the rabbit quietly hopped away and *disappeared*. When she related the incident to me the next morning, it flashed on me immediately that the rabbit was Les in *disguise* because I dreamt of him *moving house* (to another world?) and wearing white clothes that same night! What is strange but comforting, is the way the newly departed returns. Les had *prudently* came back as a lovable rabbit to say good-bye; if he had returned as a dog or even a cat scratching at the door, I bet my 'not so brave' wife would have screamed or chased Les away with a stick!

No help from scientists

Such paranormal event has been ongoing for centuries but the scientific community has offered little for enlightenment as scientists get a mental block when told to consider 'roving souls' for answers in their equation on research work! When can our top brains measure the *finely veiled* correlation for the two dimensions to help us confidently explain to our children about spirits or ghosts currently taboo in bedtime stories?

It has been well documented that sometimes dogs start to bark with wagging tails at an *invisible someone,* or the fridge and pantry doors are opened for no reason. It may be spooky but it can also be comforting that the deceased or the soul is trying to pass a message that he or she is still around. Other teachings like the Christian faith are vague after the body returns to the elements; the popular belief is that upon death, the soul is taken to face judgement day at the pearly gates where the soul either joins the angels or meets up with Satan for purgatory reforms. But whatever the case, the soul *must* return to its source of origin.

Journey Home

> *A time to weep, and a time to laugh;*
> *a time to mourn, and a time to dance.*

Ecclesiastes

When a person has passed on, the soul will make the journey '*home*' with the guardian angel. According to Dr Lobsang Rampa, a Tibetan monk-clairvoyant, the actual name for 'home' is called '*Brahmaloka*', a Sanskrit word for the highest *astral* plane where souls live in divine communication while preparing for fresh experiences in the next incarnation. This is the place with no space and time but is *not* the highest realm nor is it *heaven* as many seem to believe. It is an 'in-between plane' of earth and heaven. This is also the highest plane where your dreams or many of the occult sciences can take you. The higher planes are only accessible to a small group of accomplished spiritual masters.

Brahmaloka is the nostalgic paradise where the soul belongs: a plane beyond matter where peace and tranquillity is the order of the day and everything appears more beautiful compared to earth's standard. Why more '*beautiful?*' It was explained that when in this higher realm, the light and beauty increase materially, as does the happiness of the entities there because everything is in perfect harmony. Even the flowers are prettier and smell better! What a great place to call 'home'.

'Home' is also where some higher spirits reside including those entities that have either completed their lessons on earth or other planets in the universe. Earth is only one of the many planets the soul provides service for the betterment of the universe as a whole. This is a broad hint that there is also *other intelligence* in the universe. When back to your source, all your earthly burdens or worries will melt away as everyone lives in harmony like the golden age.

Time for celebration

On your homecoming there will be celebration and rejoicing irrespective of whether you made good or not while in lesson. You may have been a drug addict, a wife-beater, a priest or a solicitor while on earth. The lessons learned are not meant to gauge your performance or intelligence. There will be no gold medal for winners or losers as the lesson deals mainly with finding the bridge between the 'human you' and 'universal you' during your duality. You are back to a non-judgemental dimension where God is merciful and forgiving, even though you have rebelled against Him during lessons on earth. You become an entity bathed only in purity once again. Think of yourself as a love energy that knows only how to give and not receive.

The key here is to understand that you *volunteered and sacrificed* your service to improve the vibration of planet earth. The entities around you know your 'lesson' status on earth and how many times you have gone through duality. It's shown like the rings around an old tree to indicate age; you show your stripes in a particular colour where all are aware of these awards and honour you in celebration. Your job is a most difficult one, much harder and more honoured than some master spirits like Kyron because they have not gone through the process of death and reincarnation. You are very special and a hero's welcome home is only befitting.

Balancing of energy

When all the tears and joy subside in welcoming you home, you will be reunited with your soul family and all your soul mates like a normal earth event after a long trip away from home. 'Family' will be explained later. Bear in mind that upon your return, it is standard procedure to have a rest period to *rejuvenate and balance your energy* and the recovery cycle can be a long or short one depending on karma while on earth. This has to be done to pave the way for a more meaningful rebirth the next time similar to Hindu beliefs.

Some fear-based old teachings are fond of distorting this *cleansing* period as a punishment where Satan will give you *hell* using fire to inflict endless torments. I have heard of old wives' tales such as the devil throwing you in a hot pot and make delicious stew out of you or forcing 'a bad soul' to make a 100m dash over burning rocks! This is definitely not true; it doesn't conform to the teachings of reputable spiritual masters. Remember the soul cannot be destroyed by fire or slain? It is eternal and *only* our physical body can feel pain. This is probably the reason why we are so scared of dying because our forbears give us the creeps and *ignorance* is not bliss!

Master at work

> *Before long, the world*
> *will not see me anymore,*
> *but you will see me.*
> *Because I live,*
> *and you also will live.*

John 14:19

One life time experience *conditions* the setting of the next life expression. When your recuperation period is over, you will return to your 'planning room' and decide your next course of action to continue your karmic schooling in the next expression. It is here, in your godly state, you have access to the *Akashic Record* that reveals all your past lives.

Some references and questions were raised earlier in the book whether the world is really a stage for all humans to act or play out an assigned role like a 'job description'. These questions were designed not only to arouse curiosity about your existence on earth but also to cushion the most bizarre and astonishing section of this book. Do you know that *you planned your own journey to earth*? You wrote your own script, planned your role on what you wanted to be, gave yourself a 'job description' and made a contract with yourself? You *masterminded* how your next life on earth is going to take shape and planned your own lessons. The strange part is that you have all the solutions and answers to your lessons and there is no test that is beyond your knowledge or ability to walk through while in *Brahmaloka*. Your higher self is a hard taskmaster but rest assured that the next earthly lessons are all solvable and not *'mission impossible.'*

I did it my way

I had a hard time trying to accept the fact that I 'wrote my own life story' and was cynical about the whole thing. But when you sober up and reflect: what is the most precious thing in life to you? A life where you *call all the shots* or one that is *dictated* to you? The former makes more sense because freedom of expression is not only the key to our identity but also our ideas of adventure and survival. If you are part of the universe, you are also part of the planning crew who are able to contribute to the overall plan. We are a divine spark of God and possess the wisdom to choose the role we wish to play. This obviously may not materialise according to plan once on earth when we become flesh and blood, but at least our *beliefs are set in motion* and put to the test. It's music to the ear when *'I did it my way.'* You are the producer of your own life story. There is so much realism in the 'acting' because you are playing the role of yourself and no one can do it better.

Have you seen epic movies like 'Ben Hur,' "Lord Of The Rings' or low budget movies like 'The Three Stooges?' The moviemaker or film producer may require months or even years of planning especially for big budget movies to get off the ground. The producer has to select the right crew to assist him for the movie production. On top of that, he needs to work out all the plots in the movie and who's in them, pick the locations for the shooting of key scenes, *casting of heroes and villains* and all the supporting actors required for various stages of the movie. The mechanics of planning your life journey to earth is fairly similar to that of a movie producer except that the ending of a movie is more predictable. The good guys in the movie usually end as heroes and there is a happy ending. In your case, good luck to you whether you end up a born loser, a saint or a famous freedom fighter because not many will be watching your movie as it may take 99 years to end!

Memory censor

There is no predetermined outcome on your life at the end of the line. There is a *'master plan'* to resolve every problem but once as mortals in the physical world, you get a *'blackout'* and your new life will be dependent on the cultural reality of the day. Why the blackout? You can either be an angel or a sensitive human being and cannot play *both* roles when thrown to earth. Once reborn, you will have forgotten how you planned your own lessons because a *memory censor* has been *implanted* in your head. However, it is common that you have vague flashes of it through dreams or intuition but they hardly make any sense most of the time. But the main thing to remember is that although you cannot actually finesse or develop any of your earthly talents while in Brahmaloka, you planned your life with *the best of intentions to balance out karma.*

When you realise the significance of karma, it becomes easier to understand that you are on a spiritual mission on earth to become *liberated* and not a *victim*. You accept responsibilities as the gateways to freedom and obstacles in life's journey will become less stressful. Daily problems become more tolerable when you consider them as a purification process to complete the mission with the view of an early *return home*.

Man or woman?

Your higher self is a specialist in planning lessons. When reviewing the performance of human self, you are aware of your shortfalls and design a new road map to overcome them. You decide *where, what and who* you want to be to suit your *next spiritual needs*. Ready for another surprise? This is where you decide to take on the role of either a *man or woman* and become Osama or Madonna with a different personality compared to the last earthly life. Every human being has past lives experiences of both sexes as part of universal balancing. Such revelation is normally found in dreams and many are likely to feel uncomfortable or even embarrassed when recalling such dreams where they acted strangely as if they were the opposite sex. Don't feel bad about it; your soul is trying to give you a glimpse of what you were before in an earlier life.

Every incarnation is a very personal and private journey; the lessons, profession or the type of person you want to be is your choice how best to repay karmic debts. But bear in mind that when you are in your planning room as your higher self, you have *no gender* and no attachments but only freedom to act. But strangely, there are people who believe that 'heaven' is the place where they can meet up with their past lovers and indulge in endless sensory pleasures! Sorry to disappoint some cute dreamers; it is not true but *fantasies* of those hungry for love! When you have no gender, where is the urge? God has more productive plans for all of us.

The wonder of you

You are not perturbed with joy or pain, wealth or poverty, and being black, brown, yellow or white. It doesn't matter to you whether you are fat, thin, short, freckle-faced or being a boy or girl. You are at liberty to take on any realistic role as long as the spiritual experience is planned to *balance* the karmic account. This is why it takes all sorts to make the world. Your looks or next physical appearance on earth is entirely a genetic issue. It is not your fault if you have uneven teeth, small eyes, big nose or stumpy legs—blame your parents!

The preparation for the next appearance on earth is very complex, as 'heavenly matters' are not easy to grasp. The best analogy for the planning stage is like the movie producer mentioned earlier. He plans ahead and set the stage with all the answers regarding how, when, what, why, who and where, before letting the movie roll. The soul is usually as keen as ever to return to earth as the materialistic world is filled with challenges like *'an angel under the guise of man sparring with the devil'* all the time. There are also many unfinished lessons that are *'so near, yet so far,'* making the soul the more determined to finish off the job. This is the 'wonder of you.'

Your next entourage

During your previous expression on earth, you might have a shortfall in tact and diplomacy and you create new lessons to correct these traits. If lust and greed became a way of life in the past, a new road map is provided to eliminate the bad habits. You know exactly what is best for new lessons and set the stage in advance for the next expression. Like the film producer, the 'master plan' cannot be compiled single-handedly and needs a host of people to finalise it. Many 'actors' are required to play out the scene while you are in lesson. These players will be your *'family'* and including *those on earth* that are still in lesson.

Family or loved ones are those entities that came with you in your incarnations previously and 'acted' as parents, spouse, brothers, sisters or children. They are in reality your soul mates or best pals. Your soul mates or buddies are more than happy to help out as their responsibilities are to be of service to others. It's like arranging with a group of friends to go on an adventure trip.

Funny side of family

Your interaction with people or human circumstances on earth is all pre-arranged. In other words, the woman you married could be your *'grandmother'* in a previous life. The nephew you slapped on the head for calling you the' grumpy old crow' on your last birthday could have been your *'father'* from the past or the woman who jilted you at the altar was your daughter at one time! Who knows, you might have put a past son in jail for embezzlement when he was your accountant. Fascinating or bizarre? You are interacting with your soul mates all the time but the *memory censor* at birth is playing on your mind and 'distant' you from them. In this book, *soul mate* is defined as someone who had taken the role of a family member in one or many of your incarnations on earth. All are acting and playing out a role planned by you. Is there a better way other than freedom of choice to plan and choose your favourite actors to play your 'family'?

Ancestors' worship

There is also a subtle lesson to learn about family. In this new age, ancestors' worship should be a thing of the past. For all you know, you might have been worshipping *yourself* as you took on the role as 'grandfather' in a previous life! This is not meant to make fun of our forebears; it was the belief and respect for the dead of that era. Also, there is such a thing as *wandering spirits* which will be discussed in another chapter.

Even in our modern times, rituals and ceremonies for the dead appear bizarre among many eastern cultures; burning *paper* castles, BMW cars, treasure chests, plasma TVs, and so forth to appease the dead is really absurd. Idol worship should also be a thing of the past; it is meaningless worshipping idols made of gold, porcelain or plastic *manufactured* in factories whose target market is the gullible! Work this out: can *soiled human hands* create 'gods' from a higher dimension? If not, why worship them? Many people simply follow traditions blindly and blunder through the years without questioning its validity or usefulness. They give their souls away and play into the hands of *wandering* or lower spirit looking for a *'home'*. All figurines and statues should only be displayed as ornaments. What about those poor ignorant people who kissed the foot of their religious leader and treat them like gods! No living person should be worshipped. A chosen leader is only a representative for a group—a mortal with karmic debts to pay like you and I.

Another Adventure, another Life

We make our own decisions,
But the Lord determines what happens.

Proverbs 16:33

Timing of birth

As you can imagine, there is so much going on behind the scenes in planning the arena for lessons. To make it even more complicated, it is almost a standard practice that every incarnation is staged in a new environment compared to the past. You may have been a teacher in your previous life on earth but decides to change profession and come back as a doctor to add spice to your new lessons. This is all *'part of the game'* and you are provided with all the tools to reach your destiny. Advanced arrangements are made to ensure you are born to the right parents who will be able to provide you with the necessary education to reach your goal.

The timing of your birth is also planned to coincide exactly with *astrological* influence that would provide you with all the necessary characteristics required of a doctor. Because of the intricacies of timing and parenting, your *birthplace* can vary from one corner of the earth to the other, hence *the colour, the different language, new face and foreign name.* But once on earth, the game of hide and seek begins without a guidebook telling you where to start! You are in the driver's seat and your actions and reactions to various situations decide your next life.

Yummy Mums

The topic of 'birth' has brought in another interesting point although it is a slight diversion from this section. Modern spiritual leaders, including some doctors who are familiar with metaphysics, are fully aware of the reason why most pregnant women have a special *glow* during pregnancy especially when the baby starts to move or kick. Their emotions start to change for the better and they become *'yummy mums'* because their radiance—the sparkle in their eyes and natural 'innocent-like' behaviour—can be very infectious and make us happy too. Why? The *new soul*, in all its purity, has entered the body of the baby and the mothers *'feels'* the Divine origin.

Siblings

It is also not unusual that soul mates like to be together and end up as brothers and sisters as part of the contract in the 'master plan.' Do you know that it is quite common to find siblings in one family having about the same level of success without anyone that really stands out? This is because soul mates have similar aspirations and wish to be born by the same parents. The lifestyle of your cousins can be entirely different from yours because another group of soul mates formulated a different plan to experience life on earth. But the level of success or otherwise, is again well balanced among the cousins in most cases. So forget about envying your neighbours, friends and relatives because you wanted it to be *that way.*

Old soul

Contracts vary form one person to another depending whether you are a 'young' soul or an 'ancient' one in terms of number of incarnations. An old soul generally means less taxing tasks and expected to enjoy the luxury of a pleasant life for having been 'through the mill' over the ages. He has his fair share of playing the bad guys and the goodies and his mission is just about to be completed. The majority of newcomers or young souls may have to tough it out in a less fortunate environment where living conditions are not ideal in order to go through the many stages of life. However, no one is expected to be an *unenlightened* soul forever. The wisdom of Will Rogers fits well when he said,' *We can't all be heroes because someone has to sit on the curb and clap as they go by'*

Warriors and chiefs

There are more ordinary people than VIPs because we need more warriors or workers than chiefs to do the many common jobs and make the world more productive. Who's going to collect the garbage, drive the buses and trains, repair the roads, build houses, work in factories, provide us with fresh foods or be frontline soldiers and risk death to protect our country? They will not be the billionaires, professors, brain surgeons, bishops, CEO or our *friendly* politicians for sure!

Simple contracts mean simpler lifestyles but trivial issues can be looked upon as 'life and death' in various situations. A caring mother can be overcome with guilt and anxiety when her son's school grades drop from excellent to fair. She blames herself for not pushing her son hard enough in his studies and spends sleepless nights tossing in bed. In another case, an Asian mother can experience tremendous stress when her pampered daughter married a foreigner and live overseas. The mother is so concerned over the welfare of her daughter that she spends most of her time on the phone checking out whether the daughter can stomach western food, cold weather, the in-laws, etc. On the other hand, the president of a big company may experience the same type of strain when forced to sack 500 loyal staff and take a pay cut just to reduce costs to please shareholders.

Live to serve

An interesting question is how do you know whether you are on track or off course from planned contracts when trying to do your bit on earth? This is really a very tough question as the contract is prepared in another realm and you cannot pull it out from the drawer for reference all the time to check how you are faring.

Trust your intuition; your instinct is a powerful weapon in guiding you to your destiny. Are you comfortable and happy in where you are? Do you get pleasant or inspirational dreams once in a while? Are you always on the look-out to make others happy especially loved ones including *pets*? Do you look forward to the next day at the office? When you are able to *serve* and walk with a smile and never short of kind words for others, you are more than half way in fulfilling your contract. As Albert Einstein says, '*Only a life lived for others is worth living.*'

The chapter on 'The Producer' is inspired by the wisdom of Dr Lobsang Rampa, a Tibetan monk and clairvoyant and *Kyron,* the celestial entity channelled by Lee Carroll.

Humour

The best Medicine

Kenny, an overseas student, ran out of cash and sent a telegram to his father that read:

'No money, no fun, your son.'

The next day he received a response:

'Too bad, so sad, your dad.'

Chapter 3

KARMA — PART I

The Self takes on a body
with desires, attachments and delusions.
The Self is born again and again in new bodies
to work out the karma of former lives.

Upanishad

The mystics of the East became alive again during the last century when Western historians and writers discovered the many ancient Hindu texts of knowledge such as the '*Upanishshads,*' '*Vedas*' and the '*Bhagavad-Gita*'. These are the most *treasured holy books*, written in *Sanskrit* and reputed to be the earliest sacred books ever written on earth. The holy books have entered the consciousness of the West and changed their cultural and spiritual landscape in recent decades. The origin of the ancient texts is still a baffling unknown as no human is bold enough to take credit for the work. Hindu folklore is fond of claiming that Sanskrit is a *language of the gods*. The verses in all the spiritual texts were the *voices* of God dictated to the prophets. Who *dares* to question such a belief when verses and knowledge that was written about 2000 BC, is more eloquently explained than what we hear today. The same belief is also echoed in the Bible; *'In the beginning was the Word, and the Word was with God'*. If the ancient texts were not brought to light recently, words like 'dharma,' 'nirvana,' 'karma' and many fascinating and original sacred verses may forever be unknown in many parts of the world.

What is karma?

Karma is derived from the Sanskrit language which literally means 'deed' or 'action.' But the word has a deeper meaning spiritually because it is also referred to as the *'Law of Cause and Effect.'* This means that if a person performs a good deed like an act of kindness, he will be blessed with the same amount of kindness accordingly in the *present or future life*. If an undesirable act is committed such as a married man secretly keeping another woman, he will be punished accordingly in the present or next life. All humans are *imperfect* creatures and karma serves humanity as an impersonal universal teacher designed to help us to become whole. It is like accounting; the book will not be closed until all the bad debts are cleared.

The soul must balance its energy by going through all the good and bad effects of human behavioural patterns of many life times. The many imbalances of energy are the *incomplete* parts of the soul that created the personality—*you*. What you are today is the total sum of your incarnations. It should be understood that your existence today is all about clearing past undesirable traits or *karmic debts* to heal and purify the soul. The law of karma is best observed through the popular phrase of wisdom, 'what you do not want to do to yourself, do not do to others', or it will boomerang on you in unsuspecting ways!

Are there few types of karma or deeds?

Deeds are classified into three types; *physical, oral and mental.* Many people associate karma with only the physical and oral, but it's more than that. We are thrown into a society where tolerance is not our forte. Most of us are sensitive beings and get upset, angry or hurt very easily. For example; when the boss harshly treats us in front of colleagues, we may not dare to retaliate but in our mind, we said to him, 'Bugger you, shut your big gap and stop humiliating me. If I'm an idiot, you are the bigger one!' Just to *think* in anger is bad karma. It is not easy trying to stay cool in tough situations but that's the name of the game to clear karmic attributes. It is human nature to fight back whether one is right or wrong. But is that the way to react? Do you think you can look into the eyes of your boss again when you mentally swore at him? Can we accept the fact that the boss may be right and we are at fault and the issue at hand is a lesson not to be repeated?

Where is the origin of the soul?

It should be clear that the soul is a creation of God in a higher realm without time and space where there is *only* positive energy. In this realm the soul is a pure entity living in harmony with other souls as there is no greed or evil; there is no necessity for the soul to watch its back all the time like humans! But when the soul decides to return to earth as a new personality for more earthly lessons, its energy and power will be drastically *reduced* as the soul has to absorb the denser energy of earth and humans who are still not whole. It's like down grading an executive from 'upstairs to downstairs.'

The soul takes shelter in a body that is in tune with the vibration of earth and becomes *the other half* of the personality or commonly known as the hidden 'spark of God'. Every personality is only good for one lifetime but the eternal soul has to go through many rebirths of various personalities as there are countless barriers and lessons to overcome in the materialistic world before enlightenment can be attained.

What is the purpose of our existence on earth?

It may be hard for you to believe that the planet *is literally useless without you in lesson.* Can you remember 'planetary healing? How you fare in your lessons determine the 'state of health' of planet earth. When you are able to pass a test such as cultivating tolerance or give up a vice like gambling; you have attracted good vibration in the atmosphere to strengthen the health of mother earth. When you constantly failed your tests through anger, hatred or a non-caring attitude; you give out poor vibration and choke the earth. Other issues like war and terrorism, exploitation of the weak and plundering of the earth resources are also no help to sustain a healthy planet. When the planet is overwhelmed with bad vibration and starts to wobble, it will be a one-way ticket to end time and good-bye world! You may think you are only 'a small fry' in a complicated world, you are not. You are actually a part of the solution to enable the universal plan to unfold. Your existence is all about planetary healing and the grander scheme of the universe.

Is karma connected to past lives?

Yes, some gurus refer to it as the evolution of the soul. The majority of people is cloaked with emotional and psychological pains which are basically undesirable or destructive traits accumulated from how they live their past lives. The *'baggage'* you carry now and the reason for your lessons is simply a direct response to reactions and events from the past. Most of us are rarely 'top students' who are able to walk past each lesson because we *resist change.* Let's illustrate some simple examples. A person who has little regard for punctuality fails to understand why he or she is rarely invited to parties or a game of *mahjong.* Another woman was sacked three times within two years in similar secretarial positions because she wears revealing dresses and swears at the slightest irritation despite being cautioned by management. Why are people so reluctant to change? Is it so hard to be punctual for an appointment or dress appropriately in an office? Why *allow history to repeat itself* and make your life miserable? Karma teaches you to open your eyes and avoid the same mistakes. You will forever be a victim of a second-best life if you don't take action now and get rid of bad habits.

What are the main causes of karma?

I remember a hymn with the verse, 'Yield not to temptation, for yielding is sin.' Well, we will not be normal if we have not yielded to temptation at one time or another. What are these sins? From the book, 'The Teaching Of Buddha,' it mentioned that world passions stem from *ignorance and desire*. Together, they are the source of all unhappiness. When people are ignorant, they cannot reason correctly and become victim to the glitters of life and inevitably get attached to all those desires. From these two primary sources, greed, anger foolishness, vanity, resentment, jealousy, deceit, pride, contempt and selfishness will find their roots. It is the constant hunger to satisfy the five senses of sight, hearing, taste, touch and smell that lead people into the delusions of habit.

Greed rises from wrong ideas of satisfaction; anger rises from wrong ideas concerning the state of one's affairs and surroundings; foolishness rises from the inability to judge what is correct conduct. Greed, anger and foolishness are called the three fires of the world. *Everywhere these fires are raging.* They not only burn the self, but also cause others to suffer and lead them into wrong acts of body, speech and mind.

Are there many different grades of karma?

There are different grades of karma and these can be graded from a scale of 1 to 9, the heavy ones at the higher numbers. Those in lesson at the lower scale of 1 to 3 have lighter karmic attributes and clearance is designed for a shorter time frame in attaining enlightenment. The attributes under this group are generally confined to their behaviour and interaction with people. Many will be temperamental, critical, cynical and uncaring. They are people who have been abused or they themselves are bullies. They have ongoing lifetime problems with parents, relatives, friends and colleagues. These are the ones who constantly want to strike back or defend themselves. Their main lesson is to cultivate tolerance and learn to resolve problems rationally without anger in their heart.

Those with karmic lessons in the 4 to 6 categories, have to play catch up as they have to take on some of the lessons in the 1 to 3 group, on top of some heavier lessons. The addition includes dealing with human violence or using negativity to mislead people for the sake of control or profit. Lust and greed are part of the lifestyles. They cannot be trusted but their false front is hard to detect. People in this group are usually very selfish, prepared to try any thing for personal gain. These are the ones fond of instigating trouble for others, exploiting the weak or pushing people to go against one another. They are sometimes called the '*stirrers*' and their lessons are mainly to learn forgiveness for others and themselves.

The heavy karma is in the 7 to 9 groups. These are the people who seek power and can be anybody such as politicians, top executives, secret societies, entrepreneurs or unsuspecting low profile people. To attain power through normal means like being elected by members of a group or the public for president of a society or country is very different from someone who rises to power through crooked means such as rigging an election or gunning down opposition or other foul means. The latter is dangerous and decision-making can be irrational and ruthless.

Why are some leaders appeared to be unbalanced?

The obsession for power stems from past events which may have brought them tremendous fear like treason, murder or mass destruction like Hitler's holocaust to wipe out the Jews with genocide. In order to overcome this fear, the unstable person wants absolute control at all costs to prevent any uprising to safeguard his security and people like Saddem Hussein comes to mind. These smart but imbalanced few are able to put on a front to camouflage their ambitions and it is not surprising that one or two can rise to the top with hidden penchant for power. But God has eyes; the chinks in their armour are easily spotted by keen eyes that are able to detect their unstable personalities through the occasional slip or 'flip flop' decisions on crucial matters.

Tragic death like assassination and hanging, are common for those in the top bracket of karma. The lesson is to gradually work out their fear and find alternative solutions to make sound decisions for harmony and peace but it will be a tough call. Fortunately there are only a handful of such people around and hopefully current world leaders are not one of them!

Is our conscious mind an obstacle to clear karma?

Self-realisation of your duality is key to rid all your undesirable traits carried forward from the past. But making that connection is not easy because there is an *'enemy'* within; the all powerful and distracting human mind. The conscious mind is fond of focussing mainly on the external world of fun and play and many people get carried away when having a good time. The mind feeds on human weaknesses such as ignorance, greed or desire. If you fail to use your will-power, you can be swayed by the mind and get attached to the many 'undesirables' and accept them as the way of life.

The mind is more than happy to support you in becoming unfaithful to your wife; scream and shout at those who do not agree with you and spend your wages on the racetrack instead of groceries for the family. It will encourage you to drink more alcohol to get high so that you will forget about the existence of the better half of the mind, *your conscience*, a good friend of the soul. On a lighter vein, I have my fair share of laughs on drunken tales and there is this unforgettable one that I love to share with readers. A spiritual healer of yesteryears was complaining about her drunkard husband. She was trying to explain that alcohol numbed the brain and . . . *'Satan takes over from there. His head will be filled with more blood; his voice becomes louder, behaviour becomes bolder; but this is not my husband anymore but Satan!'* The healer was trying to justify why she dumped her habitual drinking husband because she was fed-up 'arguing with Satan' every night!

Can the mind be trained to tap into some of the positive energy in us?

Definitely, when there is darkness there must be light. The Chinese call it *yin and yang* or the balancing of universal energy. We must learn to balance both negative and positive forces in us by training the mind. It should be understood that the mind is a lousy master but can be made to become an excellent servant at your disposal. The mind should only be used as *an instrument* to access your inner positive power—the soul. The unstable mind should always stay at the backseat and do not hesitate to say, *'Get thee behind me Satan,'* when confronted with tough decision making.

Is it necessary to observe certain rules before making a decision?

Your inner self is the storehouse of all your creative talents and is the more intelligent side of you that can differentiate between right and wrong action. Exercise your will-power and give some work to your conscience. This means you have to think first before taking any action. *'What are the consequences of my action?' 'Where do I draw the line?'* These are some of the key thoughts or *passwords* to awaken the soul. When you think along such lines, you are actually requesting assistance from your soul before making a decision. You are trying to draw on your positive force or the *'inner genius'* to meet the challenges of life. This is what balancing the energy means when you are attempting to blend both the conscious and unconscious mind as one.

By deploying both outer and inner consciousness, there will be more clarity because you have widened your options in decision-making instead of just giving an impulsive 'yes' or 'no' in tough situations. The unconscious contents when brought to consciousness can enhance the clarity of a situation because it has not been tampered with, stays intact and is our higher level of wisdom that *works* for us.

Are there other teachings on mental balance and detachments?

It is also interesting to note that the teaching of Buddha also portrayed the importance of restoring mental balance. Buddha taught his disciples to avoid two extremes in life. They are over-indulgence in the many pleasures of life and the opposite extreme of ascetic discipline or renouncing life. Neither path is meaningful to our existence. During the course of our life, there may come a time when we have to face certain extremities. But as long as we are not carried away and get entangled with any extreme, enlightenment can still be attained. This approach is called taking the *middle way*.

The Christians are also strong advocators in the balancing of one's action. The apostle Paul wrote to the Corinthians, '*Everything is permissible for me but I will not be mastered by anything*'. Self-discipline is the art in mastery. Those who seek freedom must learn how to master their five senses.

The first teaching of mental balance comes from Lord Krishna. In one of the passages from the Bhagavad-Gita he said, '*He who eats too much, he who fasts too much or sleep too much or too little cannot perform yoga*'. Krishna's message is echoed by the teachings of later spiritual masters regarding the practice of moderation in all activities.

What do you mean by 'enlightenment'?

We have been vague with the meaning of 'enlightenment' so far. It is timely now to explain further because enlightenment is the masterpiece of Buddha's teaching. Spiritually, it means *the end of suffering and the liberation of complete freedom to act through detachment.* The bondage to karma is broken.

Is it necessary to repeat simple lessons that are not life threatening?

Clearing karmic attributes is not only complex but the variations are almost endless. A person may be here for a simple task or given easy lesson such as learning to be tolerant. But if that person refuses to hear, think or *analyse* his or her problem, the simple lesson may be repeated in the next expression until the lesson becomes a part of life. For example; Natalie is a great cook and all her friends look forward to sample the yummy dishes she is fond of preparing at pot-luck parties. But Natalie has an ego problem and thinks she is the best cook and rarely gives credit to her friends' cooking. She has a habit of making comments like, 'too sweet,' 'too sour,' and so forth on dishes that are not hers. At times she refused to try out some of the food prepared by others as if she may be poisoned!

How is Natalie going to learn her lesson? A friend took her to one side and told her that derogatory comments on the food were impolite and unnecessary. She was *insensitive* to the friendly advice and instead, took offence to it. All that is required of her is to be less critical, be sociable and enjoy the evening. She failed to understand that the 'friendly advice' is a learning stage for her to *grow* from it even though it hurts at times. She is invited to a party mainly because she is expected to be good company and not to be a wet blanket giving the host a red face. She is given all the free time to work out her problems but how long would it take a sensitive and proud woman to be awakened? This is an example of repeated cycle of karma of a very minor problem common in people who are poor listeners.

What are the consequences of a person who uses 'black magic' to hurt someone?

It is well documented in many cultures that evil people resort to *'black magic'* to destroy others mainly because of petty jealousy, resentment or misunderstanding. Black magic is like *voodoo* and comes in many forms and *lower* spirits are used sometimes to cast a spell or put a curse on a person. It can also be used to destroy or move objects into one's own orbit for self-comfort or indulgence. This is heavy stuff and the person doing it will lead a life of not only unhappiness but of haunting guilt and pain in the present and next life as part of the law of cause and effect. In such a situation, a common sign is a lack of harmony in the family of the guilty party; either tragedy will strike or there will be long separation or little love shown by family members.

Happiness will elude the sinful person and the lesson to learn is to preach forgiveness, which can be a very daunting task as admission of guilt is a difficult one for many. There have been cases of similar stories where the guilty one tries to camouflage the guilt by being generous and kind towards selected groups who have sympathetic ears to his or her *'side of the story.'* This person would openly display generosity by shouting dinner or giving expensive gifts as if to let you know that 'I am not that type of person.' This is the way out to cover up *a hidden fear*, the greatest fear in humans. The world is a stage for all.

Why are we fond of finding faults with others?

Some of the qualities and faults we see in others are none other but those that are found in us and the difference is only in proportions. Recognition of them is only possible because they are a *reflection* of us. We are here strictly for lessons because we are imperfect beings: good and bad are in all of us but in different measures. Pride and prejudice are all part of our make-up and we seldom see our own shortcomings but more than happy to criticise others for the same weaknesses that are in us. Why are there so much greed, hatred, anger and quarrels everywhere? We simply can't stand those who behaved like us! Now you know who or what is the problem—*yourself.*

In order to seek wisdom and lead a meaningful life, we must learn to look upon only on the good qualities of others and ignore their faults. Love and harmony is all about being less critical on others.

What are some of the characteristics and saving grace for drug pushers and paedophiles?

These are the slimy ones with many faces to hide their identities and thrive on exploiting the innocence. The drug pusher is lazy to find a proper job and knows only how to take advantage of the weak that are adventurous and have the means. Wine, women and song are the life blood of the addicts and the pusher ensures they are well fed in order to empty their pockets. He destroys innocent lives as '*happy pills*' is an addiction that is hard to conquer when used regularly. The paedophile is no better; he cons kids by giving them the impression of a father image through kindness and showers them with sweet talks and gifts to win them over. When innocent children start to look up to him for support, the paedophile will show his true colour.

Both have low self-esteem inwardly but put on a false front and lying becomes second nature. They are not strong-willed people and are easy prey to the negative force, the conscious mind. They yield to temptation and their minds become the '*devil*' because they can be '*bought over*' by the negative force without much resistance. The devil will feed them with more cravings of their attachments until the devil has complete control over their lives. What is complete control? The drug pusher and the paedophile are no longer aware of the existence of their duality; the higher self—the number one enemy of the devil. The higher self is the only thing that can destroy the devil.

These undesirable elements of society are also flirting with the law in all their dealings and it will be a matter of time for karma to '*boomerang*' on them which will be without doubt, a painful one. There is no escape unless they repent quickly and mend their ways. This may happen when fear sets in especially when a friend is caught or constant warnings from closed friends or relatives get the better of them. When there's life, there is always hope for all kinds of sinners. It's all about determination to see life in a new light again.

Is there a time frame for those who wish to repent or reform?

No, there is no fixed timetable for anyone to change—it may take a month or not even a lifetime as it is based on free will or choice. It all depends on the urgency of the person wanting to reform compared to stubborn people without the will to repent. But because humans are spiritual beings, 'guardian angels' are fond of coming to the rescue so that a person's life is not put to waste. The divine works in wondrous ways—sometimes a person can be awakened suddenly because of remorse such as rejection from loved ones, loneliness, loss of self-esteem or desertion of 'friends' during his or her hour of need.

A soldier who has lived unrepentantly for five years and then decided to reform and make good, wrote a touching poem about his life and it deserves a mention here:

> *Blinded by pretty material things in my possession,*
> *the taste of easy living soon became an addiction.*
> *Blurry and dazed, false hope starts to open its gate,*
> *waiting for Satan the devil to raise its ugly head.*

Somehow, guardian angels came to my aid.
Someone must really think I shouldn't be dead.
Here is my chance to move to greener grounds.
Can I make that first step to turn my world around?

Struggled out of hell and saw that peaceful ray of light.
I wouldn't have survived without that ever guiding light.
Swallowed my pride and forced to start all over again.
Thank God, now I laugh with mum, dad and friends again.

'Soldier of Fortune' by F. Jason

Why are there so much aggression, anger, hatred and jealousy in our society?

If you have forgotten the meaning of spirituality, refer to it again. The majority of people concentrate only on the physical world and are obsessed with money, power, greed, status, desires and all kinds of attachments that sometimes prepared to attain them at all costs. Their undesirable urges are due mainly to depletion of spirit. This means they get attracted *only* to what their eyes can see. When they neglect the spirit in their heart, they see only darkness or evil. It should be obvious that when there is no light, everyone will be groping in the dark and throwing tantrums.

Humans *cannot* progress without spirit; the more we depart from it because of earthly desires, we become easy prey for the devil to possess our mind and happiness will elude us. The same principle applies to a nation. If the leader has no spiritual substance in him, democracy will be dead and there will be unfair distribution of wealth, corruption, revolts and civil unrest. He will rule with an iron fist with little justice and his country and people will not prosper. Take a good look at some countries rule by dictators and tyrants.

Live righteously and 'love your neighbour as you love yourself', and the divine will fight your battles.

It is worth repeating the belief of Mahatma Gandhi when he said that mankind is so sucked up with the materialistic world that they have forgotten the spiritual side in them and needed drums to be beaten into their ears!

Is over-indulgence bad karma?

Three elderly looking men in a retirement home were sitting on a bench discussing their life and health. 'I am 90 years old today,' Sunny said, 'and I can still read and write to my grandchildren because I have never taken a drop of alcohol in my life. I drink only fresh milk and fruit juices and watch my diet to stay healthy.' The second man, Micky said, 'I am 85 and can still beat my son in golf. My fitness and mental health is due mainly to the fact that I am a vegetarian.' The third man, looking the oldest of the three because of his deep wrinkles, was a bit agitated listening to his two friends and kept very quiet. 'What about you Willy, how do you account for your ripe old age?' Micky asked. With shivering hands and a stammering voice, Willy said, 'I was born rich. I ate only the best steak or lobsters with caviar; drank a bottle of brandy every day, smoked the darkest cigar and had a different woman every night!' 'Gee Whiz,' said Sunny, 'How old are you Willy?' With a tear in his eye and a choking voice, Willy said, 'I am 37, the doc checked me out this morning and told me that I am suffering from a terminal disease called *over-indulgence* and may not see my next birthday.'

Eat and drink in moderation and don't waste. Life is meant to be enjoyable if you know where to draw the line in both work and play. Remember *yin and yang*? It's all about balancing. Don't be like some sick tycoons who flaunt their wealth by 'rinsing' their mouth with *shark's fin soup*! A president's wife was reported to own a few thousand pairs of fashionable shoes and rarely wore them twice. To top it all, she never washed her underwear. She threw all the old ones away and wore only brand-new underwear everyday. If she's not here for a good reason, her karmic debts in later life would be horrendous!

Are family squabbles over inheritance bad karma?

'I'll see you in Court', is not uncommon between siblings when a deceased parent failed to make a will. Most matured adults are able to come to an amicable settlement while others can be messy especially when there is diverse financial background among family members. Sometimes when greed comes into the picture, it can be comical to hear the poor wants more and the rich wants all!

Inheritance is supposed to be a windfall and should be settled as soon as possible to brighten up the lives of the beneficiaries instead of turning it into a family feud where there are no winners. It is almost impossible to have a perfect settlement when someone died unexpectedly and did not leave a will. But as long as it is divided fairly to the *best* of your ability and with full disclosure, no one will be punished. But if someone wants to grab everything at all costs, karma will run its course in later life. This can be illustrated by an example. Your parents had passed on but left behind ten equal shares of property for each of the children. Some of your siblings may prefer cash for financial reasons; other may be ignorant on the true market value of their shares and you *offered* to buy up the shares at a very low price strictly for selfish gains. You may have bought up all the family's shares eventually for a *song* but is that good karma? You may end up owning a big home with many cars but your family members despise you and more often than not, you prefer to shy away from family events to save embarrassment. There is no peace of mind as your guilt will haunt you.

How does karma work on a stingy person and a generous one?

It is said that a miser is a person who thinks the future is uncertain. He will not spoil himself with the luxuries of life and more than happy to save every cent for a rainy day. Charity work like helping a sick relative and socialising can be a pain as they involve spending, smiling and dressing up. When you invite *Shylock* (the miser) to your home for a party it is a norm to bring small presents like a bottle of wine, dessert, fruits or any gift. But Shylock is likely to appear with 'two bunches of bananas'! (A Chinese expression—a sarcastic way of saying that the guest came empty handed; the hands are representative of two bunches of bananas)

Stingy people normally have longer working lives than others because they love the smell of money. But their bodies and bones may ache faster making them miserable in later life. Our existence is mainly to serve; if this divine law is neglected regularly, the ugly side of karma will take its course. Misers are unlikely to have a happy ending because they are too calculating, suspicious of others and rarely have sincere friends. But though misers aren't great fun to live with, they make wonderful ancestors!

A generous person is the reverse of Shylock; he makes friends easily and feels normal to shout beers or give a treat to his mates. He remembers the birthdays of loved ones and does his best to make people happy. When someone has a problem—whether emotional or financial—this great soul is always there to lend support. His later life is blessed because a kind act is *'rewarded with tenfold'* of the original deed. A good-hearted person may not end up being wealthy compared to the miser, but his life will be a happy one as there will be plenty of family support who see to it that he is comfortable—the grace of the divine.

Why do some people appear to have little dramas in life?

I am sure you have friends and relatives who are living a meaningful life with no apparent upheaval like traumatic events or hardship. It doesn't mean that every lifetime is of significant karmic importance because the soul needs periods of light karmic work between heavy ones to recuperate and balance the energy. But sometimes you are also given a *soft life* because you are here *partly to collect a debt* instead of making a repayment all the time!

Remember karma also means 'one good turn deserves another'? Very likely you may have done some very good deeds like saving somebody's life, prevented bloodshed in a family feud, sacrificed your life to help the poor or might have been a key figure in helping your community to prosper in a previous life. But your efforts went unnoticed. Compensation for your labour was given in the next expression. This may clear the air why so many different people strike the *lottery* every week or making easy money in the stock market by simply sitting at home!

Give an example of a punishment due to lack of trust.

A poisoned arrow pierced warrior Hor in the battlefield. His friends called the surgeon to have the arrow removed and the wound treated. The wounded man objected and said, *'Wait, before you pull it out, I want to know who shot this arrow. Was it a man or a woman? Was it someone of noble birth, or was it a peasant? What was the bow made of? Was it a big bow or a small bow that shot the arrow? Was it made of wood or bamboo? What was the bow-string made of? Was it made of fibre or rattan? What feathers were used? Before you extract this arrow, I want to know all about these things.'*

The poisoned arrow circulated the warrior's system quickly before all the questions could be answered. Hor was buried the next day with the arrow still stuck on his body! Do you sympathise with our long-winded warrior? He did not trust anyone even in the face of death but preferred to *blah, blah, blah*! If he allowed the surgeon to pull out the arrow immediately, his life may have been saved. What is the lesson? The message in Buddhism is to control your mind and tackle the most pressing issue first. The Chinese sum it up well, '*Shut your gap and cut the crap!*

'Can we have an example of heavy karma in the business world?

A classic example is the senior executive entrusted with the responsibility to set up a new market overseas. When given the power to call all the shots in the buying and selling areas, temptations started to creep in to make something from the side. The executive accepted a small bribe from a building contractor initially. When he got away with it the first time, he became bolder and took more bribes from different sources. When bad deeds go undetected; discretion, fair play and loyalty go to the wind and self-interest becomes paramount. Short-changing the company becomes a way of life. Whenever there's a business deal, our executive friend's final question is always, 'What's my benefit?' It was a matter of time before all the 'wheeling and dealing' were discovered and the executive was recalled to head office and put into cold storage.

This is heavy karma for a person in a leadership position to *abuse power* entrusted to him and put the company in disrepute at the same time. He became a lonely man as colleagues shun him for fear of being tagged as 'friends' of the bad guy. What will happen to such a person? Probably its payback time; what he had unscrupulously taken from others will be taken away from him in mysterious ways. He is likely to start from scratch again and learn the meaning of integrity and do his *dharma* or to work faithfully. It may not happen in this lifetime, perhaps the next one. Karma and reincarnation go hand in hand and work together like a rotating wheel. I can't help remembering a song by Tom Jones, '*Big wheel keeps turning, proud Mary keeps burning*!'

Is there any karmic trait that is hard to clear?

It has been revealed that one of the hardest traits to eradicate when performing karma is vanity or self-admiration. Vanity appears as if it has 'a thousand claws' to dig deep into the minds of its victims. This undesirable passion starts to surface at a young age and it is very hard to suppress and usually clings onto a person until death. The vain person *overestimates* his own intelligence and ability. He is fond of exaggerating and distorting the reality of a situation so that he can enjoy the limelight. He survives on being '*one-up*' over his fellow men.

I was in Singapore some years ago and found out that the locals there have coined a new word that I found it to very humorous and appropriate to describe 'Mr Vain.' The word is '*keia su*' in Hokkien dialect; the literal translation is 'scared of losing'. But it must be emphasised that every human being has his or her own weaknesses and everyone has a time-table to resolve them in the many journeys of life.

Are we constantly being judged for what we do on earth?

Some of the examples of human traits mentioned above are purely to illustrate the many levels of karma and the lessons to be learned in order to make the planet a better place to live. It must be emphasised that the universe does not judge, punish or condemn anything you have done whether in the past or present. Karma runs its course irrespective of good or bad deeds created. Earth is a planet of free choice and you are entitled to say, '*I'm leaving on a jet plane, don't know when I'll be back again*'.

When and how karmic lessons are learned?

Karmic lessons are so subtly designed by the divine that most of the time we are not aware what is actually going on. It usually occurs at a time when you least expected it; it could take place during normal dinner time with loved ones or simply watching TV or having fun with our partner or friends. Perhaps sharing a personal experience is appropriate here. My wife and I had a rare family outing with our son, daughter and grandson. We had a great time eating, laughing and even singing because we tested out a karaoke set in a shop.

When we finally got home after a fun day, the phone rang when we were just about to have dinner. It was a tradesman confirming his appointment for a skylight installation at our home the next day. My daughter Jasmine casually asked me, 'Is the tradesman reliable? Do you know anything about skylight?' All of a sudden, a rush of blood came to my head; those innocent words sounded more like questioning my integrity whether I have hired the right person for the job. I raised my voice in an agitated tone, 'Just let me handle it, okay?' The next statement from her, 'You don't have to raise your voice at me,' triggered off a silly argument over nothing. Our dark side started to surface and it was blah, blah, blah until dinner was thrown into the bin! It only dawned on me later that it was karma at work; we were on stage to be *tested* on a special lesson and failed miserably!

Humans are well known for having a bad temper. In order to better ourselves, we have to mellow down and not over react to harmless remarks or jump into wrong conclusion. We have to learn to diffuse a potential argument by managing our emotions and be less sensitive instead of getting all worked up like adding fire to fire!

When can a karmic bubble be burst?

We have no control *when* we will be on stage for karmic lesson but the consolation is that family members are usually selected as role players for our lessons. They are our *'punching bags'* and we get away with it most of the time because loved ones are usually 'soul mates' with a special bond who understand us better compared to outsiders. Imagine what will happen if we spew our frustrations and lose our cool in the workplace all the time? We are likely to get the sack and become professional job hunters! We are sensitive and emotional beings and fond of creating our own 'heaven and hell'. They are all part and parcel of human existence to enable us to *grow* from past mistakes. Everything we do or every small incident we encounter in our life is not there by accident or mere chance but the manifestation of a divine plan designed for karmic work to change us to a better person.

However, a lesson can be repeated one hundred times to no avail because we love to fight back—whether right or wrong—to salvage our pride. We are also given many chances to observe from other sources as well such as friends, relatives, workplace and the many movies and TV programs on *'anger incidents'* and their ramifications to help us open our eyes. But more often than not, we applaud violent programs on screen as strictly entertainment and not something to reflect and better ourselves.

When anger subsides, learn to sit back and analyse the cause of the problem rationally and see whether there could be *other* better options to diffuse an ugly conflict. You have to *believe* and work on it that there is a remedy for every problem. Realising the reasons that triggered off an argument is not good enough as that's not the end of it. There will be *more* unsuspecting tests round the corner to assess how well you have digested the lesson. You are on the mend only when you have mastered presence of mind in *anger management* during future awkward situations. The best part, a karmic bubble is burst and disappears; you have passed a test and a karmic debt is cleared.

What happens to a person who doesn't believe in change?

The divine works in mysterious ways and enlightenment can come swiftly at times when you are *genuinely* concerned about your shortcomings. Life is like doctors trying to treat diseases; they conduct research and experiments to find all the cures to get rid of ailments. If you insist on being stubborn and close a blind eye to all your *ailments*, you will end up a pain to everyone till your dying days. The worst part, you contaminated the atmosphere with negative vibration with your demise and took no role in planetary healing.

Is there a short cut to clear as much karmic debts as possible in this lifetime?

Where there's a will there's a way. When you *understand* that your existence is mainly to repay karmic debt, you automatically become more conscious of your behaviour especially in awkward situations. For example: your husband got all worked up when he read in the newspaper that the government is going to increase more taxes for property investors and plans to double the amount on fines for traffic offences. He was very annoyed and shouted, 'There's a bunch of incompetents running the nation; they simply have no vision!' Being a public servant yourself, you casually answered him by saying that the government might have good reasons for doing that. 'What do you know about politics!' was the angry reply. You realised that the conversation was about to get out of hand and decided to change the subject to prevent an argument. You showed *self-restraint* as part of the lesson. If you continue to act in similar fashion in future tight situations, your anger will slowly fade away as wisdom has got the better of you.

The divine is fond of selecting simple daily events for you to learn your lesson and its best you '*don't make 'mountains out of mole hills*' wherever you are! The learning arena could be at home, in the workplace, at social functions or in the sporting ground. Controlling your mind to respond appropriately is not a sign of a weakling that crumbles under pressure but a strong willed person who is not prepared to win *just for the sake of winning*, especially on trivial matters that are not life-threatening. Can you recall some past incidents where you did not act appropriately? You are fostering a path to enlightenment when serenity in any situation becomes second nature. Words like '*Well done,*' '*thank you*' or '*what a lovely thought,*' never hurt, in fact they resonate with God.

Is it true that marriage can change a couple to better people?

All the wise men say that '*marriage is made in heaven.*' Is there a hidden message? The divine works in wondrous ways and perhaps it plays *cupid* by matchmaking couples with different characteristics so that each can learn from the *blending process* of give and take and balance out the good and bad qualities of the couple. *Love* conquers everything, especially human faults. It's more like a mutual respect of behaviour or opinion for each other but only up to the point where the pattern is *not domineering*. Realistically, marriage is an ideal period to work out karma and what better time to learn than with a loved one? Husband and wife are together most of the time and they care for each other; emotional pain is more easily learned at home than elsewhere because '*I love you*', and '*I hate you*' including break-up and make-up are all part of life and lovers must learn to *forgive and forget* on trivial issues.

When the couple decides to have children, it is a natural process that every child is a *reinforcement of love* into the family as if the divine is injecting *vitamin TLC* (tender loving care) to strengthen the marriage. Home sweet home is the best place for children to learn about love and respect. We are vulnerable beings and attaining perfect harmony can be a tall order at times but at least a 'divine plan' has been set in motion.

What are some of the causes of broken marriages?

It is a Hindu belief that a marriage should be the *beginning* of courtship and love will blossom from then on. This ancient philosophy may be outdated but it has lots of merit because statistics show that divorce cases from Hindus are not as rampant as other races. Even modern Hindus still respect their old custom of 'arranged marriage' by parents where the woman never sees her husband until marriage. In western culture the woman seldom sees her husband after marriage! In our current society of *'permissiveness,'* some of the young prefer to jump the gun by living together during *friendship* and assume its *courtship*! When the relationship gets sour or stale, they move on and hope to start another fresh romance.

The concept of having *'no strings attached'* appears to be the prevailing trend for the adventurous. A playboy by the name of Kit once said he slept with a girl because he was attracted by the dimple on her face but there was no need to marry the whole girl. His mate Hoe chimed in and added that he only believed in wine, women and *so-long!* Is so-called 'modern lifestyle' conducive to successful living when a couple puts the cart before the horse by having a 'honeymoon' first and marriage on hold to a 'maybe'? Moral conduct is so slack these days and eventually the poor kids will suffer because some parents set bad examples.

In our contemporary time, there is little sex discrimination between job positions as women have proven to be just as good as men in many fields. Role reversal between husband and wife is on the increase in our society as it is no longer the norm that the man brings home the bacon. Women are less submissive to their husbands' demands compared to the past and are able to socialise just as much as their partners. If a man has roving eyes and enjoys a romantic fling in the office or prefers to keep a rendezvous with another, so can the woman in our present world of equal opportunity.

Fame and fortune, dissatisfaction, desire and greed are some common triggers for break-ups. What's more, the media is also responsible for compounding infidelity by *glamorising* divorces and affairs of celebrities such as actors, sportsmen and politicians like they are trend setters not realising these poor souls have plenty of karmic debts to pay in later life or the next expression!

Why are there so much domestic violence and unhappiness?

Many domestic turmoils are not due to unfaithfulness or infidelity but a lack of tolerance on *trivial* matters and reluctance to change for the better. Progress in life is change. All great people are aware that they are not perfect. They always try to soften, yield and listen deeply to the views of others for greater understanding.

Karma is hard to learn if you are not mature enough to see through your own flaws. When there are abnormal conflicts in your life, calm down and ask yourself: 'Why am I always quarrelling?' 'Am I a selfish and conceited person?' 'Can I do better?' is a great start as *self-appraisal* is always the best antidote to calm the storm. So before you start complaining that the wife's cooking is worse than what you had compared to your army days, count up to ten before letting off steam! A good marriage is all about *caring and sharing*, the gist of marriage vows. True love never runs smooth—don't be too one-sided on your *'likes and dislikes.'* If you dislike lamb but lover boy loves it, cook a good lamb dish and surprise him on his birthday. Guess how he would react for the effort?

Couples are team players; their matrimony vows are based on trust to keep the home fire burning. Discipline or self-control to walk the 'straight and narrow' is God's way to maintain happiness and matrimony bliss.

Should parents be respected all the time?

Francis Bacon says: 'the joys of parents are secret, and so are their grieves and fears.' All parents have aspirations for their children to be successful in life because their own flesh and blood is their pride and joy. But when children become grown-ups, parenting can become *growing pains* especially as the young today are better educated and more exposed to the *'going-ons'* in the outside world. Many appear to have minds of their own and seldom heed advice from parents who are commonly regarded as 'conservative' or from the 'old school'. Maybe so, but it is sad to see the young displaying their arrogance or superiority to run down parents when good advice is taken the wrong way. As long as children are still living in their parents' home, they should show self-restraint by showing gratitude and respect to parents who gave them life, took care of all their needs including cleaning their bottoms!

Parents always have the safety and welfare of their children at heart and can sometimes be notoriously protective and strict, particularly with their budding daughters who are between pigtails and cocktails. Can you blame them when parents sense that their children are with bad company or developing a bad habit like regular night clubbing and mingling with shady crowds? The ideal home environment should be filled with loving energy and looked upon as a haven of restfulness. The young must not disturb this peace. It is the duty of parents to provide comfort and support while children learn about discretion and respect. If the family motto is *'learn to love,'* what better place can you find to learn and repay karmic debts?

When should parents cease to control their children?

Take a cue from nature. A bird would protect its young and looks for insects and worms to feed them. When the birdies start to grow and sprout wings, the mother would teach them to fly and look for food. When the birds are big enough to fend for themselves, they are 'shooed' away from the nest and the young birds are on their own. Likewise, the animal kingdom has a similar style of upbringing. Lions and tigers protect their cubs with their lives. Once the young are able to hunt and kill, they go separate ways and the mother looks forward to her next lot of litters for training.

Parents have the responsibilities to provide, guide and give their children the best education they deserve. When children mature to adulthood and are able to find employment or get married, parental control and attachment should be slowly withdrawn. One of the key problems with parents is that they get unduly upset when their children do not turn up the way they expect; it could be a choice of profession, circle of friends or even marriage. Everyone has to pay karmic debts in different ways, sometimes the hard way.

The many journeys of life are lessons to be learned for the traveller and they have to be experienced and *not* protected. Nature is our best teacher showing us the countless examples that nothing is permanent: a beautiful rose plant can wither away and rivers can run dry over time. Perhaps my personal experience is helpful regarding detachments. I used to love goldfish and fond of buying unusual species to beautify the fish tank. I even gave each fish a name but they normally can't last for five years and losing one of them is like losing a family member. My children shed tears when we buried the fish like a human being under my favourite plant and we had many sleepless nights. But is that right or simply emotions of sentimental people? Attachment or clinging to love ones on a long term basis is no more than self inflicted misery. It is common to see some conservative parents suffocating their children with their 'outdated views' on how the children should live. This may be one of the reasons why their sons and daughters are living farther and farther away from them!

Parents must accept the fact that every new generation is expected to be a smarter generation and that's what progress is all about. Give good advice but *'your wish is my command,'* doesn't work well any more in the new age. Follow the flow and learn to let go and *back off.* Look after yourself and pray for the children's happiness as everyone has a chosen path in life.

Can we help others to clear their karma?

Do you sometimes have a strange feeling that you are an 'observer' and not an active participant when interacting with people? You may be chatting with a friend who suddenly got agitated over a casual subject or event and started to lose his cool. You sympathised with him and tried to offer good advice knowing that his reasoning was illogical and very uncharacteristic of him to behave like he was possessed by a demon. In such a situation, it is likely that you have been specially selected as the 'angel' to help your friend clear his karma. Whether your friend accepts or rejects your advice is entirely up to him because either way, karma runs its course. The strange part with such situations is that you don't get offended even though when your friend gave you the 'thumbs down'; in fact, you get a happy feeling when everything sinks in.

Must we go all out to help someone in need?

The irony of life is that although to be kind or generous is an admirable quality, it is unnecessary to *go overboard* in helping others. To give an analogy: imagine that a log blocks the flow of a running stream. As a responsible person, you lifted out the log and allowed the stream to flow smoothly again. But how the stream runs its course should be of little concern to you because nature takes over from there.

'A friend in need is a friend indeed,' doesn't mean you have to take over your friend's life and allow that person to laze around and enjoy life while you do all the hard work. The friend should take the initiative to approach you when he or she needs help and ancient wisdom of 'ask, and you shall be given,' should be the way to go. Don't make decisions for others when your advice is not solicited.

Being a '*busybody*' may be a harsh word, but this is a fact of life. Every person should learn to resolve his difficulties as much a possible in order to learn from experience and fend for himself. Don't fall into the trap of *misguided* responsibilities that everyone needs your help as you may have an ego problem! Enough has been said that everyone has different spiritual journeys to repay karmic debts. When too embroiled with another person's state of affairs, you are actually trying to take over his or her karma on top of your own and that is *double trouble*!

Humour

The Best Medicine

A handsome but lonely Kevin decided to see a fortune-teller and find out when he will get married.

'Your stars are really shinning today', said the gypsy. 'What's more, I am so excited for you because you are going to meet your future wife today. But be warned; this woman only wants a husband who is generous and you have to shower her with expensive gifts on your first meeting to impress her. She will be in Gabbie's café opposite the road in ten minutes time and you have to hurry. She will be wearing a white dress and carrying a red handbag.'

Kevin was very excited and gave the gypsy a fat tip. Immediately after he left, a voice from a hidden tape-recorder under the table screamed; 'Ma, what's wrong with you? I'm supposed to be wearing black today and now I've to change all over again!'

KARMA — PART II

Did Jesus Christ absolve the sins of the world from his crucifixion?

If yes, why are we still having wars, terrorism, sufferings, crimes and poverty everywhere? The Bible says that the last breath from Jesus on the cross was: '*Father, forgive them for they know not what they have done.*' Those are very saintly and touching words that could melt a cold, cold heart. But *who* heard those final dying words or were they simply the concoction of gospel writers intending to play on the emotions of simple people of earlier times?

The Bible is filled with countless quotations and sometimes it makes one wonder whether tape-recorders are a recent invention or have existed during the time of Jesus. The reality of life is that '*crime does not pay,'* and that is why we have law courts, prisons, detention centres, electric chairs and firing squads to punish criminals, murderers and evil-doers. Jesus Christ, despite all his glory, *cannot* take away your karma because universal truth is such that every person is given a *choice* to choose the life he or she wants to lead. Do you believe in *Santa Claus* or is it just a myth to bring some joy to the world?

Is there such a thing as national karma?

In my opinion, yes. Look at the Jews today; they are still fighting for a country to call their own and have been either driven away or at war. Through the centuries, the kings, tsars and conquerors alike, have made sporadic attempts to stamp out the small but stubbornly burning flame of Jewish culture. Why? If you go back to biblical times, Moses was given the instruction by God to build a special temple as a *House for God.* Moses made the pledge to God and his people of Israel were able to escape from persecution by the Egyptians through God's guidance.

Remember the story regarding the *parting* of the Red Sea (which may not be entirely true) to enable the Jews to escape? But when Moses and his people were led to the promised land, Moses was too involved defending his people from the Romans and Egyptians. His son David could do no better as the Jews were always under threat and David did not have the time or resources to upkeep his father's promise to God. But finally David's son, Solomon, was able to build the long awaited Temple for God. But Solomon was like a modern day *playboy:* he had many wives and allowed his women to do as they pleased. The women worshipped all sorts of deities in the temple and forgot that the temple was meant to be for *God alone.* The sacredness was gone, and the temple was like a *playhouse* for the women! This is *probably* one of the main reasons why the Jews until today are faced with hardship as their forebears created the bad karma through a broken promise.

It grieves me to relate the history of the Jews because I have worked for a Jewish company previously and those I have known have proven themselves to be highly intelligent people with good business sense and integrity.

Has any nation taken the initiative to build a 'new' Temple for God?

It may be of interest for those who are not aware that Japan has taken the initiative to build the *'Main World Shrine'* or *Suza* for Almighty God after the failure from the Jews. This project was mooted by *'Sukuinushisama,'* (Great Saviour) the founder of *Mahikari* in Japan since 1959, a true light spiritual organisation where the humble founder receives direct revelations on Divine Principles and the greater Divine Plan for the world. Strangely, prophecies by clairvoyant Edgar Cayce, Jesus Christ and various religious texts have predicted that the world would flock to the East to seek universal truth. Nostradamus said: 'And from the East a Great Initiate will be seen who will bring a new light. He who is awaited so expectantly will never return to Europe, but will appear in Asia'.

Suza was completed in the 1980s in the tranquil and peaceful mountain city of *Takayama*, meaning *sacred high mountain*, in the district of Hilda, in central Japan. Takayama will become the new 'Mecca' for all religions because God's Light or energy is *enshrined* in the Suza for humans to have *direct communication* with God. Sukuinushisama pointed out that when Suza is completed, Divine Light will increase enormously throughout the world as part of *cleansing* of the old energy and the planet will become a better place to live. Suza only reveals *universal truth* for human enlightenment and all are welcome because it has nothing to do with religion, race or colour but a *unifying force* for the population of the world as part of the Divine Plan. Sukuinishasama has passed away and is currently succeeded by his daughter, Oshienushisama, as leader of Mahikari.

Many will agree that because of the initiative taken to construct Suza, God now *guides* the destiny of Japan and it will only go forward as a nation. For starters, Japan has *to stoop to conquer* after the defeat in the Second World War. It started from scratch again and despite the lack of natural resources, it is now the biggest exporter of cars, computers and cameras. It has one of the best transportation and education systems coupled with the fact that Japan has the lowest crime, divorce and hard drug cases in the world, making it very difficult for lawyers and conman to survive there. Respect for the elders and self-discipline are the many strengths of the Japanese: they courteously bow to all and look after their health well by eating mostly natural food. I was told that Japanese seldom overeat and obesity is looked upon like almost committing a crime! The police force don't see much action as drug trafficking, robberies, riots or unruly demonstrations are rare in the land of the rising sun. Obviously the children are well brought up to respect parents and the law and such desired qualities are fast disappearing in many societies. This is probably one of the key factors why many nations are bogged down with violence and economic woes as discipline is not taught at grass roots to show constraints in lifestyle.

Sukuinushisama is one of the very few anointed persons in the modern age to unite all races through direct revelations of divine principles to enable the world to strive for peace and harmony. Such revelations conform with *celestial messengers* like Kryon as both sides of the veil bring the same message of heavenly love. It will be a matter of time for many religions to become a thing of the past as they contain *only fragments* of universal truth that do not resonate with human psyche. The various religions today are based mostly on 'man-written' doctrines and *not* the teachings of *true* prophets or messengers of God. Jesus Christ was undoubtedly a great soul as he taught his followers that only humility and non-caring of wealth (greed) would bring mankind together as *one* because human survival is all about *love*. Unfortunately the importance of living a simple but caring life faded away like passing clouds. Greed and power got the better of leaders who took advantage of their positions and exploited the gullible with false teachings and many became slaves of religious leaders. A true prophet like Buddha was able to see the steady decline of religion and prophesised that Buddhism would fade away over time as future generations will have the intelligence to know what's best for them.

Is there also such a thing as 'community' Karma?

If there is karma for a nation, there is also state, provincial or community karma. This is all about leadership—if the state premier, mayor or sheriff does not practice what they preach, the state or community under their charge will suffer because of broken promises or obligations. There will be unfair taxes to keep the economy going and normal facilities for better living such as proper transport, education and hospitals will be inefficient and the people will have to bear the brunt. Lip service appears to be a peculiar trait among inefficient politicians and the world is littered with them. Karma is all about cause and effect. Greed, power, deceit and an uncaring leader are the quickest ways to bring down a nation or community and Saddem Hussein is a good example. Without mentioning names, look at some of the countries going to the dogs today because the rulers are more interested in *grabbing* as much as they can instead of *doing* as much as they can! Why? Not many people have the guts to fight back because they are too scared to change the system because they might be jailed or killed.

Is freedom of expression good karma for a nation?

Definitely—many nations are showing signs of prosperity when the people's voices are heard because success is two-way traffic. As long as democracy is not dead and there is no rigging in voting during election time, that country is expected to enjoy peace and harmony because a clean nation deserves clean living. A glaring example is China: there was a cultural revolution in the late 1980s when university students revolted against their government in Tiananmen Square because there was no freedom of expression at work and play. The Red Army took stern action by either putting the students behind bars or shooting defiant students and threatened to run them down with tanks as seen on TV world-wide. The students were prepared to die as martyrs for their country and the ruling party cannot continue to shoot their own unarmed 'sons and daughters' and show the world the barbaric ways they adopt to curb national unrest.

Political power is no longer through the barrel of a gun. The dissension and shame are on those who abuse their authority by ignoring the needs of the people who have lived in silence for too long. Why can't the people be allowed to have their voices heard instead of crushing them into muteness? Traditional *fear-based* policies need reforming to meet the changing pattern of modern society. The bulk of the population is better educated today and are entitled to higher expectations and values. Reforms on strict laws that used to tie down freedom are being rectified and it soon becomes evident that such drastic changes are short cuts to national progress. It is all about restoring balance and uniting the people in a fair and just method to keep abreast with changing times. Look at China today—the old '*bamboo curtain*' is now the most sought after market in the world and businessmen and tourists want a piece of the action in Beijing, Shanghai, Quandong or in any major cities there.

Humour

The best medicine

The politician decided to change his campaign strategy by canvassing in the remote areas populated by the African natives.

'The time has come for all you hard working people to have control over your destiny,' he started off his speech. From the crowded field came a responding chorus, 'Sokitomi, sokitomi!'

Sensing an enthusiastic crowd, he continued, 'If you vote for me, I will make sure the railroad and the bus lines will be connected to your land. I will build schools and hospitals in this forgotten place.' There was a thunderous roar from the natives again, 'Sokitomi, sokitomi!'

After the speech, the local chieftain invited the politician and his guide for tea at his nearby home. While walking there, they had to climb over a fenced up area reserved for the bulls to do their studwork.

'Bwana, be careful, sokitomi everywhere,' the guide said. The familiar word rang a bell and the politician asked what it meant. 'In your language,' said the guide, 'it's called bull shit!'

Chapter 4

MYSTICS

Creation

*The universe comes forth from Brahman
and will return to Brahman.
Verily, all is Brahman.*

Upanishad

Daylight comes, night falls, the season changes. Rain appears in big drops; all living organisms come to life. Wind blows, storm ends, cleansing for earth is done. What's more, on a moonlit night, away from the glare of city lights, look up to the sky and silently admire the awesome array of stars. They sparkle like diamonds lighting up the sky in the stillness of the night. Sometimes words simply cannot describe the exquisite splendour of nature and you have a strange feeling that there is a more powerful force up there as if smiling down on you.

The wonderful chi

Why do city folks fond of going to the countryside to take a break? Is it an inner urge to get away from a man-made world of buildings, polluted air and 'grab-cash' society so that they can recharge their batteries by connecting with nature that is forever alive and vibrant? Are we part of nature? Try this; stop thinking for a moment and empty your mind for a minute until you hear *only* buzzing sound of insects. Hold that sound and you are likely to become more aware of the wonders of nature before you; the heavenly sound of the running stream, the caressing breeze, friendly chirping of birds, sweet fragrance of flowers and the majesty and sacredness of the mountains and sea. By restoring and invigorating the natural awareness in the heart of our being, we transform life into a sacred expression of our unity with nature and all aspects of the universe. All living things are composed of primal energy, sometimes also known as universal energy, divine spirit, life force, *prana* to Hindus, *ka* to Egyptians, *ki* to Japanese or simply *chi* in Taoism.

When you are able to appreciate and pay tribute to nature, you become part of it as the blending of *oneness* is felt within you. Give this holy essence from within to surface more often by switching off the mind and immerse yourself into nature's world of *light and sound*. Nature is harmony and balance; it correlates to all living things like orchestrating its own symphony. *'The hills are alive with the sound of music, with songs they have sung for a thousand years . . . My heart will be blessed with the sound of music, and I'll sing once more.'* Those lyrics were beautifully sung by Julie Andrews.

God does not play dice

> *Why does the sun go on shining?*
> *Why does the sea go to shore?*
> *Why do the birds go on singing?*
> *Why do the stars glow?*

Lyrics from 'End of the World'

No 'big bang'

Some scientists are still confident that the universe came about because of the *'big bang.'* They will get grey hair at a young age because it will be a hard struggle to substantiate the endless 'missing links' of the theory which are wider than the sea! They may have vague clues on certain physical aspects of life, but what about DNA, complexities of brain cells, the five senses and especially the existence of the soul and afterlife? Chance evolution or life originating by accident is so remote that it prompted even Charles Darwin to admit: *'I can never regard the immense and admirable universe to have emerged merely by purposeless chance.'* The most famous statement against the big bang theory comes from Einstein when he says; *'God does not play dice.'*

Treasure Hunt

Creation has long been completed before mankind walk the earth. This means that the entire contents of all time and all space in our planet are fixed in advance *unknown* to us. Nothing new has been created, they are there all the time, only waiting to be discovered or manifested. What is called creativity is only that process of becoming aware of what already *IS*. You simply become aware of increasing portions of that which already exists. It is like a game of *'Treasure Hunt,'* where all the treasures are hidden in different places and you have to search for them and finders are keepers. It is all there for you to create what you want with nature's five elements of mineral, wood, water, fire and earth. It is only a matter of whether you have the *know-how* to blend the elements with one another in perceived patterns to bring out the imbalances as by themselves, each element is quite empty.

The Chinese *fung shui* is based on blending the elements for harmony and prosperity at home and at work. Consider the marvellous *aloe vera* plant, the nutritional mushroom *lingzhi*, all the minerals, gases, oil and natural resources on earth; they have been around since ancient time but its up to the modern herbalists, doctors, scientists, geologists and engineers to *research* and blend the products with the right ingredients or materials to ensure all the benefits are available to mankind.

DNA

In the past, it used to be common for criminals to walk away free from charges because of lack of evidence for conviction. Look at what DNA has done to put guilty parties in prison. Many previously unsolved crimes are back in Court as new evidence has surfaced, thanks to DNA. Is this discovery something new? It's in our blood cells all the time but we were not smart enough then to understand its significance. Behold, dreams are still beyond the thinking of man and the complexity of the human brain remains a biological frontier for our scientists to pool their knowledge and sort it out.

But don't despair; many *unknowns* still surrounding us are part of the grand plan of the Divine. This is where slow and steady wins the race. The unknown is fertile ground for mankind to continuously explore and search for knowledge to enable us to find our real strength. If everything is *known* to the world, why are we here? They will be no challenges to test our knowledge or curiosity, no adventure to unmask the mystery or any excitement to keep our adrenalins flowing.

Born Free

> *Born free, as free as the wind blows,*
> *as free as the grass blows,*
> *born free to follow your heart.*

Lyrics from 'Born Free'

Saints and sinners

We have heard of common phrases like, '*We are all born to be slaves,*' and '*all men are born equal.*' The formal sounds very demoralising and lazy bones take it literally by refusing to get up early! The latter is encouraging as there is hope for the action minded because all of us is given a gift from God the day we are born: *the divine soul* that is endowed with the same creative and imaginative power for everyone. There is no such thing as someone is given a 'smarter' or better soul compared to another during birth. We are born equal; this means the *inner self* of everyone possesses the same essence or intelligence irrespective whether we are saints or sinners.

All saints and sinners have visions or dreams. The subtle difference is that they see the *same truth* from various aspects. Every person has his or her own believe system. It's all about rationalising; what is good for one may appear bad or evil to another. For example: the sinners, false masters, conman and all sorts of crooks see their truth in exploiting the gullible for abundance and power. On the other hand, the saints, the virtuous or the good guys have a different approach to work ethics; they work with a *conscience* and are guided by their heart to ensure justice and love for mankind. The simple *truth* about life is this: what you are is what you *believe* you are. Your life is not determined by what you have done; but what you *expect*. The quality of your life on earth is dependent on your imagination how best to survive. It's all about how well you are able to bring forth the consciousness from within to work out things for you. Your destiny is dictated by your *beliefs*. Such simple truth is rarely taught in religions because mystery holds power.

The Human Brain

If paranormal phenomenal are genuine,
the key to understanding them may lie
in the study of the human brain.

Unnamed doctor

Of late, medical experts are starting to open their eyes on the supernatural as more unexplained phenomena are beginning to surface outside the realms of medicine. Psychologists and doctors have discovered that some of their patients are able to 'cure' themselves without medication when they put their mind to work. A medical expert says, '*The human body experiences a powerful gravitational pull in the direction of hope. That is why the patient's hopes are the physician's secret weapons. They are the hidden ingredients in any prescription*'. It should be clear by now that certain ailments are all in the mind and the power of suggestion to change the mood and emotion influence the health of a person.

The natural forces surrounding us have impacted human behaviour and the focus now is on the biological make-up of people; the conscious and the unconscious mind. There are simply too many paranormal events happening and the workings of the mystics cannot be ignored. Because of many unresolved events, people from all walks of life are starting to turn to *metaphysics:* the study of situations that are not yet fully understood, and which perhaps, have a spiritual connection to them. What about *clairvoyance?* Its common knowledge now that many police work including espionage, in the international fronts relies on clairvoyants for answers in mysterious cases. If it were 20 years ago, the layman may laugh at this because of ignorance as such information is rarely made known to the public and is a closely guarded secret. The police chief would be quick to deny suggestion of 'psychic help' that may undermine their intelligence work or put the clairvoyant at risk.

Today we have many TV programs such as 'Medium' and 'Ghost Whisperer', linking police work and ghost busters.

Magnetic Energy

A heartening breakthrough only took place not long ago when researchers discovered that magnetic waves or vibrations are constantly penetrating and bombarding the atmosphere from outer space. All living organisms: humans, animals, plants, including minerals, cannot be shielded from this 'downpour' and they have telling effects on all life forms on earth An astonishing discovery was made when it was found that a complex magnetic field not only establish the pattern of the brain at birth, but also provided *direction and lessons* to be learned during our entire lives.

It was further ascertained that our nervous systems are superb receptors of electro-magnetic energies enabling the ten million cells in our brains to form a myriad of possible circuits through which electricity can channel. This discovery has triggered the likelihood that the combination of minerals and chemical elements, together with the electrical cells of our bodies and brain, do respond to the magnetic influence of every sunspot, eclipse and planetary movements. There is no doubt that planet earth is actually a gigantic magnetic field working in unison with other planets. In a nutshell, the universe *controls* our lives.

Hippocrates

As Hippocrates, the Greek father of medicine observed, *'From the brain and the brain only arise our pleasures, joys, laughter and jests, as well as our sorrows, pains, grief and fear'.* The brain is indeed the master organ, controlling all other organs and systems in our bodies. Many people have likened the brain to a computer. But computers cannot laugh and no computer has ever fallen in love. If, by some strange chance, we had never seen a computer and had found one on the Moon, we would soon have unravelled its mysteries, awesome as they might seem. Nothing found in the universe compares with the complexity of the human brain, which remains the great *biological frontier.*

Without our brain we could not breathe, process our food, get rid of wastes. How precisely it works—what in the brain does what—we are only beginning to discover. Neuro-scientists hope to plot with the precision of finest mapmakers or cartographers, the millions of micro-contours of this uncharted world. The voyage of discovery is enormously challenging, inside the brain are some 100,000 million cells or neurons. The cartographers' job is to identify how—when we retrieve a fact from our memory, for example, which piece in the puzzle come into play. But at present, it is not even clear what it is that has a path until one sees the subtle order. How long do you think our experts can jump and scream, *'Eureka'?* To pose another question: is *somebody* up there or *somewhere* controlling our progress for some unknown reason?

Dreams

> *Memories, light the corners of my mind.*
> *Misty water coloured memories,*
> *Of the way we were . . .*
> *Memories, may be beautiful and yet*
> *What's too painful to remember,*
> *We simply choose to forget.*
> *So is the laughter . . .*

Lyrics from 'The Way We Were'

When we start to snore and wander off to dreamland, we are at once both observer and actor of that disoriented theatre of the sleeping mind. Heavily influenced by memory, dreams are plainly much more than memory, for they regularly deal with events that have not happened, in places that are not real. Dependent on imagination, dreams are yet more vivid, emotionally intense and *uncontrolled* than any waking fantasy. And though dreams are not like everyday reality, they often seem strangely real and tangible. Small wonder then, that people have persistently felt that dreams could be understood as messages. But messages from where? From ourselves? From other minds? From the gods? From the dead? And, perhaps, most importantly of all, from whatever source, how best might such messages be interpreted?

It is without doubt that that there is a connection between the dream state and the waking state, for the dream is put together from the *materials* taken during the waking state. But *how long* have we been in the *waking state*, or events going on in our lives since the soul keeps coming back to earth for incarnation? The human brain can only retain memory of this life but the soul keeps all the *records* of past lives. Dreams are often a part of the subconscious memories and need careful analysis and understanding. Literal interpretations are of little value in the majority of cases because dreams are clothed *in symbolism*. We have to piece them together like a puzzle before they make sense most of the time. When a person starts to dream, the *soul* becomes the key player in a *timeless arena* where we are still struggling to find the *bridge* to a part of the mind that is hidden from a waking world.

Dreams can be divided into the following groups:

a) *The sensual dream*

Sigmund Freud once argued that the strange creatures and confusing events in our dreams were symbols of thwarted desires too frightening or shameful for conscious thought and we disguised fulfilment through dreams! Modern analysts tend to disagree and maintain that pleasurable dreams are connected with anything that gives pleasure to the body, including eating, drinking and a good massage! Such dream may make us blush but spirit does not hide: it only *reveals* our true nature. Our deep secrets and actions are exposed in dreams but the revelations do not mean that we are all sex maniacs at heart!

b) *The projected dream*

This is the type normally studied in the mystery schools. A spiritual master is able to use the forces of nature and appear in the dream of an individual, sometimes a student of the master, and instruct or communicate in the dream state. This can be referred to as *'soul to soul'* communication. It is well documented that spiritual masters prefer to instruct their *'chelas'* or students through dreams because they (the souls) share the same energy and instructions are better understood.

c) *The memory dream*

This is probably the most relevant for this chapter. It consists primarily of past lives. This type reveals *karma* now in our life and tells us *why* we are here. The dream is trying to reveal the cause of your psychological or emotional fears in your present life. Take stock from memory dreams for they are there to show you past mistakes so that change can be made to improve your life *now*. There are many people who laughed or get upset with dreams upon waking, 'I had a stupid dream,' not realising that they were actually stupid in some past lives! The message is, 'stop making the same mistake!'

d) *Spiritual dream*

This type consists of precognition, soul projection and clairvoyance. It opens the future time track so we can see into it. Such level of dream is confined to prophets, sages, shamans and those very high up on spiritual matters who can predict the fortunes of their people like impending drought, natural disaster or war. Some have also excess to the *Akashic* records or Divine Consciousness; a complete record of each person's history of past lives. The Akasha is comparable to tiny files or a deck of cards that can be spread out like a fan where each card contains the record of a *single* life experience on earth with vivid details.

When you request a spiritual master to look into your Akashic records, he would normally pick out one or two *cards* that have bearing or relevance to your present life. For example: you wanted to find out why you have such a rotten life—broken marriage, job switching all the time, longing for good friends and hardly any fair share of the good life. The Akashic record may reveal that your miserable life is due to *karma* at work. During one of your past incarnations, you were a tribal chief and a great warrior. You conquered new land and accumulated great wealth but you were very selfish; you kept all the wealth to yourself and allowed your people to starve. You were feasting every night with your many wives and did not even bother to save the crumbs for the poor because your pet dogs had the first bite! Your unhappiness in this life is all about *payback time* for the miseries you have caused to others during a past life.

But be warned; there is *only* a handful of living spiritual masters who have excess to the Akashic records. Rumours are rife that a *scam* is going on where certain charlatans claimed to have the ability to act as a channel for an ascended master or even 'spiritual master' from another planet, who is able to access past lives of individuals. There is a code of conduct among *true* psychics not to meddle into people past lives as it is like an intrusion to privacy. If the code is not diligently observed, his or her gifted power will either diminished or completely taken away. True psychics live humbly and rarely advertise their gifts. The frauds are fond of telling their clients of colourful past like being a king or princess in a former life to keep the gullible client interested and happy to part with a fee. Most false masters have an uncanny talent to play on the emotions of insecure people and cash in on them.

e) *Creative dream*

This is one of those dreams that can change our lives completely and we wish to have more of them! This is usually a *flash* of brilliance or a new idea to resolve a problem. Sometimes it can be simply inspirational to keep you going. Such dream is normally manifested when one has been concentrating very hard on a situation *as if subconsciously* asking for help from the divine.

The richly documented phenomenon of the creative dream illustrates the mystery that even today surrounds the sources of dreams. The lore of dreaming is replete with examples of poets dreaming verses, writers conjuring up plots, musician discerning melodies and scientists discovering truths that had eluded them during their waking labours. The result, apparently a kind of synthesis of thought and unconscious reverie, has often been a gloriously original burst of creativity and inspiration.

A strange dream by the 18th century Italian composer, Tartini, is a point in case. He dreamed that he made a deal with *Satan* for knowledge in exchange for his soul. He handed his violin for the devil to play. 'How great was my astonishment,' he wrote, 'when I heard him play with consummate skill a sonata of such exquisite beauty as surpassed the boldest flights of my imagination.' When he awoke, he grabbed his violin and 'tried to retain the sounds I had heard. But it was in vain. The piece I then composed, however, '*The Devil's Sonata*,' was the best I ever wrote, but *how far below* the one I had in my dream!'

Sitting Bull

What about the mystical *vision*? Of all the richly documented reports about people praying and hoping to see a vision for guidance, perhaps the best classic is the legendary tale of the spiritual and great Red Indian chief, *Sitting Bull*. During the days of the wild, wild west in the 1800s, General Custer of the US army discovered vast amounts of gold in the Black Hills of Dakota, the sacred ground and home of Sitting Bull and his people. When there's gold there's greed; prospectors and white settlers swarmed into the Black Hills like hornets, bullied and killed the Indians who crossed their path. The army gave an ultimatum that Sitting Bull and his tribes must evacuate to a reservation or their land would be taken by force. But the Indians refused to budge and were prepared to defend their sacred land and hunting ground with their lives. Sitting Bull was aware that the hard decision taken could be the end of his people; they were simply no match for the US army who were better equipped with cannons and automatic guns compared to their outdated rifles and bow and arrow, so the story goes.

The troubled chief retreated to a mountain, performed the ancient *sun dance* ritual and prayed to the *Great Spirit* for guidance and protection on the plight of his people. He did not eat or sleep for two days and nights trying to induce a vision and was losing strength quickly. The Great Spirit finally answered his call and in a trance, Sitting Bull '*saw hundreds of white soldiers and horses leaping over him and falling like grasshoppers from the sky!*' It dawned on him that his vision was a *new war strategy;* in order to see *leaping horses,* he had to fight from underground to win the battle. With news of the coming attack from General Custer, the Indians dug holes and trenches, camouflaged them with shrubs and stayed underground. When the unsuspecting cavalry troops were within shooting range, a surprise attack was launched from all directions and the US army suffered its worst defeat with more than 2000 men killed in what has come to be known as '*Custer's Last Stand.*'

Cate and Jo

What about modern day inspirational dream of two sisters, Catherine and Jo whom I know very well? They were staunch Sai Baba devotees and occasionally had to play hosts to overseas visitors.

On one such occasion, the sisters decided to change the standard program of having the usual get together dinner and a tour of the local Sai Baba Centre to something more entertaining. They thought of a musical program with spiritual songs and local dances to liven up the evening. But who was going to supply the music and there was never a song written by anybody in the group. While still very focused on how best to entertain the visitors, Jo had a strange and inspiring dream. She heard *music and lyrics sung by a heavenly voice* as though encouraging her to memorise the tune. When she woke up, the dream was still very fresh in her mind and she took out a pen and wrote down every verse of the song. When every word was written down, the dream started to fade away.

Jo began to hum along with the words and was astonished when she realised there was an '*inner voice*' helping her to sing and the tune got better and better until it was too good to be true! Inspired and happy as a lark, she rushed to Catherine's place and told her about the dream. Cate was a piano teacher and within hours, they were able to compose a melodious song backed up by the right music. When they performed as a duet for the visitors that night, the audience was not only spellbound by the *heavenly* sound of music that touched their heart, but also fully convinced that the memorable evening was a gift from Baba! The song is now tape recorded and circulated to most Sai Baba centres throughout the world. Is this a reward from the divine to the sisters because of their *dharma* or strong commitment to serve well?

Death and Babies

Why dreams that appeared to be prophetic should often be the bearers of tragic tidings, particularly death, is a baffling unknown. Perhaps it is because the most vividly disturbing dreams are the ones that linger longest in the memory. French actor, Champmesle, for example, was stunned by a dream in which he saw his dead mother beckoning to him. Instantly divining that the scene foretold his own death, he mentioned it to friends and promptly organised and paid his own funeral Mass. At the conclusion of the Mass he walked out of the church and dropped dead.

However, dream analysts are quick to mention that dreams of death should not be fearsome all the time as they can also mean the end of a habit like smoking and gambling or severing a relationship, retirement, giving up a job or business which has been stressful and unproductive. Dreams of dead relatives in various situations are common too but their appearances are usually loving and gentle as most of them are your soul mates or guardian angels trying to say 'hello,' or hoping to pass a message to you. They are your loved ones, don't have to wake up with cold sweat unless they squeeze your neck or kick your bums for something you did to them!

Some dream analysts say that if you dream of babies, it could mean a new start to anything ranging from job, fresh romance or added responsibilities. You may decide to improve your appearance by slimming down, crowning your teeth, go for a face lift or getting rid of outdated clothing to upgrade your image. Baby dreams can appear because of your new personality. Can all these be true or simply intelligent guesses or dream symbols for everyone are different?

Big Dreams

Are you aware that some dreams come in full colour while others are in black and white? Those in technicolour are referred to as *big dreams* that come in vivid form and easy to remember. They are usually *meaningful* dreams and the dreamer is able to grasp the subtle message which normally come as a form of enlightenment in the waking state. It could be a warning about the consequences of certain action or behaviour and quite often, a scene in past life is shown to alert you not to repeat past mistake. Such dreams do not come often and strangely, those appearing in the dream are usually in their *pure state* with rosy, healthy-looking complexion as if they are angels! *Small dreams* or plain dreams are not in colour and appear to be flighty and come in fragments making little sense due mainly to concoction of the subconscious of previous waking activities like after watching a movie, playing a sport or any event that hold some attention.

Invoking Dreams

Dreams provide a wonderful and mysterious source of information. A close friend of mine, Kramer, has always been afraid of heights and vowed he would never live in a high-rise apartment. He was puzzled why he was so *chicken* with heights but intuitively understood that it had to do with something in his past life. He was dead set in getting to the bottom of this and concentrated hard for many nights before going to sleep to *invoke* a dream to satisfy his curiosity. About a week later, he saw in his dream that during one of his past lives, invaders attacked his village and he and his tribesmen had to run to the mountains to escape. While scaling the mountain to reach a valley on the other side, he lost his footing and *fell* to his death. The memory of this incident is still embedded in his mind and Kramer cannot run away from the fear of heights.

There are some people who are scared of water and swimming in the sea would be close to telling them to commit suicide! This is the same problem with Kramer. He loves the beach, but prefers to feast his eyes on all the scantily dressed beauties, and would not budge from his lazy chair to go for a dip or take off his dark sunglasses. Kramer's inquisitive mind started to work again and he focused on a dream for answers. The revelation came: it was like watching a war scene in a movie where Kramer was a soldier in a past life. He was in the battlefield but his people were losing the war and had to retreat and cross a swift river to escape the onslaught of the enemies. While trying desperately to wade through the swift current, an enemy on horseback caught up and *speared* him to death.

Can Dreams Be Analysed?

Since the last decade mankind has made tremendous progress in technology, medicine and the intricate functioning of the human body but little headway is shown on the workings of the mysterious dream. Perhaps the laborious research work of modern day dream analysts like the eminent Carl Jung and Calvin Hall have found some answers in lifting certain dark clouds in the dream world. Jung stated that the many characters, plots and images the dreamer encounter, whether fearful, sad or pleasant, are all part of the dreamer's personality connected to past lives. During an interview with the BBC, '*We are not simply of today,*' he stated, '*we are of an immense age.*' According to Jung, dreams are concerned mainly with the present situation and the subtle message is for the dreamer to balance off certain characteristics of his outer and inner selves in order to attain *wholeness*. Obviously there is a spiritual aspect in dreams and Jung is a firm believer that past lives are '*the organs of the soul.*'

Strangely, most dreams have the tendency to deal with the opposites—message and messenger. For example; if a man is fond of dreaming of a woman who panders and worships him, the dream message is more to alert the dreamer to mend his ways for mistreating his wife in the waking state and be less egotistic. If such dreams occur regularly, it's a clear sign the dreamer fails to recognise his own shortcomings and prefer to fantasise and risk losing touch with the realities of harmonious living. Take heed, when you are fond of dreaming that you are a great guy—throwing parties and giving money and presents to all your friends—check out the next morning when was the last time you took the family out for dinner or bought them presents.

It should be understood that all dream figures are not only our *allies* but also part of ourselves that work *for* us. Dream messages are personalised and the dreamer is the only person who understands his own circumstances. A person has to learn and integrate the good and the bad of both worlds as part of universal balancing to attain wholeness. Notable analyst Fritz Perls defined dreams as '*the royal road to integration.*' However, there is still much work to be done by dream analysts as computer print-out is still unable to ascertain whether the figure of a dragon in our dreams is actually a blessed creature of wisdom or simply a grotesque and evil giant snake hissing flame on anything in its way!

Snake Symbol

The *snake* is probably the most familiar symbol in dreams. The ancients regarded the snake as the guardian of the earth and associated it as a wisdom symbol because when the snake rises, it shaped like the human spine as if capable of opening up the *chakras*, or energy points of the body. Gamblers are fond of believing the snake to be a 'lucky' symbol. Many have allegedly made a bundle after having a dream on snakes while there are also unreported stories of gamblers selling off their homes, cars and mistresses when lady luck did not smile on them in the casinos or race tracks! Dream analysts are of the opinion that the snake symbolises a *new awareness* or a *change* is required of a present bad habit. For instance, if you are a compulsive gambler and dreamed of a snake, the message is to quit gambling and save your job or family and definitely not a case of *doubling* up your bets! Another interpretation is that a positive change is forthcoming, something to do with a conscious thought of a change in your life; perhaps a decision to spend more quality time with family or the start of a new hobby.

Conclusion

And so the mystery of the essential nature of dreams abides. Even if a dream is merely a message sent from the self to self, and the subject matter deals solely with the problems and themes that dominate the waking life—human relations, sexuality, security, self-esteem, illness and death. Yet if this is so, why are waking dilemmas manifested in such persistently perplexing and bizarre form? If dreams are merely self-generated messages to us, why should they be in codes that are obscured and often barely decipherable?

What's in a dream? Are they real or fantasies? The Taoist version is both intriguing and amusing when a sage related a story. Once *Chuang Tzu* dreamed that he was a butterfly, flitting merrily through the flowers. When he awoke he was not sure if he was Chuang Tzu who had dreamed he was a butterfly or a butterfly that was dreaming he was Chuang Tzu! Did the story provide any insight to the dream world? Perhaps the question should not be confined to dreams alone. As Havelock Ellis once said, '*Dreams are real while they last. Can we say more of life?*

Spiritual Guides

Soft as the voice as an angel, breathing a lesson unheard. Hope with a gentle persuasion, whispers her comforting word . . .
Whispering hope, oh how welcome thy voices, making my heart, in its sorrow rejoice.

Lyrics from hymn 'Whispering Hope'

Soul mates

It was mentioned earlier that planning your own lessons is not an easy task as the 'when,' 'where' and 'who,' have to be clearly defined before the lesson could begin. But implementing them is even harder because when thrown to do battle in the materialistic world, the gap between planned lessons and actual performance can be as wide as a mile. It's like a huge assembled jigsaw puzzle suddenly falling apart, thanks to the memory censor. But take heart, even though you are likely to slip, stumble and fall along the journey, you are smart enough to bring along at least *two soul mates* to guide you.

You are fully aware that it is no easy task to accomplish all your spiritual needs in your next rebirth. To give yourself a better chance to succeed, you brought along two *specially selected* soul mates to help you out and they are aware of your heavenly plan and have the necessary expertise to expedite your karmic lessons. Every incarnation means new lessons and starting from scratch again. Soul mates accompanying you are likely to change because of specific needs. This is similar to the business world; it's all about getting the right people to achieve the best results on a given project. But whether you are a rich man, a poor man, a beggar or whoever you are, there are *'friends'* always waiting to guide you. They are your *spiritual guides*—your invisible care-takers.

Unsuspecting Helper

They are the *invisible ones* who stand next to you or behind you and holding your hand most of the time. They are the ones whom you occasionally feel that there's a shadow or someone close by, but somehow appear invisible and out of reach. You don't feel fear in situations like this because they are your guardians. When you have lost your way in life's struggle or when you are down, your guides will lift you up and provide direction again in an *unsuspecting* way. Sometimes it could be a piece of good advice from a friend or a memory of a past incident that provided you clues to resolve a nagging problem. Be alert to inspirational messages and listen to your instinct. In case some of you may not be aware, the word 'inspiration' is coined from 'in spirit', the *hidden beings*. It is very common that a simple solution to an old problem is right under your nose if you pay close attention.

The observations and actions taken by your guides are done with complete love for you. They remain silent most of the time, especially in the early part of your life when you are still in the development or 'grooming' stage. They are fully aware that infancy and childhood are pre-requisites of your contract to experience motherly love, spontaneous reaction, handling of likes and dislikes, excitement, injured feelings and more importantly, rapid learning. Strangely, most babies in their carefree and pure states are able to connect with their guides. Have you noticed why some babies seem so happy playing alone laughing and mumbling away as if there are 'invisible guardians' playing with them where adults can't see?

Making the bridge

Their presence is more strongly felt when you start to become spiritually inclined, as communication is two-way traffic. For example, while in lesson and you questioned yourself such as, '*Am I doing the right thing?*' or '*Why is it that I have so few friends when I am so rich? Have I been harsh and mean to others?*' These are some of the 'golden words' your guides love to hear, as they are the springboards for them to take action and do their real work.

When the conscious mind seeks advice or clarification from the heart, it is an indication you are beginning to understand the duality in you. You are actually trying to knock at the door of your higher self to tap for inner wisdom in decision-making. When such a connection is made, the guides would switch from quiet observants to active participants by helping you to make the bridge between physical you and *godly you*. When you continuously question your actions, you are indirectly seeking divine guidance and that's the way to go.

The many faces of angels

The saving grace by spiritual guides comes in mysterious ways and everyone has experienced the good fortune of being 'saved' at one time or another; it could be a lucky escape from a potential accident, close encounters with dangers, sudden reminder to rush home and switch off the gas stove, slipping from stairs, just missed by being struck by lightning or a flying golf ball, etc. Your saviour can appear at the blink of an eye in your hour of need and able to take *strange forms* too depending on the circumstances. The following well documented experiences are enlightening and worth mentioning:

(1) Frau Elsa

A German woman, Frau Elsa, related her experience while on holidays in the Bavarian Alps in the 1950s. She joined a group on a mountain climbing tour but while on the trip down, the group took off a bit earlier as she was slow in packing up. She had to do catch-up to join the party when she accidentally took a wrong turn. She realised she was lost when the path disappeared and it was getting dark. When she was just about to panic, all of a sudden she saw an unusual ball of light that slowly condensed to the shape of a tall, Chinese-looking gentleman. Strangely, she was not the least scared by this manifestation and the whole event appeared quite natural to her. The gentleman bowed, spoke a few soothing words and led her to the proper path back and disappeared as a ball of light.

(2) Starlitt

A five-year old girl Starlitt was sitting at the back of a van while her mother was driving up a steep gravel country road in Oregon, America, in 1986. It was a dark night and the mother lost her sense of direction and took a wrong turn and the van went off the road and plunged into a 100 feet ravine below. But while the van was rolling half way down the slope, Starlitt was thrown free. At the bottom of the ravine, the mother was badly injured and lay unconscious. Starlitt was also badly bruised and bleeding but somehow, barefooted and in pain, managed to struggle and climb her way back to the top of the cliff where she was later found by passer-by Ellen.

The good Samaritan Ellen took her home and when she and her husband questioned Starlitt about what happened, they quickly organised a rescue team to search for the mother. The cliff was so steep that the rescuers had to call for a helicopter to bring up the unconscious mother in a rescue basket and then rushed her to hospital where she later recovered. But the rescuers were puzzled how a badly injured five-year old could climb a steep cliff in total darkness? When questioned, Starlitt said something to this effect: 'Well, I was not actually alone. When I was trying to climb in pain, a young boy, holding a puppy, came to me and comforted me. He gave me strength and direction how to climb.'

(3) *Karen, George and Jason*

What about the three cousins who went to the beach and nearly had their last swim? Karen, George and Jason grew up in Malaysia but migrated to Sydney at different times. When they finally met up in Sydney as teenagers in 1988, they decided to have a 'get-together' by going for a swim at Bondi Beach. They laughed and talked about old times in the unsuspecting warm waters of summer, unaware that the silent moving currents were sweeping them deeper and deeper into the sea. A sudden big wave swept over them and the three suddenly realised that they were too far out from the beach. Karen, the eldest, sniffed danger and shouted, 'Let's swim back!' Karen was a natural water bird and managed to power through the waves and made it to shore. When she looked over her shoulders, her two cousins were unsighted and she panic and screamed for help.

Meanwhile, young George and Jason were struggling to stay afloat against the roaring waves that was getting fiercer all the time and pushing them to deeper waters. The boys were fighting for dear life when the fury of nature took its course; they were swallowed by the raging water and somersaulted like flies as if destruction was the name of the game. Their only chance of survival then was to kick up with all their might and hoped for the best that they could bounce to the top and gasp for air. They lost count how many times they had to go through those painful lung-bursting ordeals.

Jason recalled that when he was swept to near bottom at the last time, his legs started to cramp and was about to lose the spirit to fight. But somehow, there was that *unexplained* faint inspirational voice encouraging him that he still had the strength for one last leap for air. It flashed on him that it was either bye-bye world or *pray*. With purity of heart, he screamed mentally; 'God, save me!' In spite of his cramped legs, he used all his might for the final kick and made it to the surface—and the grace of God was at hand to greet him too; a surfer saw his plight and brought Jason back to shore on his surfboard. His cousin George shared the same faith in God at the time of need and was saved by another surfer.

Respect for higher intelligence

What was that ball of light that can transform to a Chinese gentleman who could guide a strayed climber down a mountain? Who was the boy with a puppy that gave encouragement to barefooted Starlitt to climb a steep hill on a dark night or how Jason 'mayday' call or prayer answered? Guardian angels have special ways to react with all of us; they always appear in friendly images or speak in comforting words to suit both young and old depending on the circumstances. In the case of Starlitt, her guardian angel *prudently* manifested as a young loving boy of her age to *reassure* rather than frighten her.

Such intelligence is not from our world; it lies *beyond the frontiers of reality* as we know it. They (soul mates) are entities from a higher dimension that intervene in our affairs when there is a need to give comfort and aid especially when our lives are in danger. We are fortunate to have them as our protectors and guiding light because they are buddies of our being—the soul. But how many really understand and appreciate them? Worse still, some either laugh or get agitated when told they have a soul.

Team Spirit

Learn to speak to your guides and treat them like team players when confronted with problems. They are always more active when instructions come from you instead of giving you hints all the time. Many of us are unable to see the hidden messages in certain sacred phrases like '*ask, and you shall receive,*' because they sound too simple. Don't be afraid to ask them what you want; confide in them, they are your '*buddies*', remember? If you find it hard to be alone, speak to them in your car, in a quiet spot or even in the shower. Keep your voice down of course, or you may be branded a *sicko!* Speak to them like old friends such as: 'Spiritual guides, I am getting very restless and bored with my present job and am planning to put in my resignation. Please give me advice and guidance whether I should quit or hang on.' There may be other problems bugging and you can say to your guides: 'I have foolishly insulted my best friend in front of her relatives and regretted my action. Find a way for her to forgive me.'

Answers can come in mysterious ways when spoken from the heart. It could be a gentle nudge to alert you to visit a certain person who can help you, flashes from the mind of some action to be taken, or a soft whispering voice telling you what to do. Your guides are part of you; they are most effective when made active participants working as *a team*. Speak to them like fighting for a common cause and wondrous things can change for the better.

Communication

Spiritual guides are fond of communicating through dreams because it is a *universal rule* that humans are given the *free will to act* when performing earthly lessons and guides are only allowed to *subtly* assist without direct involvement. But many are not aware of the '*hidden message*' given to them when asleep. Sometimes you are made an observer on scenes where a friend or relative resolves problems which are similar to your own but you failed to understand the significance or pick up the cue and allow spiritual help to slip away.

It's worth relating an example of the mystical dream message. Kirk is a decent person but has a nasty temper when provoked; especially when his integrity is questioned or when someone is trying to pull a fast one on him. One day after selling a property through a real estate agent whom he has dealt with for many years, he discovered from a statement that the agent charged him 3.3% commission fee instead of the agreed 2.2% rate like previous transactions. Kirk was hopping mad because the difference works out to the tune of $5000, an amount he wanted to set aside for a vacation with the family. His initial reaction was to charge into the agent's office and have a showdown. But Kirk's hands were trembling with anger because when he's hot, *he knows* he is really hot! He took a beer to cool down and came to his senses that if he stormed into the office in a rage, fists may even start to fly and he might regret it later. He decided to see the agent the next day to enable him to calm down. While tossing in bed that night, he said to himself, 'Temper, temper, that's me. Can someone teach me how to be more dignified?'

You guessed right; he had a dream. It was an ancient scene: he was walking on a stony road with a heavy load on his back. Struggling with his steps, he heard a very *familiar voice* telling a story to a happy crowd and they were laughing all the time as if wanting more from the storyteller. The voice was very clear, relaxed and soothing with the occasional humour like a good salesman and Kirk followed every word that was said when he got nearer to the storyteller. '*What clarity and confidence this guy has and I know that voice*,' Kirk said to himself. When he was within range to size up the storyteller, he was shocked to find out it was his father who had passed on! '*This can't be, my dad knows only how to scream and shout and I inherited all his traits!*'

Kirk immediately woke up and it took him a few hours to digest the dream and understand the subtle message. If his father could change for the better in his dream why can't he? His current life was burdened by a heavy load as depicted in his dream simply because he was unable to control his temper. He went to see the agent the same day, no longer fiery but cool as a cucumber, told the agent to explain the higher charge of commission. The agent apologised profusely blaming his oversight as the culprit. The agent even bought an expensive bottle of whisky for Kirk the next day to make peace with a valued customer.

Kirk is a changed person after that dream and is now enjoying the role of a cool-headed diplomat. Your spiritual guides are prepared to burrow through time and space to pass a message of wisdom to you if you consciously use them as *team players*. Soccer superstars like Ronaldo or David Beckham would not be able to score goals by themselves if there's no team work from their players.

Alicia

Alicia is a family member and her experience with spiritual guide is enlightening and worth sharing with readers. She reads the heavy stuff and attends workshop sessions whenever she senses that a particular one could enhance her spiritual knowledge. She related that her spiritual guides are her daily companions when her husband is off to work and she is alone. She has come to the level where she can communicate with her guides and have fun with them. She says it's hard to describe this strange but wonderful feeling when in the presence of the guides. 'You are enveloped with pure love and bliss and don't want to let go,' she said. Sometimes when she sweeps the floor in her apartment, she sees strange feathers scattered on the floor and would jokingly say, 'You again!' She mentioned that she met her guides many times in dreams and one of them used to be an American Indian shaman from the past. The shaman was just trying to give a sign of his presence with the feathers from his warrior's headgear!

Alicia is not a working person but she travels a fair bit as her husband is based overseas. Sometimes she needs to visit relatives or to attend special spiritual workshops around the globe. When she is short of cash, she will '*SOS*' her guides for assistance. Somehow, her '*sceptical*' husband would top up her bank account and give his blessing for the wife to travel.

Alicia's passion is rock painting. She says that when she was a schoolgirl, art was not one of her favourite subjects. Today her new interest in rock painting is really something to be admired. They are not only beautifully done but also creative and lifelike and even experts of the craft are prepared to pay good money for a piece of her work. A piece of rock can come in any shape and size and turning it into a treasured ornament requires artistic skill and imagination as none of the original rock is chipped away. What is the secret of her success? '*Before I start to paint, I co-create with the spirit of the rock, and together we churn out beautiful rock art.*' she said.

Helper Spirit

I find it very enlightening and grateful to be given the insight by spiritual masters regarding the active participation of *helper spirits* to keep us motivated in our quest for knowledge. Helper guides need not necessarily be our 'personal guides' and can be new spirits coming in to give us a helping hand especially in our new endeavours. Renowned psychic medium James Van Praagh, says: '*These beings are drawn to us through the universal law of affinity: Like attracts like.*'

When we have a special interest in a particular subject or work, a helper spirit with *expertise* in that area would assist and further stimulate our interest in artistic creativity. Alicia's rock painting is a fine example of spirit guidance. The same is true for my sister's Irene neat and 'four season' blooming garden as if nature spirits or *gnomes* are her regular helpers! An amateur writer can be pinned down with mental blocks in the initiate stages of writing, but more often than not, he or she will attract a helper guide for inspiration to keep the person focused. As for myself, I am certain there is a helper spirit gleaning over my shoulders and giving me with ideas and words to complete this book—my first one. The best part, I can feel that there is a mutual attraction; my invisible friend likes a good laugh too. Every time when I write something funny, I can *sense* laughter in the air—especially when the humour or jokes are *not* mine!

What about scientists, musicians, entertainers and architects? The list is endless. The appearance of helper guides is connected to our determination and *passion*. When we are passionate in what we do, there is no frontier for success. But it must be quantified that helper guides will only appear when our work is of good intent like a service or enlightenment for mankind.

Attaching Spirits

> *When there's a positive force,*
> *there must be a negative force.*
> *It follows that if there were no devils,*
> *there will be no gods!*

> Lobsang Rampa

What are attaching spirits?

They are wandering or *unevolved* spirits that are still earth bound and yet to move on. Their presence is usually a sad one associated with untimely death such as people involved in fatal accidents, violent demise like being murdered or killed in disputes or wars. According to the masters, when a person dies in unusual circumstances, the *etheric double*; the *energy* existing between the physical and the aura—the absolute counterpart or image of the dead—refuses to *dissipate* and instead, remains on earth with the behaviour or habit of the dead but without a physical body and without a *brain*.

Does 'ghost' exist in our environment?

Unfortunately yes. The mindless etheric energy is what we commonly call a *ghost* and *not* the dead person returning for vengeance or to haunt somebody! What we know as ghosts is in reality quite harmless. It is only the image of the deceased in energy form and wanders about according to the past habits of the dead person. For example: a ghost may be attached to its previous home because all the things and people the dead person used to love are still there. In another case, the ghost may have an obsession for its former sports car. It is possible that the new owner can experience a strange feeling that an invisible *someone* is in the car at times or get the occasional 'slap on the head' when driving too fast!

But it is human nature that we run for dear life when confronted by a ghost and unwittingly we make the ghost *feels* as if it is superior to humans! It is said that there are certain methods that can make a ghost disappear. A common one is to remain calm and say the protective words to the ghost: 'Are you from the *light*? If not, please deflect.' But during such a spooky encounter with a ghost, how many of us can calmly recite the golden words freely without wetting our pants first?

It is true that most ghosts are pranksters?

It is well documented that ghosts are more mischievous than monkeys and love playing pranks on humans. I remember an incident in Malaysia where a taxi driver picked up a female passenger on a rainy night. When asked where she wanted to go, the well dressed lady directed the driver to take a short-cut and made him stop at a cemetery. The driver was concerned for her safety as it was dark and raining but a $100 note and 'keep the change' shut him up. When the taxi driver got home to count his night's takings, he nearly got a heart attack when he discovered that the still wet $100 note was not legal tender but 'hell bank money' used by the Chinese to '*burn wealth*' for the dead!

One of the favourite tricks of ghosts is to attend séances or take over from mediums and *give messages* from the grave. Most of the screams and groans including silly messages you hear are unlikely to be from your grandmother or dead spouse but our mindless ghosts having a good time with insecure humans!

Are there 'attaching spirits' that can play havoc to our lives?

Weird as it may sound, there are *'attaching spirits'* roaming in our midst that can turn our earthly lessons into living hell! These are usually unhappy entities with longings to 'relive' the comforts or pleasures of their former earthly lives and *unaware* that the physical body has passed on. In order to satisfy their cravings, they have to get attached to humans because of their bodiless forms and lower vibratory rate as such entities are from a lower realm.

How do attaching spirits invade our body?

Remember that everyone is well armoured with a magnetic energy or auric field commonly called *aura* that surrounds the body? The aura will glow and appears healthy and strong when we act with *love*. But when we over-indulge, react with resentment or with the intention of hurting others, the aura turns dull and likely to have ripples or holes in it as if needing repair. This is where our body is most *vulnerable to intrusion* by lower entities because we have lost sight of our spiritual self by living unrighteously. Good examples are drug addicts, alcoholics, liars, and those with strong obsession in vices or living in a world of *fantasy*.

Another simple way to ward off attaching spirits is to learn to live a balanced life. You are entitled to enjoy life as much as you can but do it in moderation and don't forget about responsibilities or losing touch with reality. You are on the right track when your actions or chosen path are strongly supported by those closest to you. When there is harmony, there is approval. When you try to bulldoze your way to do what you want to do against good advice, you are playing with fire as there is the likelihood you would attract only the devil to become your 'friend'. What sort of success or friendship do you expect when you listen to lowly spirits?

What can attaching spirits do to us during our period of weakness?

Attaching spirits thrive on negative behaviour and emotions and can possess you like the devil and take full control of your mind if you do not know how to change your attitude. They can *instigate* and create problems to generate anger and rage during your moments of weakness or loss of reasons. They will sidetrack you to only one direction: how to win you over and absorb your energy and *weaken* you in order to *strengthen* them. They are from a lower dimension and can only be stronger than you when they absorb your energy through worship. It is well known that when a person is too involved with idol worship at home, especially praying to various 'gods', *wandering* spirit can *mimic* your god or deity in order to find a '*home*'. In such a scenario, it becomes a case of *mistaken entity* when the person is actually praying to a wandering spirit and not the deity! When a lower entity takes over your energy, it can control your life. Your wishes then—likely to be laced with blind passion or greed—could be granted as a payback to appease the worshipper. Eerie as it may sound, this arrangement becomes mutual attraction as both sides benefit. But beware; most of these low-minded entities take pleasure in giving pain mentally and emotionally and how you end up is not their concern because love and compassion are *not* in the make-up of lowly spirits.

Domino effect

Attaching spirits have strategies too like fighting a war. In order to control your mind, they can invent problems to sour up your good relationships with friends and colleagues hoping for a *domino effect* where you passed on the pains to those closest to you such as family members. Domestic strife can become the order of the day and the devil will hoist the victory flag when you have no one to turn to for help. What do you expect from negative energy anyway?

Is it true that most of us are 'stuck with these ugly friends?'

You may get a running chill in your spine, but it's true. It sounds bizarre but its part of nature as lower spirit has lessons to learn too. But controlling their manifestations or allowing them to turn to full bloom is entirely up to us—our lifestyle. They are not easy to get rid of once attached to humans. The best way to steer clear from attaching spirits or make them 'inactive' is to live righteously, be healthy, stay sober and live in harmony with everyone. It is well documented that such entities can manifest in spooky fashions like crying out loud in pain or screaming in great discomfort when *strong prayers* are directed at them to disappear and return to their source. Remember the movie, *Exorcist* on spirit possession? For Christian readers, the Gospel of Luke says that Jesus cured the mentally unsound Mary Magdalene by casting out seven demons in her including other women who were also cured of evil spirits and diseases. Attaching spirits are real and have been destroying people since ancient time.

Why do we need a complicated world of evil and devils for karmic work?

The law of nature is such that when we have a positive we must also have a negative; otherwise the positive could not exist. If you have a battery you cannot have just a positive terminal because no current would flow. You must have a negative terminal in order to complete the circuit. Remember planet earth is only the arena for karmic lessons. Earth is a work-place for us to learn to shrug off evil and *spar with the devils* at the same time to free ourselves from the bondage of karma.

The negative force is not entirely bad; in fact it is a necessity for human survival because without it, we would not be able to differentiate what is good or bad. There is no denying that the presence of evil and devils is not only our incentive to be do-gooders but also the yardstick to measure proper behaviour and thought. It follows then that if there were no devils, there will be no gods!

Is there any nation or leader that condemns idol worship?

Yes, in fact the most notable one is China. In 1927, a young government official by the name of Mao Tse Tung went to the countryside in Hunan to check out personally how the peasants lived. It did not take him long to understand why the backward community there were regularly requesting for government assistance. Mao found out that there was little agriculture planning and worst of all, every family in the village believed in ancestor worship and prayed to various 'gods' like Lord Kuan Kung, Goddess of Mercy including various 'house gods,' for prosperity and protection. Probably young Mao couldn't help chuckling to himself when the 'gods' appeared better fed than the locals because of daily offerings of 'fresh food' from the ignorant peasants! Trusting that superstition and traditional beliefs were the downfall of the peasants, Mao declared: 'The gods and goddesses are miserable objects. You have worshipped them for centuries, and they have not overthrown a single one of the local tyrants or evil gentry for you! Now you want your rent reduced. Let me ask how you will go about it? Do you still believe that the gods can lower your rent or are you at the mercy of government officials?' Mao's tough stand on superstitions had changed the mentality of the illiterates and the maxim: 'action speaks louder than god,' is being taught to the young to embrace *reality* for productivity.

Some of the above material about 'Spirits' are partly inspired from the book, *Wisdom of the Ancients* by Dr Lobsang Rampa, a renowned Tibetan monk-clairvoyant and the book, *Heaven and Earth*, by James Van Praagh, who is arguably the most famous and successful psychic-medium of our time. Some of the examples quoted were from what I have witnessed, experienced or heard from reliable sources over the years.

Indigo Child

> *He could have added fortune to fame,*
> *but caring for neither, he found happiness*
> *in being helpful to the world.*

Epitaph of George Washington

The emergence of the Indigo children was foretold by the ancients and Edgar Cayce long before the appearance of New Age books on this subject. The term *'Indigo Child'* was coined by psychic Nancy Ann Tappe, who specialises in classifying personalities according to the colour of their auras. Everyone has a *life colour* or magnetic field encasing the body. Personalities or character traits can be grouped according to the colour of the aura in the same way as astrology that relies on the planetary influence during birth. However, the average person is unable to see the human aura or has the ability to size up another's personality; but 'colour workshops' are getting popular to enhance knowledge of this *'new found spiritual science,'* and high-tech computer cameras are able to capture the colours of the aura. But this technology is still in its infancy and needs fine tuning.

Purpose

According to Tappe, the Indigo phenomenon is recognised as one of the most exciting changes in human nature ever documented in society. The Indigo label describes the energy pattern of human behaviour which exists in over 95% of children born around the late 1980s. This phenomenon is happening globally and eventually the Indigos (*violet blue*) will replace all other colours. As small children, Indigo's are recognised by their unusually large, clear eyes. Extremely bright, precocious children with amazing memory and a strong desire to live instinctively, these children of the new millennium are sensitive, gifted souls with an evolved consciousness who have come here to help change the vibrations of our lives and create one land, one globe and one species. They are our bridge to the future.

The new earth cycle and the emergence of the new breed are all part of the divine agenda to slowly *change* the human genetic code or DNA and further increase the positive vibration of our planet. The presence of Indigos is different from us as some *do not carry karma* and bypass 'the many lessons' we have to go through. They come as *productive beings* aware of their purpose, which is mainly to expedite new knowledge and complex issues that eluded current experts in various fields.

Marketing maestro

Our current science, medicine and technology are so advanced now that almost all our material needs are fulfilled. But are we using all the new knowledge for constructive purposes all the time or wasting the knowledge on unproductive projects like weapons of mass destruction or secretly utilising them for selfish means like spying, fraud and intrusion of privacy, for example. The new breed will enlighten the old guard with the 'leadership through example' approach and undertake new projects that can benefit all human beings. Some of the priorities would be getting rid of nuclear wastes, saving the environment, immunity of certain common diseases and all the new techniques to utilise natural resources for power, heating and better living.

The Indigos will revolutionise changes and thinking of present humans and awaken the spiritual side in them to accelerate righteous living. Working in harmony and integrity and honouring God has always been the divine plan of creation. God has the answers to everything if He wants the human race to continue. He is the marketing maestro because when mankind gave a deaf ear to all His prophets generation after generation, He employs a new strategy by sending down countless Indigos to work side-by-side with *parents or their elders* and patiently waits for the unfolding.

Characteristics

There have been countless reports about young parents and nursery teachers losing their cool because children under their care are hyper-active and hard to control. Indigos are '*no cool dudes*,' one of their traits is to scream and shout when they can't get what they want. Parents and carers should be made aware of the sensitive nature of the new breed and hopefully the media and maternity wards are encouraged to provide more information on Indigos and how to handle them. The problem is; how many doctors *believe* in Indigos? They are not *misfits or imperfect* children, they just have to be treated differently because they possess a new type of energy that is different from us.

Some parents get stressed out easily with abnormal behaviour and resort to punishment or requesting doctors for prescriptions to calm the child. Such actions only amplify the problem as the poor child is being drugged at a tender age! Learn to understand and love them or seek counselling on how best to deal with the situation. The following are common traits of Indigos extracted from various sources:

- They come into this world with feeling of royalty (and often act like it).

- They have difficulty with absolute authority (authority without explanation or choice).
- They simply will not do certain things, like waiting in line is difficult for them.
- They get frustrated with systems that are ritually oriented and don't require creative thought.
- They often see better ways of doing things, both at home and in school, which make them seem like 'system busters.'
- They seem anti-social and prefer to mingle with their own kind. School can be tough for them socially.
- They will not respond to 'guilt' discipline such as,'No more chocolates for you because you screamed at me!'
- They are not shy in letting you know what they need.

Ethan

I have not learned how to see the human aura yet, but I think my grandson Ethan, who just turned three, is an Indigo child because the above characteristics are almost 'spot on' in describing him! He is a handful for family members but we have to learn to play his game. Nobody can *insist* that he must say 'thank you' on anything given to him whether its food or toys. His answer is always a screaming 'No!' But when grandma *quietly* takes off his wet nappies or gives him his bottle of milk, he would react normally and say, 'Thank you grandma.'

When you take him shopping, be prepared for trouble! His eyes move very quickly looking for toyshops. When he sees one, he will lure you there by throwing tantrums. The *strange* part, he knows *exactly* what he wants whether it's 'Spiderman' or a car. He screens all the toys and makes his own selection. His new toy is always different or a new model from those he has at home. His memory is quite uncanny for a three-year-old. When you are not careful and start to swear in front of him, angry words like, *'shut-up' or 'go to hell,'* they will come back to you like a boomerang! He can also be a bit of a *sadist* too; he is fond of repeating those swear words in front of your friends and giving you a red face on *how* he is being brought up!

Change of Guards

The earlier Indigos in our society are either in their teens or beginning to enter the workforce now. Their colleagues and even superiors or seniors will sense a different approach by the new breed on work ethics. It is not surprising and very timely too that recruitment company, Drake International, 'has warned employers they need to make their workplaces more fun, interesting, flexible and full of variety to attract the up-and coming 12 to 26 age group' who will be our stars of tomorrow. Drake's research went further adding that salary alone will not attract the new breed because they also want flexibility and are concerned primarily with outcomes or *solutions*, not process which is mainly rigid rules and regulations. There will be higher turnover of staff in the workplace because the young will continue to look for 'better pastures' not because they are compelled to leave, but because there is no compelling reason to stay on.

Do you regard it as a coincidence when feminist Dr Germaine Greer echoed the same message when she urged young women not to work too hard but to take time to smell the roses? 'Look for joy, pleasure, satisfaction—don't think solely in terms of ambition. Even if you've a seat on the board of directors, it isn't necessarily where you want to be,' she said during a youth forum in Queensland, Australia.

Our world is full of surprises since the turn of the new millennium. While young parents and teachers are still learning to cope with Indigos, words are out that another new breed; the *Crystal* children are *now* emerging! What else, angels coming down to teach us how to fly soon? Whatever the make-up of the *Crystals*, they are here for good reasons. The message should be quite clear: learn to *love* and accept the new breeds—they are the catalyst to a more enlightened world. Indigo and Crystal children are not suffering from *brain disorders* but are here on a *divine mission*.

Astral Travel

> *We are already immortals.*
> *We only have to recognize ourselves*
> *as the true spiritual beings that we are.*

> *Taoist Text*

Astral travel is nothing new in modern time as psychics and spiritual gurus have reported *out-of-body experiences* in vivid detail. Are such trips real, or are they hallucinatory responses to crisis? Some sceptics ridiculed the phenomenon as 'expressions of man's perennial quest for immortality; a deliberate challenge to the threat of extinction!' Such a statement will receive little support today as soul travelling is no longer confined to the sages, yogi or those in near death crisis. A normal person is able to do soul projection when properly trained by a spiritual master. But the divine law is such that both parties must have *absolute humility* about such knowledge or power to ensure they are not seeking only *glamour* to project themselves like a *special* breed or the chosen few. The guiding light for spiritual growth is all about humility and passion for enlightenment and not, 'I know better than you.' But beware, *false masters* are everywhere! Why are we not aware of our hidden power to check out the twilight zone? A living master says, '*Spirituality is not meant for the multitude, only true seekers*'.

Nuri Sarup

The concept of the astral body, '*the starry envelope of the soul*' known as '*nuri sarup*' (light body) to Hindus '*merkabah*' to others or simply the etheric body to most, is one of the oldest and most universal of man's ideas about himself. It is a perfect replica of the physical body in which it is housed. The astral body is made of far lighter stuff, *sparkling stardust-like*, translucent and eminently suited to the out-of-body travel of which it is allegedly capable. One of the main functions of the astral body is to transport the soul at the moment of death where it will become the next instrument of expression in the astral world.

The astral body coincides with the physical body during the hours of full, waking consciousness, but in sleep the astral body withdraws to a greater or lesser degree, usually hovering just above it, neither conscious nor controlled. In trance, being unconscious, while fainting or when under the influence of an anaesthetic, the astral body similarly withdraws from the physical. The astral body can also flee from the physical in times of crisis like near death situation or actual death itself. Such cases of withdrawal constitute instances of *automatic or involuntary projection.*

However, conscious or voluntary projection is also possible in which the subject *'wills'* to leave his physical body. He is then fully alert and conscious in his astral body; he can look upon his own physical mechanism, and travel about at will, perhaps viewing scenes and visiting places he has never seen before. Under conscious projection, the astral and physical bodies are connected by the popularly known *'silver cord,'* along which vital cosmic current or life force passes. Should the cord be severed, death instantly results. The cord constitutes the essential link between the two bodies.

Movement out of the physical body is often accompanied by a clicking sound or the popping of a cork from a bottle. The person will lose consciousness and the emerging soul will start its journey normally assisted by its guardian angels. The projected form is immune to gravity and able to walk, glide, float or fly. It can hover lazily in the vicinity of the physical body, and fly great distances beyond the limits of time and space. It is also able to pass through matter with ease but is very seldom capable of *touching* or *moving objects;* the main reason why there are sceptics even among our top brains as *proof* of a heavenly flower or fruit is unavailable for examination!

Clinical Death

Author Ernest Hemingway felt his soul depart from his body after having been badly wounded. *'I felt my soul or something coming right out of my body, like you'd pull a silk handkerchief out of a pocket by one corner. It flew around and then came back and went in again, and I wasn't dead any more.'* The sensation of seeming to travel out of the body is virtually impossible to explain to those who have not experienced it, believers feel, because it is so unlike normal conscious existence. Nonetheless, a sample of comments from respondents in a study conducted by Celia Green, a British parapsychologist, provides some insight of what *'being out'* has meant to different people:

* 'What seemed to have escaped was whatever made the physical body m*e, i.e. whatever gave me personality or character.'*

* *The part of me that was out of my body was the real me, as I knew it, the part that sees, thinks and feel emotionally.'*

* *'It wasn't weird or frightening, in fact if there is a reaction, it is one of feeling superior.'*

* *'I have never been so wide awake or experienced such a wonderful sense of freedom before.'*

* *'All movement was instantaneous. To think was to have acted.'*

What about the countless documented reports from those that visited the astral plane and came back? Some who have returned from the brink of death reported the sensation of floating down a dark tunnel leading to a *beautiful* place or being met and welcomed either by friends or relatives or by a sort of guiding light. A five year-old child came back from clinical death and said, *'I went to a nice place and the people were nice too. I don't mind going there again.'* I am sure even hardened sceptics would blink for a second after hearing such pure and simple words from an innocent child.

In our modern time, doctors and psychiatrists are still unable to come up with answers regarding the existence of the soul despite documented evidence from their patients' uncanny experiences. Like in astrology, no one is prepared to 'play god' and endorse or denounce it because convincing scientific proof is not at hand despite of very compelling evidence. If somebody raises the question: *'Have you been to heaven?'* How are doctors going to answer? It is impossible for scientists to 'trap' a soul in a test tube and dissect it in the laboratory and find out what this strange energy or *'thing'* is. Who knows, it may be God's way of giving us a glimpse of the other side of the veil and comforting us *not to fear death* at the same time.

Don't Think Like Humans

Do not allow your soul to fall.
For your soul can be your friend or enemy.

Lord Krishna

The core of humans

The *core* of humans is spiritual as our source of origin is not earth but of a higher realm. In order to be successful in life, we must first be able to *realise our identity* as separate from the body. We have to come to terms with the fact that we are masters of the body and not as servants. This is where it takes two to tango and the reason for our *duality*; but we have to remember who the *boss* is. When we fail to realise this truth, our progress and success in life will be limited; it's like a diseased apple tree that can bear very little apples or none at all. We will be confronted with obstacles most of the time and be dragged down by disappointments and frustrations in our endeavours instead of hoping to make good in life. When we think like humans, we become humans and lose control of our senses and fall prey to earthly desires.

Contemplation

How can we awaken our spirit to guide and protect us from the many pitfalls of life? Start by directing your attention to what is good and useful and ignore the rest. This means you should get rid of selfish thoughts, bad habits or attachments by *nipping them in the bud* before they blossom and become your lifestyle. If we are regular drunks and abuse the family most of the time, what are the chances of having 'a yarn with an angel' when there is no spiritual substance in us? The next step is to have *self recognition* that there is a spiritual consciousness within us. In order to harness recognition of our being, we have to constantly contemplate *what* we are to bring forth what we *might* be. Make it a point to spare a few quiet moments a day by being still and quieting the mind. The real point of being still and doing nothing is to empty the wandering mind entirely of all conceptual thought to enable spirit to abide in the emptiness and silence or *separation* from the physical world. This is called 'returning to the source,' in Taoism. Through regular practice in contemplation, there is likelihood we can begin transforming ourselves from our low, often troubled states into higher, more refined stages of spiritual life.

Contemplation is different from meditation or yoga that requires full concentration for *long* periods with the various sitting, breathing and even dieting rules which are not ideal for those who are always on the move. Let meditation assist your life; but do not use it to spin a cobweb around your life! Contemplation can be done anywhere whether sitting in the comforts of your home, office, garden and even in the bathtub and not necessarily in places of worship, attend workshops conducted by so-called gurus who charge hefty fees or live like hermits in the mountains. When there is purity of heart in contemplation, there will be *unfoldment* of our purpose on earth and eventual self realisation that we are all a piece of God.

The Power of Affirmation

> *Oh, what a beautiful morning*
> *Oh, what a beautiful day.*
> *I've got a wonderful feeling*
> *Everything's going my way.*

Lyrics from 'What a Beautiful Morning'

'Nay' or 'yea'?

'Please help me God, my boy friend Bill left me for another woman and I am just about to crack up because my whole world is crumbling down. I think I am going to die because I can't sleep, eat or work without Bill. Please use your power and return Bill to me.'

The above affirmation was from broken-hearted Sisi; a typical example of a desperate woman who has little understanding on the mechanics of how spirit works and turns to God only as a last resort. She was requesting God to perform not only *'black magic'* on Bill and his new love for selfish reasons, but also made God an *accomplice* to the whole scheme! Is it going to be *'nay' or 'yea'* from God for Sisi to be back in the loving arms of Bill? Imagine, if God is always so accommodating, there will be no sufferings, ill health or loneliness and everybody will be holding hands singing and kissing one another!

I came across an article in the newspaper recently where a metaphysical healer said, 'What you tell yourself creates your reality.' I was expecting to read more but that was it. Some of the stuff we read regarding the benefits of affirmation are fond of pampering our greed and focus on the idea that God gives us anything we desire if we pray long and hard. Don't you think it is a dishonest approach to solving problems of those who are emotionally disturbed or in hardship? Such advice only brings distress and disappointment to many because their wishes are not fulfilled, making some an emotional and mental wreck. This is probably one of the reasons why so many have forsaken God.

Honour God

Some research work and consultation with experts on this subject points to a common belief that the power of affirmation is workable only when there is *God-realisation*. This means that you must be totally convinced you are part of creation and the real you is the soul and not fleshy you. It must be vitally clear that the only path for divine assistance to our earthly needs is to accept the fact that we are divine beings. When you have this belief, the next step is to observe self-discipline in all your actions whether at work or at play like a long-term commitment. The chances of your wishes being answered are good provided they are of an *unselfish* nature and for the service or good of others. In other words, honour God and maintain integrity.

Key Players

The soul is only a minor player and not entirely responsible for the outcome or result of your prayers. When you speak from the heart, you automatically switch off your conscious mind and use your higher self as the instrument to link up with the *cosmic spirit* to answer your wishes. The cosmic spirit (Holy Spirit or Universal

Mind) originates from a *higher* plane than the soul and possesses the power to say *'yes' or 'no'* to your prayers.

It is important to understand that when requests for worldly ends such as petty little cures, job promotions or seeking 'beautiful partners' for marriages, they do not reach the Holy Spirit but only to those lower *deities* who deal with such restricted spheres simply to enable the *'living **weak** to live!'* It doesn't necessarily mean that when petty wishes are met, you are the chosen few who are deeply loved by God! This is fairly similar to the real world: when an employer sees the potential of a loyal, efficient but *insecure* employee, he gives that worker a small promotion or more responsibilities to butter up that person in order to motivate the good employee to continue his or her productive work. But all prayers arising from pure love to render *unselfish* service will reach the Holy Spirit; the *embodiment of love*. If it is hard to comprehend, just work this out: is it not true that we can see the moon only through moonlight? So too is the Holy Spirit that can be realised through love.

Meditation and prayer

It must be emphasised again that meditation, prayer or invocation is the *catalyst* to form the *channel* for all spiritual communication or services for help. They are the channels to contact the cosmic spirit; any *resulting effects* are in the power of that spirit or deity alone and *not* the lower soul or the personality as many seem to think. Affirmation—like self healing—is only an *extension* of the spirit and has nothing to do with *human* power; the common theme of those fond of seeking glamour and projecting themselves as 'gifted beings'. When 'certain gurus' play on your emotions and tell you in colourful words that they are the heavenly masters who are able to get rid of all your woes, hang on tightly to your wedding ring or wallet and run!

Mystics at work

When requests for spiritual help are answered, they usually come in mysterious or indirect manner. Spirit will '*burrow*' through your body like a drill to find out what are your *actual* problems or needs which you may be unaware of most of the time. You may have requested for a better job with more pay because you wanted to improve the quality of life for your family. But instead, the cosmic spirit did something to your health like getting rid of your drinking problems, tiredness or nagging back pain. Why? You need good health first before you can concentrate and work diligently on a higher or more responsible position.

You may be longing for '*Mr Right*' to appear to beat loneliness and perhaps get married. But if you are the sort of person who hardly leaves the house and prefers to wear pyjamas or old clothes and no make-up most of the time, what are the chances of meeting Mr Right other than in a mental institution? Spirit '*prepares*' you in many instances without your knowledge and this '*healing process*' may take time, as it cannot be done overnight like magic. This is one of the main reasons why patience is necessary for affirmations to come close to the mark. Who knows, perhaps the divine may specially '*arrange*' for a very pleasant cosmetic salesgirl to win you over regarding beauty treatment. You might start to doll up a little and socialise. After a few months, you might transform from a caterpillar to a butterfly and very likely the nosy men will follow the scent! It is a fact that when you look good, you feel good. In other words, never underestimate the *power* of good grooming as it is not only one of the ways to attract the opposite sex but a definite booster for self-confidence and respect.

No risk, no gain

Love, good health and the manifestation of abundance are there for the taking provided you see the signs and capitalise on opportunities given to you. Your true love or a bagful of money will not simply fall on your lap after affirmations are made; you have to be alert to opportunities thrown at you and work towards them instead of just dreaming about the results.

For example: you happened to bump into your school sweetheart Jennie, whom you haven't seen for 20 years. Both of you had good laughs over drinks catching up on lost time. Jennie mentioned that she was a property developer and about to market a block of apartments with waterfront views located in a sought after suburb. For old time sake, she offered you a corner apartment with great views coupled with a discounted price of 5%. It dawned on you that this was a chance in a million to see big bucks and you were dead serious to take up the offer. But the enthusiasm faded immediately when your wife angrily said you didn't have the means for that kind of investment. Like a timid rabbit, you gave up the idea without a second thought.

What went wrong? You did not take the trouble to *analyse* your situation properly; you were not prepared to do some ground work to ascertain existing property values nearby to your friend's project. You could have easily made a profit of 200K if you had thought about re-financing your home for a loan; shared the investment with someone or work out some easy terms with Jennie, your *'choi sun,'* or 'money god,' in Cantonese. The lesson is to 'make hay while the sun shines' and the *'no risk, no gain principle'* also applies in affirmations. We are referring to *calculated* risks here and not like a blind gambler going for a 100 to 1 punt!

How to make affirmations

What about making affirmations to sweeten up our lives? The following are examples for different needs and occasions.

Begin with 'Divine Spirit . . . '

Fear

- *. . . protect and defend me from evil, no matter what it is or how it is done.'*

- *. . . I want to say goodbye to fears, worries and anxieties. I want to face life with courage and love from now.'*

Wealth

- *. . . let money come to me in abundance from different channels.*

- *. . . I want my business ventures to succeed from my hard work.'*

Health

- *. . . I want excellent health and wealth to be inseparable in my life.'*

- *. . . I feel wonderful. Every part of me vibrates with vitality and health. I feel stronger everyday both mentally and physically'*

Career

- *. . . I have total confidence in my abilities. I want a job in the marketing division of a manufacturing company.'*

- *. . . I am respected in what I do and I am ready for promotion now.*

Love

- *. . . give me love that is easy and safe. I want a partner who shares my passion for gardening and cooking.*

- *. . . find me a good person who loves me completely in sickness and in health and turn a blind eye to all my wealth!*

Timing

Some people make affirmations like a shopping list and their wishes rarely come true because they are mainly greed. Remember wishes are best answered when they are of an *unselfish* nature. Is there any affirmation that works most of the time? Feedback from many say that affirmations like: 'Divine Spirit, surprise me with unexpected good tidings today,' rarely fail when spoken from the heart because the request is not demanding and *faith* in the divine goes a long way. Who knows, your boss may brighten up your day by giving you a compliment or a good looking guy buys you a drink for no reason and end up playing an important part in your later life. Unselfish affirmations made for others such as: 'let my visiting friend have a wonderful time,' not only encourages you to do your best but also resonates with God.

The mind is most receptive to affirmations when awakening or just about going to sleep because 'problems for the day' have either not started yet or begin to end. 'Command the morning' is wise advice. The novelist Barbara Cartland tells us: 'My first thought as I awaken is to give thanks for the gift of sleep, and for the fresh opportunities of the new day for happiness and usefulness.'

When you say your affirmation daily, you automatically raise your energy level and positive vibrations will flow inside you. The power of words when spoken with conviction not only sets in motion a true magnetic field of positive vibration within your mind, but also acts as a catalyst for spiritual communication with your higher self, the linkage to cosmic spirit and the universe.

What's your choice?

Affirmations appear to be so simple and almost sound stupid to some readers. Well, they have transformed the life of many because all it needs is understanding the dynamics in the workings of spirit, faith, and an unselfish nature. They *cost nothing* because they are gifts from God. Learn to enjoy the many gifts of life; when you think positive, you attract positive vibes. If you think like a loser, you will end up as one. Is that so hard to accept? If you have to decide whether you are a divine spark of God or the son or daughter of Satan, what's your choice?

Time to say 'Thank You'

We take it all for granted that the sun would keep on shining, always giving light and *never* asking for anything in return for *millions* of years! Have you ever wondered what will happen if there's a '*blackout*' from the sun and it cannot give light to our planet for just a *single* day? The earth spins on its axis with a constant speed of 1040mph at the equator since the beginning of time. Can you imagine what will happen to the length of our day and night if the earth spins at an unpredictable speed or wobbles in space due to lack of consistency or imperfection? What about the air we breathe? If our naked eye is able to see the ugly bacteria, dust and pollen including polluted fumes floating right in front of our noses, do you think we feel like breathing? Think about that. Don't you think it's time we say a *prayer of thanks to God for creating a perfect world?*

The topic on astral travel is condensed from the book, *The Projection of the Astral Body*, first published in London in 1929. The authors were Hereward Carrington, an Englishman, and Sylvan Muldoon, of America, who not only claimed to be a habitual astral traveller but was convinced that astral projection was within anyone's capability.

'The Power of Affirmation' is inspired from the many teachings of Sai Baba of India and the wisdom of Paul Twitchell, the modern-day founder of *Eckankar.*

Humour

The best medicine

Little Red Riding was walking through the woods on her way to visit her grandmother, when suddenly a wolf jumped out from behind a tree. 'Ah-ha!' said the wolf, 'Now that I got you, I am going to eat you!'

'Eat! Eat! Eat!' Little Red Riding Hood said angrily. 'Damn it! Doesn't anyone make love any more?'

Chapter 5

THE MANY FACES OF RELIGION

Religion

Religion without science is blind
And science without religion is lame.

Albert Einstein

How did it all begin?

In the book, the *Golden Bough* by James Frazer, a Scottish expert in ancient folklore, Fraser argued that religion grew out of *magic*. According to his theory, man first tried to control his own life and his environment by imitating what he saw happening in nature. For instance, he thought that he could invoke rain by sprinkling water on the ground to the accompaniment of thunder-like drumbeats or that he could cause his enemy harm by sticking pins in an effigy. This led to the use of rituals, spells, and magical objects in many areas of life. When these did *not* work as expected, he then turned to placating and beseeching the help of the supernatural powers instead of trying to control them. The rituals and incantations became sacrifices, dances and prayers; and thus religion began. In Frazer's words, religion is a 'conciliation of powers *superior* to man.'

Another English anthropologist, R. Marett who specialises on beliefs of primitive natives, stated that religion was mainly man's emotional response to the unknown. The witch-doctor or shaman performed rituals which mostly involved with matters pertaining to danger and uncertainty in life such as birth, death, disease and hunger. The circumstances of actual or potential danger vary with the preoccupations of each society as the focus of rituals for some could be fertility of crops or domestic animals while others could be life-crises rituals or rites of passage, because they involved the passing of an individual from one status in life to another. Marett left his mark and let the world thinking when he concluded that religion was 'not so much thought out as *danced* out.'

What are some of the differences in religions today compared to the time of the wandering cavemen?

In every part of the world today, however primitive, there is some form of religious practice and belief. Religion is basically a belief that the world is inspired and directed by some superhuman power and intelligence. This power, whether an unseen and abstract spirit or a personal god, is seen as having the will to provide a *law* for mankind to live in harmony. Thus religion, under the guidance of an unseen force, goes hand in hand with morality for peaceful human existence.

Today we are able to express religion in a rich variety of ways. Hinduism, for example, embraces elaborate rituals and a hierarchy of gods. Christianity and Islam, which both have roots in Judaism, offer a universal God and a direct personal experience between God and man. Buddhism offers not gods but a code of moral conduct and inner enlightenment through righteous living or take the *middle way*. All the world's major faiths have proved remarkably durable. But the best development so far among religions is the rising belief that every one has a soul with *inner* power; a part of creation, a part of God that *is* everlasting. In other words, we are all *mini-gods* walking the earth like raw diamonds that only need polishing!

How do we assess people who do not have a religion?

It must be pointed out that even in our modern society, there are also millions of *atheists* or those who do not believe that there is an all mighty God that rules the universe. Then there are others like the *agnostics* who believe that God is unknown or beyond our comprehension. But it does not mean that they are people without principles or ethics compared to the religious ones. A dictionary defines religion as being 'devotion to some principle; strict fidelity or faithfulness; conscientious; pious affection or attachment,' giving rise to the fact that most people, including atheists and agnostics, do have some form of religious devotion in their lives.

Who is the first prophet in our recorded history?

The first saviour on earth to preach the path of God was *Rama* who appeared from the forests of Northern Europe. From there, he travelled to Persia and taught righteous living to the Persians through trust and faith in God. Rama's teachings was later reformed by *Zoroaster* who continued to spread the message of Rama and won many followers. There is little historical record on Rama's movements after Persia except that he finally settled in India. Rama taught early man that *life is eternal* and everyone can have the experience of God in his lifetime.

After Rama many spiritual messengers came from time to time and notable ones were *Krishna, Buddha, Jesus Christ* and *Mohammad.* They continued the same teachings of Rama regarding eternal life and it is important to note that they were *not* propagating a faith or religion but enlightenment on certain '*truths*' about the hidden powers of the inner self. 'Truth' was all about the connection of humans with

God and the beauty of living. But are we hearing the *same truths* as Rama or what Jesus used to preach at this present time?

Who is Abraham?

One of the most neglected giants in religion is Abraham as not many people seem to remember how he changed the world as a religious innovator by proclaiming that there is only *one* universal God. Abraham is best remembered when he heard 'the call of God' that gave him a shock of his life when told to sacrifice his son as proof of his love for God. He was forced to choose between the love for his precious son and God. In the end his heavy heart went with God and he took his son to the mountain to be slain as instructed. When he was about to slay his son, the angels came and stopped the painful ordeal as Abraham had proven his test of faith in God. His purity of heart has led to the promise that his descendants would ultimately occupy the land from the Nile to the Euphrates but they have to wander in the desert for many years as slaves before his children can be free.

The legacy of Abraham is endearing not only to Christians but is beloved also by both Muslims and Jews as the Koran and Hebrew Bible sing the praises of Abraham for his unwavering faith and the pioneer of a universal God. No one can really tell which century Abraham existed. However, it is said he lived before the formation of the main religions because Abraham is embraced by Judaism, Christianity and Islam as the 'Father' who served only one God. In fact, excluding God, Abraham is the only biblical figure who enjoys the unanimous acclaim of all three faiths; he is referred to by all as 'Father'.

Why the conflict over the centuries when there is a 'common Father?'

Historians are certain that early religious leaders have been trying to put claims on the identity of the 'Father' that he was a Jew,

Christian or Muslim and this move has probably done more harm than good for peacemakers. Despite the early bond, the three faiths appear reluctant to accept one another as part of a big family.

How and why Jews and Muslims split up?

The *family feud* between the two groups is further compounded by the fact that Abraham had two sons and both the boys were conceived in unusual circumstances. Abraham's wife Sarah was barren and persuaded Abraham to sleep with her Egyptian slave Hagar—a Muslim, who became pregnant and gave birth to the first son Ishmael. But because of Abraham's strong faith, God promised that he will have an heir from his blood-line and this was where the aging Sarah was able to conceive Isaac through a miracle birth at the age of 90. While the boys were growing up, Sarah sensed the jealousy and competition from Hagar and Ishmael. She forced Abraham to send them out into the desert. But through the grace of God, mother and son were saved and God made a promise to Hagar that Ishmael will also sire a great nation through 12 sons, which according to tradition, to be the 12 Arab tribes but stipulated that the Covenant with Abraham will only flow through Isaac's line. The Koran says Ishmael and Hagar travelled to Mecca and the prophet Mohammad was a descendant from Ishmael's blood-line. The Hebrew Bible says that Isaac's second son, Jacob, later became the founder of the nation which is now known as Israel.

It didn't end there as hostility between Jews and Muslims start to get petty; who was the loving and obedient 'sacrificial lamb' Abraham wanted to slay? Ishmael to Muslim and Isaac to the rest, with each revised religious book fantasising their hero with all his good qualities and running down the other the way they want to believe.

For generations both Jews and Muslims are at loggerheads as their knowledge or 'truths' about Abraham are coming from different texts based on the whims and fancies of scripture writers. But are simple *technicalities* such as who was being sacrificed a key issue? The fact remains that they were once all part of a big family and are 'cousins' as all of them are either sons of Ishmael or children of Isaac.

Who's to blame for present conflicts between Israel and Palestine?

At time of writing, both nations are still squabbling over their ancestors' land and are prepared to fight for their 'rights' to the very end. Are such nations the stumbling block to make the world a better place to live today when they threaten world security all the time with possible nuclear and biological warfare? But many shrew observers are quick to add that weak leaders can be easily bought these days and perhaps it is not insane to suggest that there may be *war stirrers* outside the two nations who thrive on wars because of a secret agenda.

It is of interest to note that the name 'Abraham' itself can be a unifying force because it means 'ancestor of multitude' in Hebrew. The Islamic pronunciation of Abraham is 'Ibrahim' and Ishmael and Isaac are also popular names in the Muslim world but written as 'Ismail' and 'Ishak'. The early connections among the various faiths are very clear but what are the chances of reconciliation if faith in a universal God founded by Abraham is brought back to *light* again? Perhaps a *charismatic negotiator* with the calibre of former president Gorbachev of Russia who united East and West Berlin, should be sought to mend fences and prevent a bloodbath in the Middle East. Abraham may be the only *realistic resource* available as the unifying force for interfaith in present troubled times of political mistrust. Peacemakers should know that firepower or corruption is no longer the answer to settle sensitive issues; it's all about *finesse* now where everyone wins.

Christianity

And what does the Lord require of you?
To act justly and to love mercy and to walk humbly with your God.

Micah 6:8

Why were early Christians in deadly conflict with their own Church?

Religion is supposed to be the basic foundation of morality and a friend of mankind. Unfortunately it was not the case with medieval Christians when the Church especially, was all-powerful and feared upon as if God resided there. But when there's power there's usually greed, indulgence and deceit.

Many good Christians today are not aware of centuries of doubt and in-fighting among their own church leaders and theologians over the truth and teachings of the New Testament that focused on the message from Jesus Christ. The origin of the sacred book is still a baffling mystery because the first New Testament conveniently disappeared after they were composed! What you read today are merely collections of *hearsay of storytellers* from different generations and regions. Exaggeration and distortion from basic truth by gospel writers are only expected.

Is the Bible influenced by early ruling Romans?

Scholars are almost unanimous in suggesting that the *New Testament,* composed more than 300 years after the death of Jesus, was the fusion of Christianity and the *main beliefs* of the ruling Romans who were pagans and worshipped nature like their *Sun God* and others like Neptune; lord of the sea. Our *'Sunday'* is obviously a mark of respect for the Sun God. The Romans' influence came to a crisis when corruption and immorality became a way of life and 'the nearer people are to the Roman Church, the head of their religion, the less religious are they,' says Machiavelli, a famous Italian philosopher of the 16th century. Moral living started to decay when the conquerors did not treat marriage vows seriously and regarded it as a social and economic convenience. Prostitution, abortion and divorce became widespread. In short, the Roman Church followed the footsteps of the Roman state and not the teachings of Jesus Christ of that time.

It has been said that the Bible was initiated by Emperor Constantine as a 'quick fix' mainly to avert a religious civil war among growing Christians and Romans after the death of Jesus Christ. Early Christians did not see eye to eye with their leaders who approved the Bible mainly to suit themselves for selfish reasons and distorted the teachings of Jesus Christ and perhaps, even his background as a person. The discovery of the *Dead Sea Scrolls* in the late 1940s adds more cracks to the credibility of the New Testament as there are more discrepancies to biblical knowledge against authentic old writings.

How did the all-powerful Roman Church acquire its riches?

'The real tragedy of the medieval church is that it failed to move with the time . . . . Far from being progressive, far from giving a spiritual lead, it was retrograde and decadent, corrupt in all its members,' says the book, '*The Story of the Reformation,*' giving accounts of church activities from the 5th to the 15th century.

By the end of the 15th century, the Church became the biggest landowner in Europe owning numerous plots of land including parishes, monasteries and convents throughout its domain and collecting taxes on properties that were leased out. The focus on land became an obsession and reportedly the greedy Church abused its power and took over half the land of France, Germany and any property it could grab to increase its assets. The steady flow of income eventually led to greed and church history of that period was what a historian called 'a succession of worldly popes.'

Greed and immorality from church leaders came to a ridiculous state when a common saying of that time was: 'If you want to ruin your son, make him a priest.' The situation became almost bizarre—but laughable to modern readers—when the church introduced the *sale of indulgences* which was like an insurance policy signed by church elders against punishment for any sinful act such as cheating or womanising, for a *price!* A reformist of that time, Erasmus said, 'The remission of purgatorial torment is not only sold, but forced upon those who refuse it.' Its like 'live it up and heaven awaits you' *if* you can pay. Church confessions became strictly for the poor but *charged* for a lower price! Such despicable acts were the main catalysts for *Reformation or Renaissance* mooted by German monk-scholar, Martin Luther who was against mercenary and sleeping popes basking in personal power and glory. Luther believed that forgiveness is granted solely because of God's grace and *not* by the authority of priests and popes. It was because Luther *protested* against the sale of indulgence, the word *'Protestant'* was coined for the Reformation movement in Germany.

Why are there so many factions in Christianity today?

It should be clear by now why there are so many divisions of Christianity today; we have Roman Catholics, Methodists, Mormons, Protestants, Jehovah Witnesses and *hundreds* of other groups with the same Christian faith breaking away from the Vatican like new political parties with different agendas how best to run the country! Church leaders from the past were not leaders in the real sense, but a stumbling block to religious unity of not only Christians but also to a troubled world deep in religious conflicts. Christendom was like an enemy to the outside world as it was well known for greed and religious hypocrisy. The Vatican was scorned by all during the medieval period and some staunch believers in Jesus wanted to break away from the moral corruption of the Vatican to start their own groups to re-establish the teachings of Jesus—whether rightly or wrongly—as each group had its own interpretation on the true message of Jesus based on their level of understanding.

Can Jesus Christ react to the many false teachings?

Remember in the 1990s where there was a sensational report about *real tears flowing* out from a figure of Jesus in one of the churches in Europe? Prominent scientists and psychics were baffled by the very strange occurrence as investigations showed that there was no evidence of trickery from the crying statue of Jesus Christ. Isn't that a loud and clear message that Jesus *is in pain* as his teachings on universal truth is misled and distorted by many Christian groups?

We have heard of living spiritual masters today but why are they not well known?

Prophets, enlightened or spiritual masters that walk the earth today are *few* and far apart. They are a humble breed that practice austerity like Jesus and Buddha. Jesus used to eat and sleep with the fishermen and Buddha and disciples find shelter in the forest and begged in the street for food. Mohammad used to mend his old clothes and did not believe in wastage. Some living masters are found either in the remote snow-capped Himalayan Mountain or some outback areas soaking up the sun instead of worrying about which attractive robe and headgear to wear in their next public appearance. Moses humble shepherd's stick has been changed to a sceptre made of gold or stud with jewels used by so-called 'regal popes'!

It is unfortunate that the majority of people kow-tow to money and colourful images first and seeking God is a low priority. Modern men and women are well noted for having a strong ego and it will be difficult for them to connect with the real masters or prophets who speak with the authority of God because egos are attracted to higher egos. They are more prepared to be drawn by false masters that are able to offer pomp and regality as witnessed in many religious ceremonies.

Our world is such that people get carried away by the messenger, not the message. This is one of the reasons why new religion, occultism, philosophy, metaphysics and spiritual organisations are on the rampage today because many people wanted to break away from past beliefs that were either outdated or questionable. This trend will continue because of changing times. But beware; there are also *fanatics* and 'false masters' in our midst with fat Swiss bank accounts!

Why are church crowds getting less all the time?

Our world is filled with uncertainties with potential nuclear wars and natural disasters that could wipe us out and bring end time. The church offers little to relieve our fears and probably the reason why so many have forsaken God. Jesus Christ declared that 'the Kingdom of God is within everyone,' during his famous sermon at Mt. Sinai. Does that mean everyone is a divine spark of God and possesses the power from within to connect with God? Are we here on a mission and it will not be finished as long as we are alive? Is there life after death? Is it true that we can serve God even at home or at the office as long as our minds are pure?

Many of the sermons we hear today are devoted to social conscience and little of the eternal life previously expounded by Rama, Krishna, Jesus Christ and Muhammad. The church is becoming more like a social institution these days and the crowd on Sunday is getting thinner all the time. We are all spiritual beings by nature and there is always the inner urge to seek a spiritual path or be connected to a group. But are we given the right directions by some churches and the reason why previous churchgoers are spending more time at home reading new age books which stimulate their minds and resonate with their souls.

Jesus Christ

> *When narrow pride and ignorance defiled mankind,*
> *Jesus came as the embodiment of love and compassion and lived*
> *among men, holding forth the highest ideals of life.*

Sai Baba

Please bear in mind that it is not the intent of this section to make any judgement on the Christian faith as mainstream Christianity today has integrity, love and tolerance. Some of the old Scriptures are filled with wisdom and are most inspiring. The *Ten Commandments* and the *Lord's Prayer* are not only timeless wisdom but also very humbling. We are only questioning *the accuracy of facts* in some sections of the Bible.

What is the significant on the discovery of the 'Gospel of Judas?

This discovery is not only amazing but will definitely add more controversy to the authenticity of the Bible. The *'Gospel Of Judas'*, previously unknown to the modern world, was discovered in a cavern in 1978—sold twice and stolen once—was authenticated through radio-carbon dating by Swiss experts in 2005 confirming that the writings on tree barks were ancient, going back to about 1,800 years ago. Latest findings have vindicated Judas from betrayal and deceit to a hero; Mary Magdalene—depicted as a prostitute in the Bible—exonerated from working in the world's oldest profession to possibly the right hand person and consort of Jesus and probably more influential than the head apostle Peter.

The *Gospel of Thomas* was also unearthed but never got a mention in the New Testament. Thomas was one of the 12 disciples of Jesus and his words should be respected as what he wrote was like a personal diary with nothing to hide regarding his time with Jesus. He had no doubt that Jesus was a highly evolved soul and a man of great wisdom. But he doubted the divinity of Jesus and did not mention anything about the crucifixion or resurrection leaving more controversy that *truth* was destroyed by the church or the ruling Romans. How are modern day Christians going to separate facts and fiction or conspiracy and ideology from the Bible when honesty was *not* the best policy in earlier time?

Has the New Testament given us enough information on the early life of Jesus Christ?

The truth about the life of Jesus Christ—his early whereabouts, crucifixion and place of death—is under the microscope and serious Christians like to clear the air and get to the bottom of it. Many sections of gospel writings are incomplete and one of the most disturbing missing links is the lack of report pertaining to the early life of Jesus. The Christian world places so much emphasis on the virgin birth of Jesus; remember the three wise kings who made the long journey from the East following the stars to Bethlehem and brought many gifts because Christ the *Saviour* was born? But strangely, very little was known about the childhood of Jesus; the saviour had conveniently *disappeared into the wilderness* at about age 13 according to the gospels and did not return till nearly twenty years later!

Many priests and pastors are having red faces and likely to suffer from ulcers as questions are hotting up by history and religious students who wish to know more about the missing years of Jesus' life that were not mentioned in scriptures. Curious students like to know whether Jesus was dark-skinned, short like Napoleon, fat like the Laughing Buddha, strong like Hercules, jovial or married and where did he go as a young man and why the secrecy?

Is the resurrection of Jesus Christ a myth?

The Bible says Jesus was '*resurrected*' or rose from the dead on the third day after his 'death'. This information does not hold well with modern day historians and theologians because Jesus did not come from the clouds and was *not* a celestial entity. Jesus was a mortal; a living person in flesh and blood with brothers and sisters and his physical body cannot be restored after death without human remains like skull and bones. Christians should be cautious taking the Bible word for word without knowing the truth about early church leaders fond of deceiving the simple-minded multitude of that time. If you believe in *karma*, it should be understood that no one can reincarnate as his previous physical self with the same brain or memory; otherwise the world would be very chaotic with 'dead people' walking again! Many theologians are prepared to challenge the authenticity of the resurrection as stated in the New Testament.

It is *without* a doubt that Jesus was a great teacher; he was the chosen or *anointed messenger* of God like many before and after him. The 'last days of Jesus' as explained in many gospels is losing credibility and people are questioning the integrity of early church elders whether they *fabricated* the crucifixion and resurrection of Jesus as a cover up. Is it a ploy the Church exalted the status of Jesus from a human to 'Son of God' to prevent further speculations on the tomb or remains of Jesus because it cannot be substantiated? Can you blame historians when they say that there are so many discrepancies that '*most objective New Testament scholars today dismiss the gospel accounts of the conception, birth and lineage of Jesus as a mixture of contrived fictions and demonstrable myths?*' (D. Joyce, 1972—*The Jesus Scroll*).

Where are the missing links in the life of Jesus?

Legends are rife in the East that Jesus was always on the move as a young man and there are records to validate his whereabouts.

Scholars and historians are certain Jesus left Judea at an early age to further his spiritual knowledge. Jesus was guided to travel to Egypt and learned from spiritual masters in the *Great Pyramid* where universal truths and eternal life were taught. Such teachings were supposedly the legacy of the *Atlantean* passed down to the Egyptians. When Jesus 'graduated' from the Pyramid, he moved on to *Persia, Nepal, Tibet and India* to learn as much as he could on spiritual matters from different ancient masters.

History may have to be rewritten because historians and researchers have gathered sufficient evidence to overturn history in a most intriguing and controversial issue; Jesus *might not* have died on the cross but managed to escape from punishment and took the 'Silk Road' through Asia and *landed in Japan*, the least expected place, and spent his final days there. Admittedly there are some discrepancies on the actual places Jesus visited during his early and later days but most historians agreed he went to Japan twice. Jesus appeared to be more like a saviour for the world venturing into many Eastern countries instead of confining his teachings to his people in Judea.

Are there proofs to substantiate Jesus living in Japan?

The most astonishing part about this new twist on Jesus' demise on Japanese soil is the fact that a *grave* was erected there as well as a signboard giving an account on his life and death in Japan. The signboard explains that Jesus first arrived in Japan at the age of 21 and after studying ancient Japanese *Shintoism* for 10 years, he compiled a doctrine and made his way back to Judea to teach his people. But the authorities there opposed the '*foreign teachings*' and decided to crucify him. But Jesus' brother, Isukiri, (Jacob) volunteered to die on Jesus' behalf. Jesus returned to Japan at the age of 37, made Japan his home and died at the old age of 106.

Until today, the burial site is well looked after by the 'Sawaguchi family'—locally known as the descendants of 'Kirisuto', the Japanese way of saying 'Christ'—in a remote village called *'Herai'* in Northern Japan but the name of the ancient village has now been changed to 'Shingo.' According to scholars, the name 'Herai' is a derivation of the word *'Heburai,'* the Japanese pronunciation of *'Hebrew.'* When I first came across this somewhat whimsical information, I thought it was all a hoax. But later research shows that there are pictures to prove and the grave and signboard are still there coupled with the fact that the history is well documented in the Japanese archives where *all* are welcome to examine. The details about the life of Jesus from Japanese sources are well chronicled with fresh, intriguing revelations and definitely deserve further investigations. The Japanese have nothing to hide, its all part of history to them. They maintain a low profile on the burial site partly because only a fraction of the population is Christians. They are also discreet as any publicity would only create religious turmoil for the Christian faith in the Western world.

Is it God's will that the grave be preserved in a foreign land so that the truth would eventually surface? If I am a historian, I'll be taking the first flight to Japan to verify the truth regarding the life of Jesus Christ despite objections from the Vatican!

How should the Vatican tackle this astounding and disturbing news?

This unexpected discovery will obviously stun the Christian world. But why shouldn't the truth be taken in a positive light instead of an ill wind that blows nobody any good? Isn't it true that God is for *all* the races of the world? Jesus should be glorified all the more for his tireless efforts to preach the Kingdom of God as far as his feet could carry him without fear, prejudice or discrimination but only love. *If* ancient Japanese documents bear any semblance of truth, past ill-judged decisions designed to silence the public must be rectified immediately as *facts* are stubborn things that won't go away.

Church leaders must clean their house before they can do God's work and theirs. The embarrassing cover-ups of the past is history; current church leaders are not to blame. It's time for 'spring cleaning' and making amends for past mistakes where good Christians would understand and forgive and forget. If such a revelation is necessary, it offers the Vatican the unique opportunity to transform and reform like the start of *a new beginning* instead of being dragged down like a victim in a sinking ship. It is never easy to right a wrong but when Vatican's correctness is humbly made, it can breathe a 'freer, religious air'—the conscience is clear and productive work becomes easier and faster. More importantly, it shows the true strength and character of a leader who is in tune with changing time and as upright as a tower instead of being part of an *ancient dark system* that couldn't heal itself.

Are there other persuasive evidence supporting the fact that Jesus did not die on the cross?

Yes, facts do not go away even though you are a master in cover-ups. It was the *written words* of a Jewish historian called *Flavius Josephus* who lived during the time of Jesus that provided very compelling evidence. The gospels had led us to believe that Jesus was '*arrested*' by a mob sent by the High Priest to put Jesus on trial. But Josephus recorded that the High Priest Ananus (Annas) 'convened the judges of the Sanhedrin (Jewish Council) and brought before them a man called James, the *brother* of Jesus who was called the Christ, and certain others.' (Jewish Antiquities, XX, 200-ix,1). The name 'James' or 'Jacob' is supposed to be the same person and brother of Jesus according to gospels.

I also find it very intriguing when ancient scripture mentioned that the reputed seer Daniel who served the great Babylonian king

Nebuchadnezzar around 600 BC, predicted that Jesus would be *'cut-off'* from his people 500 years ahead of his time. Daniel was the ancient Nostradamus as he accurately prophesised the destruction of Jerusalem and its great temple in amazing detail. The highly respected seer *did not say* that Jesus *died* on the cross as we were led to believe from later gospels. I am of the opinion that the word 'cut-off' is more likely to mean *'excommunicated,'* or *'banished'* and not 'death,' as assumed by simple people of olden days. The confusion is probably due to lack of appropriate word in describing the fate of Jesus in ancient time coupled with the difficulties of scripture writers in translating *ancient* Hebrew writings to the English language.

Can we improve the image of religions?

A good name is better than riches. Perhaps the time has come for the restructuring of religions to keep pace with the ever changing world. Forward thinking leaders like the Pope, Dalai Lama, respected Muslim and other ethnic leaders should start now by having dialogues like 'knights of the round table' to thrash out differences for common goals and agreement on basic *universal truths.* They should not be glued to their comfort zones as the new generation is no longer discussing their *authorities* and *lack of actions* but debating the existence of God as last resort to save a corrupt world! For starters, the lessons on karma should be taught in schools to enable the young to understand the consequences of good and bad behaviour. When karma is understood at a young age, there is a tendency for more people to live appropriately instead of recklessly in later life.

Perhaps the UN can initiate such a move to keep the different faiths fighting for a common cause. More productive work can be done when religious leaders are actively working as a team to unite the world. There is so much work to be done if people are prepared to put their heads together to change and improve the image of religions. More importantly, such a move will result in some basic *control* on religious activities for the first time and probably a much needed *catalyst* for more reforms to expedite harmonious living for all cultures.

It is said that a big beautiful garden is the result of many hands responsible for watering, fertilizing, pruning and clearing the rubbish. Likewise, the joint efforts of leaders in the various faiths can work together to *differentiate* the trees from the wood. Obviously it is easier said than done but look at the business world today: It's all about restructuring and looking for fresh ideas, getting rid of unmarketable products or services and bringing in new personnel with expertise to enhance productivity and growth. There is no denying that it will be mammoth task but if leaders show little urgency on religious reforms, our history would slip further downhill waiting for 'end time' to take its course. Complete religious freedom as we see it today, is no good thing as it breeds only *fanatics* with outdated beliefs not conducive to progress for a fast changing world of new technologies and sciences.

A Glimpse of God

It is a joy to be hidden but a disaster not to be found.

D. W. Winnicott

Are the main religions of the world worshipping the same God?

We have come a long way to respect the religions of the world today by realising that the *essence* of the message in various religions is all the same, the difference is only in the wrapping. The name '*God*' is the most universal word today although many races use different names such as *Brahman* for Hindus, *Sat Nam* or *Aum* for some Indians, *Allah* for Muslims, *Sugmad,* and various names for the sake of identification. They all mean the same *Divine Reality or Universal Spirit.*

What actually is God?

Not many dare to answer this question because the *absolute truth* is not known, even to all the organised religions. Other than knowing that God is love, our knowledge of God appears to be a big blur. Have you seen a picture or statue of God in any place of worship other than Krishna, Jesus Christ, Buddha, Mohammad, Goddess of Mercy, Sai Baba and other deities?

Paul Twitchell, a spiritual giant and the modern-day founder of *'Eckankar'*, repeatedly mentioned that for those who have not experienced soul travels, it will *stagger* the human mind to understand God and the workings of timeless perfection or the universal concepts of the *spiritual* science. God's presence has to be *experienced* before it can be understood. Our level of consciousness in the physical plane is attuned mostly to shapes and material forms like land, forests, animals, humans, money, houses, cars, and the lot. Our world is *'seeing is believing,'* and anything that is abstract or invisible is banished to the weird, absurd or twilight zone because of our lack of imagination and understanding. Humans are strange creatures whether religious or otherwise: we all pray to God in our moments of need. *Who or what* we are praying appears unimportant. Is ignorance really bliss?

For the sake of simplicity, God is not a law, nor a person and has no form. Twitchell explained that *light and sound* are the basic elements and *representation* of God on earth. His universal energy (life force) or *chi* is everywhere. It may be easier to explain that God transmits His light like blowing a conch shell: a swirling, soothing and lively sound is generated from His breath and the *chi* expands like a blanket and vibrates into space as sound waves. The divine *chi* is composed of very fine and invisible particles called *atoms* to make our world and other worlds. The sound waves or vibrations become the stream of life in the universe. Those who are familiar with physics would understand that sound waves are actually electro magnetic waves and you are not wrong to say that our planet works like a gigantic magnet. All living organisms are composed of atoms; humans, animals, plants, including the air we breathe and everything in it. Strange as it may sound, scientists today are still baffled by the origin of atoms.

According to the spiritual group Eckankar, light and sound is the Holy Spirit of God and the two aspects through which God appears to our physical world. The light is the *reflection* of the atoms of God moving in space and the *sound* is the audible life current caused by interaction or bumping of trillions of atoms that will carry souls back home to God. This is not something easy for many to comprehend but suffice to say that the greatness of God is not meant to be understood by *unevolved* humans from the third dimension.

How does God rule the universe?

If *anybody* knows, he or she must be the right hand person of God! When we gaze at the sky, we will be struck by the exquisite beauty and *orderly* fashion of the universe that supported the galaxies, stars, planets, nature and the functioning of the human mind. There is no denying by scientists that there is structure and order in the laws of nature that underlies all things but nobody has the faintest idea on the dynamics of its perfection. Many authors of new age books have plenty to say about this but do they really know or simply put their theories to book and wait for the gullible to believe? The best part: who is going to prove that what they claimed is right or wrong regarding heavenly matters? We are only here for lessons; God's work is beyond our comprehension because we are *far, far* from whole.

Are we created with the image of God?

Definitely, you are a divine spark of God and other than your physical make-up, your main elements are also light and sound. Your light is represented by the *aura* encasing your body. The sound is your heartbeat and breathing. When the light and music in you disappear, what do you think has happened? Remember, '*Verily, all is Brahman?*'

Humour

The best medicine

A church notice-board says: 'If you are tired of sins, come in and rest with God.' Below the sign and scribbled in lipstick: 'If not, call friendly Madonna, 12155'.

Chapter 6

MEGA TSUNAMI, WAR AND PEACE

Asian Tsunami

> *Under heaven nothing is more soft*
> *and yielding than water.*
> *Yet for attacking the solid and the strong,*
> *nothing is better; it has no equal.*

Lao Tzu

'*It's an extraordinary calamity of such colossal proportions that the damage has been unprecedented,*' a journalist said about the catastrophic tsunami disaster that occurred off the coast of Acheh in Sumatra on Boxing Day in December, 2004. A pilot conducting aerial survey made the chilling remark that some villages appeared to have *vaporised* and were completely wiped out! The fury of nature affected 12 countries and the death toil came up to 230,000 and a few million people became homeless within minutes.

My stomach churned when I watched TV and saw families searching for loved ones among the corpses lined up on beaches, fields and roadsides. The living co-exist uneasily with the dead and struggling to withstand the nauseating stench of decomposed bodies at the same time. Haunting scenes of grieving parents cradling their dead children are unforgettable. Dead bodies start to decompose very quickly and the authorities have little choice but conduct mass burial immediately to safeguard the spread of diseases. There is no dignity in this kind of death where bodies are thrown into a big hole like a *rubbish dump*. As parents carefully laid their children down, a bulldozer shovelled sand on the corpses and the parents moved aside for the next family to do the same. Mothers and relatives could only grieve, lying on the side of a giant sand mound as if the light has gone out of their lives. The tears in their eyes they can wipe away, but the aches in their hearts will always stay.

Mega Tsunami

It is part of nature,
part of history
and part of the future.

Prof. Bill Mcquire

'*Tsunami*' is a Japanese word for giant tidal waves hitting harbours and commonly called 'killer waves'. The initial energy may be so vast as to drive a series of waves at high speed across the Pacific Ocean from Japan to California and *back* again. Is the worst still to come? The Asian tsunami in 2004 coupled with the many earthquakes in recent time have shocked the world and questions are mounting up whether there were *mega tsunamis* of catastrophic and unimaginable force that could change the landscape of planet earth and swallowed up legendary cities like *Atlantis* in prehistoric times?

Our scientists and geologists made a chilling discovery when trying to figure out the reasons on the disappearance and appearance of many islands in the world particularly in Hawaii. This popular holiday resort has been scarred by many tidal waves occurrences which swept away villages and countless lives. The dark history of Hawaii started to surface when it was discovered that two million years ago, mega-tsunami had struck Hawaii before; part of ancient Hawaii is still buried *underneath* the sea. A single giant rock, believed to be the equivalent to 10 times the volume of Mount Everest, is buried in the ocean. It is very hard to imagine the size of waves that can wipe ancient Hawaii off the map. As if this scary information is not enough, it has been calculated that what happened in ancient Hawaii was a *thousand times* more powerful than the event that took place in Sumatra!

The size of tidal or storm waves which Hawaii and other parts of the world experienced in recent time is a far cry from the past. Tidal waves, no matter how high they are, the length rarely exceed 100 metres from front to back. This is because they are created merely by the effect of the wind on the surface of the ocean. In mega-tsunami however, the wave moves the entire body of the ocean right down to the seabed several kilometres below. The size of the wave is directly related to the size of the *landslide,* and not under-water earthquake as experienced in Sumatra. When gigantic amount of rocks and earth come crashing down, enormous volume of water will be shifted; the size of the wave can be hundreds of kilometres in length from front to back and capable of travelling thousands of kilometres in the ocean. The sheer magnitude of its size makes mega-tsunami particularly devastating when they hit the shoreline with unimaginable power!

Search for Volcanic Islands

This scary discovery is a real potential catastrophe for our time and geologists all over the world concluded that the biggest threat is large volcanic islands which are prone to landslide because of the way they are built. Volcanic islands began life millions of years ago when lava erupted in the ocean floor. As it cooled and hardened, layers built upon layers, until it formed a land platform of volcanic rubble above sea level. Scientists realised that every few thousand years, the volcanic rubble would collapse and fall into the sea.

After extensive research on many islands, a British geologist, Dr Simon Day, identified the island, *Las Palmas*, in the Canary Islands off North Africa, as the location for the next *'big bang'* on land and will be the *biggest natural disaster* in recorded history! According to Day, the island Las Palmas has all the precursors for a colossal landslide. He discovered that part of the west-side of the island is *slipping and sliding* off to the sea. Baffled by this occurrence, Day decided to investigate the cause of the mystery by using a tunnel into the extinct volcano hoping to find some answers.

This was the first time in history that researchers have the opportunity to explore the 'the dark side' of a volcano going a few km inside horizontally and 2 km below the surface for a better understanding of the rock structure. What was discovered inside the volcano was unexpected: *water*! Over thousands of years, rainwater has sipped into the heart of the volcano through the loose rubble—mainly earth—which is permeable and act like a collection tank for water. Alongside the permeable rubble, is a different type of rock structure, vast *vertical* columns of cooled lava which form hardened *dykes* or solid walls, and is not permeable. The formation of the dykes act as dams responsible for trapping columns of water in the heart of the volcano. But further studies revealed that water pressure alone cannot collapse a volcanic island. It needed another element of nature: *heat.* It was discovered that when a new vent of magma starts rising and erupt, water trapped between the dykes would be heated up. This will make it expand creating enormous pressures within the volcano. The flanks of the dykes and the rubble would be greatly weakened by the extremely high pressure. This, according to scientists, will trigger off a *giant landslide* where the west of Las Palmas will collapse and plunge into the sea as a single pulse of energy never seen by humans before.

America, going, going gone?

> *To everything there is a season,*
> *and a time to every purpose under the heaven.*

Ecclesiastes

Biggest disaster on earth

But what is most alarming from the discovery of Dr Day is the magnitude of fractures in the current active volcano in Las Palmas. A detailed rock study showed that about 20 kilometres of the volcano are under tremendous stress and showing signs of weakening due to water pressure making it *critically* unstable. If this were to collapse, an unimaginable half trillion tons of rocks would come crashing down into the ocean! Bear in mind that the island originated from thousands of years of piling up of volcanic rubble underneath the sea. What you can see of Las Palmas today is like the tip of an iceberg. The length of this mega-tsunami would be at least a few hundred kilometres in length from front to back and heading directly to the East Coast of America like a torpedo at a great speed of 720km/h! It would take about 8 hours before all the cities from New York to Miami would be engulfed; how far *deep inland* the wave would sweep is any body's guess as it is dependent on the contours of the shoreline whether it is flat, hilly or with high cliffs to break the wave. It would appear unreal to see a wall of wave between 700-1000m high, charging from the coastline at tremendous speed and hitting land with not only one deafening roar but *many times* because of the building up of the giant wave from the back when nearing shallow water and upon impact.

Part of Nature

Historical records estimated that earthquake in Las Palmas occurs once in every 200 years and the island may still stand for decades to come. But smaller summit eruptions will continue to weaken the flanks of both rubble and dykes. It may take another five or even 20 volcanic eruptions before the 'big bang' goes off. There is no time frame to expect another giant landslide because our Creator is not in the habit of giving out deadline. But as one scientist, Prof. Bill Mcquire puts it, '*It is part of nature, part of history and part of the future.*'

The predicted disaster for America is heart stopping because even powerful nations can always negotiate and compromise to prevent a nuclear or chemical war but have absolutely no control over the fury of Mother Nature. Because we have not experienced mega-tsunami, we don't think it will happen in our time, we ignore it and many would even dismiss it as another myth like Atlantis. But speak to the geologists and scientists; they are certain it will happen, the only difficulty is *when?*

Warning Bells from God

The golden moments in the stream of life rush past us,
and we see nothing but sand;
the angels come to visit us,
and we only know when they are gone.

George Eliot

Breaking up the holy agreement

Is heaven offended with human transgression and plans to take off another slice of the world? Through the many classical texts we have come to learn that the people during Noah's time did not live righteously and revelled in indulgence where wine, women and song were the order of the day. The people repeatedly ignored the teachings of the prophets on repentance and gave a deaf ear to follow God's way to live righteously. They went against the prophets and were subsequently destroyed by the great flood. Are we going to allow history to repeat itself? Are we going to heed the testimonies of written scriptures and pay attention to warnings from living prophets on the dangers of greed and sins? What is most disturbing and scary now is the chilling warning in the scripture for America:

> *And now, we can behold the decrees of God concerning this*
> *land, that it is a land of promise: and whatsoever nation*
> *shall possess it shall serve God, or they shall be swept off*
> *when the fullness of his wrath shall come upon them. And*
> *the fullness of his wrath shall come upon them when they are*
> *ripened in iniquity.*

(Eth. 2:9.)

The Chambers dictionary defines *'iniquity'* as—want of equity or fairness: injustice: wickedness: a crime.

Apparently the land of promise has tremendous potential because God sanctioned it. However, its success and prosperity are subject to a very *clear condition*—the people must follow the teachings of God through His messengers and live righteously or be 'swept off' when warnings are consistently ignored. It's almost an identical message compared to Noah's time and many Americans reading this should get goose bumps.

How are Americans faring today?

I honestly believe that the majority of Americans are highly intelligent and wonderful people. The world used to look up to America as a great nation: it is the land of plenty with all the glitters and well known for producing quality products. Many dream of living there or at least visit America during one's life-time. Our lives have been spiced up through America's influence: we laugh and cry watching big or small screens as the American entertainment industry is second to none. Americans are great innovators but what about their *leaders*? Are they fond of pulling wool over the eyes of others? Do they see only evil in their enemies and not themselves? Are they following the footsteps of their founding fathers like Washington and Lincoln who believed in justice and faith in God? Are they acting righteously as trustees to preserve the American heritage of a firm reliance on Divine Providence?

The American constitution is being amended all the time to suit ambitious new leaders who trust themselves more than the principles of good governance laid down by great leaders of the past. Since the new millennium, it's all about world domination and being the greatest superpower on the planet. To be continuously obsessed with might and power and achieving them at all costs is an early invitation for God to display His wrath.

America is branded a *corporation* and not a country because it will say and do anything to sell its products especially fighter planes, missiles, guns and bombs that are not conducive to world peace. Don't allow *iniquities* to ripen. 'Abandon ship' on unproductive projects that are life threatening or exploiting the weak—give priority to some key issues like preventing corruption at the top, global warming, dangers of nuclear wastes, looking after the common people, raising the quality of life in third world countries and last but not least, educate the nation about universal truths.

'Fiat justicia, ruat coelum'

It is difficult for a powerful and glorious nation to switch to reverse gear and change established political and economic philosophies that gave them the 'big brother' tag though simmering of discontent from locals are hotting up by the day. It's all about power and winning an election. But for how long before their leaders start to falter with answers that needed immediate verifications or caught in the wrong act? Other nations are getting smarter all the time too.

The fate of America lies in the hands of its policy makers. Nobody has the answer on the timing of the biblical prediction or whether the *potential* demise of America will be put on hold indefinitely as God works in mysterious ways. The religions of the world share a common principle that if a person is earnestly prepared to repent on past sins, the all forgiving God is more than happy to give him a new lease of life when he consistently shows positive changes. The children of God are not all angels; they are also *reformers* who finally see the light.

Policy makers should learn to soften or retract certain harsh actions that are one-sided and follow the guiding light of the Latin maxim, *'Fiat justicia, ruat coelum.'* (Let justice be done, though the heavens fall.) Science and technology are so advanced these days that God has provided almost all the physical or material needs of the people. The only shortage now is the hidden spiritual needs as human survival is all about the balancing act of *yin and yang* or the balancing of the physical and spiritual. America must change its 'warring foreign strategy' so that the wise and honest can repair the damage before it becomes the river of no return.

The former great leader of India, Mahatma Gandhi, once said that humans are so sucked up by the materialistic world that they lost sight of their spiritual side and ignore the signs that God sent to them from time to time. They *required drums to be beaten into their ears* in order to open up their eyes.

Are Wars Mostly Cover-ups?

The great masses of people . . .
will more easily fall victim to a big lie
than to a small one.

Adolf Hitler

Are there suspicious underlying reasons for wars and terrorism?

It is hard to believe that The United Nations is still unable to stop years of on-going wars in places like the Middle East and Africa. Is the UN exercising its full power or has it succumbed to the voices of the powerful? Are many such wars '*stirred up*' because some so-called superpowers are fond of cover-ups to fulfil their hidden agendas?

Some of the biggest industries in the world are the production of war planes, submarines, warships, tanks, missiles, bombs and guns. Production must continue and obsolete stocks *must be sold* to enable new lines to be added to *sustain the industry*. It's like selling motor cars; if there is no sale, the production line or factory will be closed and workers displaced. Any shut down of big industries will obviously have a negative impact on the country's economy; smaller businesses connected to national defence will be affected and investments in stocks and properties will slide while unemployment rate will climb. Poor nations appear to be the target to incite wars as they are not only easily controlled, but also excellent dumping grounds for outdated weapons that are rusting away at the yard. But more often than not, things can get out of hand and planned strategy can backfire because God has eyes.

Has the world been taken for a ride on Iraq's WMD?

Are there *really* weapons of mass destruction (WMD) in Iraq and connections of Saddem to al-Qaeda or merely lies to justify further expansion of war from Afghanistan to Iraq? What's more, it was also a timely option to *experiment* and test out new weapons and getting rid of old ones at the same time. I remember watching on TV where an uncomfortable Colin Powell, former US Secretary of State, made a presentation to members of the UN Security Council with *blurred* satellite pictures showing the location of the Iraqi's hideout for their WMD to justify an invasion. A French investigator said that Powell's presentation was *'unconvincing at best.'* When actual invasion took place on the ground, the Americans were *unable* to find the site as shown on tape other than a feeble excuse that the enemies have moved!

Is it possible that a supposedly modern plant of WMD could disappear into thin air? The funny part was the audacity of US troops to 'hide' protective chemical suits in the ground so that they could be *discovered* as proof that there was a plant for WMD as shown on television! Sometimes the American leadership has no respect for its allies and treated them as if they would more easily fall victim to a big lie than a small one. Some political analysts speculated that Powell, a former four-star general and commander of the Allied Forces during the Gulf War, was made a scapegoat to front the UN Security Council. Powell was obviously a man of honour and decided to have no part in dirty politics by retiring before his term was up.

Isn't it true that current wars only promote terrorism?

Why did so many nations back out from joining the Allied Forces to invade Iraq? The world is not blind. The carnage of war only brings death to the innocents and inflicts grief, sufferings, poverty, hatred and revenge to the living; the hatching ground for terrorism. When a son, daughter or parent is killed in the crossfire of war, retaliation on the offender cannot be ruled out to avenge the dead. This is an option, especially in poor nations where many have lost their livelihood; revenge has given survivors a cause to live again. Eventually there will be a payback time for the *stirrers* for causing the painful miseries of wars on others.

At time of writing, the Allied Forces led by the Americans are drowning in the quicksand of Iraq because they are responsible for more civilian deaths than opposing soldiers. Innocent women and children have their heads and limbs blown away and we hear little of these because the dead were not Americans and cover-ups for *mistakes* and controlled media reporting to hush up controversial issues are the specialty of the Bush administration. The locals will not stand by and watch their people and country destroyed by invaders. I find it very sickening when Time magazine reported that in Nov. 2005, near the town of Haditha in western Iraq, a roadside bomb exploded and killed an American Marine. However, the next day the local American Marine newsletter reported that an American and 15 Iraqi civilians were killed by the blast and that 'gunmen attacked the convoy with small-arms fire,' prompting the Marines to return fire, killing 8 insurgents and wounding one other. But the truth of the incident was inaccurately reported by the military to deceive the public: the details of the report contrasted greatly with eyewitnesses and local officials who were interviewed. The locals claimed that the civilians who died in Haditha were *not* killed by a roadside bomb but by the aggressive and trigger-happy Marines themselves. They went on a rampage in the village on a cold-blooded revenge after a colleague died, killing 15 unarmed Iraqis in their homes, including seven women and three children. A living witness to the slaughter; a nine-year girl called Eman, who was tightly held by adults that died in the process for shielding her from bullets, said: 'I watched them shoot my grandfather, first in the chest and then the head. Then they killed my granny.' War atrocities are rarely made known until journalists go beyond borders to seek the truth. Time magazine and staff should be saluted for its fair and balanced reporting on world affairs.

Take a good look at the on-going border wars in Gaza between Israel and Palestine. The innocents are dying almost daily for years and what has been done to resolve the pains? Why are the Americans so wrapped up in supporting Israel and have done little as peacemakers? Why can't Americans leave the Middle-East problems to the UN and mind their own business? There must be some amicable solutions for a win-win situation for both nations. Analysts strongly believe that negotiation on financial compensation appears to be the only solution for a 'New Jerusalem' as money talks. Who's going to pay? Stop the war and withdraw the foreign troops and the mammoth expenditure saved should be more than enough to cover all agreements. But is peace between the two hot headed countries the answer to American foreign policies?

The innocents, especially loyal soldiers, unaware of the secret agendas of their ruthless leaders, will continue to die as withdrawal of troops means 'defeat' or loss of face for their masters. Sacrifices of lives, under the guise of a righteous war, appear a better option than admission of an ill-judged war from egoistic leaders. Some so-called world leaders—past and present—are not speaking their minds; they are trying to poison our minds simply for their unquenchable thirst for world domination. What have leaders learnt from the 'Holy War' of the middle Ages, the exploits of Napoleon, Hitler or even the not so long ago 'Vietnam War'?

What are some of the causes of internal war within a country?

It's the same old story about greed and power that has been entrenched into the human mind for thousands of years. Look at the situation in Congo, Africa today in 2007. About 5 million civilians, rebels and soldiers are reported dead in the last decade because of fighting between the Government's army and rebels over the free-for-all mineral resources of the country. Experts on the Congo's situation are of the opinion that the 'defender of Congo,' General Nkunda, wanted to have a monopoly on the revenue of the lucrative exports of cassiterite tin ore which is in great demand by electronic manufacturers like Japan. The renegade general is prepared to shoot and kill anyone who hinders his short-cut to riches. What about African diamonds? They are no longer girls' best friends but a source of survival for some African men and women who risk death to extract the white stones in exchange for food and shelter or, in some cases, barter for guns and ammunition for protection from raiders. The government had issued stern warnings on the extreme dangers of illegal prospecting for gold or diamonds; but many turned a deaf ear as a starving stomach doesn't have ears.

The tragic assassination of Pakistan's Benazir Bhutto in a country plagued with sporadic wars and coups is another example of political struggle for power. It will be a long road for poverty stricken-countries like Zimbabwe to end sufferings when under the ruthless leadership of Mugabe who laughs at human rights and treat his people like slaves. It was reported that a can of ham cost a week's pay and an average teacher is considered a high earner when paid $10 a month while Mugabe moves around in a chauffeur-driven Mercedes car. Cambodia is also worth mentioning: the army rules the country while elected leader of the people, Aung San Suu Kyi, a Nobel Prize winner in 1971, is under house arrest for nearly two decades. Some of the Cambodian generals live in palaces while the hard working farmers who made the country 'the rice bowl of the world,' live in huts and battling rain and storm in the rice fields with children who cannot read and write. The list is endless.

What is the main cause of the Afghan war?

The Afghan war was mooted by America after the surprise attack by terrorists on the Trade Centre in New York on 9/11 in 2001. The world sympathised with America and supported it to crush the terrorist organisation, al-Qaeda, masterminded by the world's most wanted terrorist, Osama bin Laden. After more than seven years of fighting, killing and destruction of properties at the expense of the poor locals in the rugged hard land of Afghanistan, the elusive bin Laden is still at large. Common sense should prevail by now that Osama will not be hiding in one of the caves in the mountain waiting to be captured. He is probably enjoying his Kentucky fried chicken in Saudi Arabia or living in a 'castle' somewhere with his many wives!

It was reported that long before the arrival of American troops, the Korengal Valley in Afghanistan was once a relatively rich land and timber was the main source of income for the population. According to local lore, war with the coalition troops started in *earnest* when the Americans, acting on a tip-off from a rival tribe, dropped a bomb and destroyed the timber mill of a local chief, killing his workers and relatives that lead to a trail of vengeance. It must also be understood that *'Taliban'* these days, no longer refers only to the regime that once ruled the country; the word has become synonymous with those who are against foreign and government's troops. A tribal elder, Sham Sher Khan had this to say: 'The Taliban say they are fighting because there are Americans here and it's a *jihad*. But the fact is, they aren't fighting for religion. They are fighting for money,' he says. 'If they had jobs, they would stop fighting.' In another part of Afghanistan, U.S. troops are gunning down the Taliban because they argued that it was necessary to eradicate the opium trade. Such action will only inflict more financial woes to the mountain people and fuel more aggression when 'job strategy' or alternatives are not considered to sustain the survival of the locals. Who wants to fight or kill another human being when one has a steady job and money to feed the family? It should be clear that as long as the Taliban are hunted down like animals and forced to hide in caves and live in rotten conditions without electricity, proper food, sunshine or even the luxury of a proper bath, their only motivation to stay alive is *revenge.* The question is: 'Are Americans stopping terrorism or spurring it'?

Is there any prophecies regarding the fate of Osama bin Laden?

We are side-tracking a little from this question. But a 21st century prediction made by Nostradamus made 500 years ago is too good to be ignored:

> *On the midnight hour, the army's leader*
> *Will run away, disappearing suddenly.*
> *Seven years later, his fame undiminished*
> *Not once will yes be said to his return.*

If you are prepared to reflect maturely on his famous quatrain of four liners, Nostradamus is referring to Osama that is *eerily* accurate so far. The bearded one has given the world the slip but will play mischief to tout his foes.

Is the War in Afghanistan justified?

The media reported that the death toll of foreign troops is getting higher by the month and civilian deaths and sufferings are also mounting. Local Afghans complained that the soldiers 'were meant to save us, but they are actually killing us,' when more than 1200 civilian deaths were recorded in 2007. The commander of the NATO coalition, Brigadier-General Richard Blanchette said that 232 soldiers have been killed in combat in 2007 and the 2008 death toll is expected to surpass that figure. He added that the Taliban militants was mounting more attacks on the foreign forces and acknowledged that the use of improvised explosive devices or roadside bombs, are constant threats to foreign troops. More importantly, the commander was frank enough to admit that winning the war greatly depended on the capacity of the *local* Afghan army and police, the key to the nation's long-term security. It's a broad hint that NATO troops are ineffective in crushing the well organised militants who have a distinct advantage fighting in their *own backyard*. Remember why the Americans had to pull out from the Vietnam War?

In mid 2008, it was reported that American commandos were blamed for causing civilian casualties due to 'wrongful raids' of suspected terrorists' cells in Pakistani villages along the Pakistan and Afghan border. The Pakistani Army Chief confronted its American ally and accused them of not only 'intentional raids without consultation,' but also *irresponsible* fighters who are trigger happy to heighten tension and justify their presence.

The time has come for foreign troops to pack up and go home after seven years of hide-and-seek in a senseless war that not only accelerate pains and hardship on both fronts, but also the billions in foreign funds that have been wasted. Instead of waging wars, 'a little America' can be built in any poor country and what can be more appealing and challenging than that if you are a *genuine* leader who wants to unite the world? The issue of troops' maintenance and high death tolls have sparked fresh debates in France, Germany and Canada about their continued presence in Afghanistan.

Are certain deadly diseases created by an evil group with dark agenda?

Is it possible that disease such as 'AIDS' and 'SARS' are *manufactured* to disorient the world for dark reasons? We were initially led to believe that AIDS was transmitted through monkeys because of some sex starved Africans or is it merely an experiment that got out of hand on an *expendable* nation who is unable to see the sinister motives of the dark group and too weak to fight back?

After 9/11 in New York, the American economy took a dive and the tourism industry there was at a standstill and the East became the sensible alternative for rich travellers to splash their money. Business in most Asian countries skyrocketed for a while but all good things must come to an end. Out of the blue, the deadly and infectious SARS virus has devastated Asian markets, ruined the tourist trade of an entire region, nearly bankrupted airlines and spread panic in

Asia. The mechanism by which SARS works is still unclear giving rise to a growing suspicion that the life threatening virus might have been cultivated from a secret lab somewhere, mainly to balance power and trade between East and West or perhaps, the work of an unknown group not meant for us to know?

Any reason why 'sudden death' of certain people is becoming common?

Modern science is so advanced today that it is no longer necessary to secretly hire hit-man to bump off any menacing person or leader. 'Undetected food poisoning' is high on the suspicion list to get rid of anyone. The strange demise of former Palestinian leader, Yasser Arafat, and the sudden critical illness of former Prime Minister Sharon of Israel, are making more people to wonder that *perhaps* modern science can have a dark side when fallen into wrong hands.

Is the American CIA an asset or liability for world peace?

Probably only the Bush administration can answer that question. But in the eyes of the world, the CIA is a can of worms and should be the first to be blasted away! They are branded as the 'secret trouble-makers' that is well known for stirring up small wars, espionage, corruption and security to keep the American armament industry afloat as any collapse of this lucrative business will cripple the American economy.

It is not surprising that even the fragile democratic government of Pakistan headed by Zardari—the widower of Benasir Bhutto—had plenty to say about the Americans. 'The terrorist threat is a cancer eating my country. The germ was created by the CIA.' When questioned about Osama bin Laden and gang hiding in Pakistan, he denied supporting al-Qaeda. 'They were pushed into Pakistan by your great military offensive in Afghanistan . . . I've lost my wife, my friends, the support of my countrymen . . . and in eight years you haven't been able to eliminate the cancer,' Zardari said sarcastically.

Time magazine reported that 'American secret commandos' were fond of carrying large amount of US dollars in small steel boxes hidden in their jeep. The plan is to bribe greedy 'traitors' willing to stir up trouble amongst local factions of Shites, Sunnis or Kurds in Iraq to incite hatred and eventual civil wars to justify the presence of Americans as peacemakers and not trouble makers! When a person is dying of hunger and has nothing much to look forward in life; easy money like 50K goes a long way not only in feeding the family but also the catalyst for change—good or bad is secondary in difficult time. When there is security coupled with the satisfaction of 'secret work' for a master, role playing such as setting fire to buildings, screaming false accusations, throwing stones and hurting neighbours become less offensive as survival is paramount.

Why are many countries unhappy with prisoners in Guantanamo Bay(GB) in Cuba?

This is supposed to be a prison camp and the CIA interrogation centre for terrorists. But many prisoners are *labelled* as terrorists based only on flimsy evidence that does not tantamount to long imprisonment and torture. It is common knowledge to many that this place is also the testing ground for new interrogation methods such as using torture, drugs and new technology such as embedding tiny computer transmitter to the body to break prisoners. Bad hats like terrorists are excellent guinea pigs to test out new techniques. Some selected prisoners are rumoured to be brainwashed to follow the master's instruction making them very dangerous as potential trouble shooters and killers. Such a scenario is like a replay of the main theme of the movie, 'The Manchurian Candidate,' played by actor Denzel Washington where a former black American war hero was mentally deranged through torture by his masters and *unknowingly* tried to kill the President of the United States.

But GB has given cause for alarm; it is controlled by the military and not judges or Court giving rise to speculations that prisoners are not given fair trials. Pardon or release of suspected terrorists is up to the whims and fancies of those in command as proofs of guilt are not made transparent to the public. The American Democrats even accused its own government for cover-ups in erasing certain 'torture tapes' in GB as if guarding its secrets or destroying evidence to hide the truth or reliability of its words and work. The main problem: what or who gave America the absolute power to make judgement of 'suspected' terrorists of the world without consultation or dialogue from countries where the terrorists originate?

Why some powerful nations appear to be dragging their feet in resolving the many conflicts of the world?

It is disappointing to learn that the 8 permanent members of the UN War Council are not doing much to promote peace and the world appears like a stage for them. The mighty 8 are reported to be responsible for selling 80% of the world's arms such as war planes, tanks, guns and bombs to other countries. As mentioned earlier, production must continue or risk stupendous costs in shut-downs giving rise to high unemployment that are detrimental to national growth.

I find it very disturbing to hear from a BBC program, 'Hardtalk', in 2010 when Mexican President Felipe Calderon reported that during his 4-year in power, there were 30,000 deaths caused by the ruthless drug cartels in Mexico. Isn't such atrocities just as bad as 9/11? What is also alarming is the seizure of 90,000 weapons belonging to drug traffickers and all the weapons came from America! How is the local government going to stop the easy flow of both firearms and drugs when there is a 'higher authority' working in the shadows and as if in league with drug cartels? In a later Fox News report, it mentioned that gun dealers in America have no qualms in selling 600 firearms to a person without any question or accountability other than making a fat profit. What is most shocking comes from the fact that the powerful drug cartels in Mexico were *not* using ordinary hand guns or rifles to rob, kill or exchange gunfire with police but were heavily armed with US *military* weapons of 100-bullet magazine and high powered guns that can go through bullet-proof gun vests or vehicles to take on enforcement officers! Law and order are almost forgotten words in rural Mexico as no one wants to join the police force as it would be suicide to tackle criminals who are better armed than policemen. The only difference between guns used by US military and Mexican drug traffickers was the obliteration of serial numbers for issuing purposes leaving high speculations that firearms manufacturers in America that are likely to be government owned or contracted out, *intentionally* supplied arms to the Mexican drug traffickers. It appears to be more like a barter trade where millions of dollars worth of drugs are going in to America—and the world—and millions worth of firearms are going out of America. Why culprits are not made known or punished? Are gun runners a closely guarded trade or the CIA and FBI are simply blind? It's time that ordinary Americans take action against policy makers with dark agenda and heed the warnings in the scripture that the nation could be 'swept off' if *iniquities* are allowed to ripen. Meanwhile, God is watching from a distance.

Many people are fond of reading only the headlines in newspapers and seldom read the details. They give praise to countries like America, Britain or France that donated aids to suffering nations worth millions of dollars without knowing what exactly were given out as aids. Sometimes a rich nation may give away a billion dollars worth of aids to a third world country and it sounds great in terms of humanitarian reasons. But it could be only strategic aids for defence purposes like obsolete rifles and tanks which are all unnecessary other than to incite war. Have you heard of a rich nation sending tractors, bulldozers, electric saws, wheel-barrows, spades and shovels including corn and wheat seeds or livestock to the poor?

Ken Foo

Where do we draw the line to punish law-breakers?

Where are all the hard drugs of the world coming from? Are current drug laws tough enough for suppliers, runners and users? Are short term jail sentences of one or two years for drug traffickers, hard core criminals and corrupt officials more effective than capital punishment? Should high profile personalities be treated differently when they break the law? Countries like Japan and a tiny island like Singapore rarely have drug issues or even graffiti problems on public walls as such activities are considered serious offences. Obviously law and order are strictly observed in such countries to bring down crime rate and vandalism. I remember a senior politician in Singapore was found guilty on corruption charges and was immediately sentenced to do *humiliating* community services like sweeping floors and cleaning toilets in public places. In another case, a drug smuggler had to face the electric chair. Corruption conjures up images of secret deals among corporations, lobbyists and crooked government officials. If early actions are not taken against corruptions, they can destabilize a nation as *official extortion* erodes trust and nation building will be a very slow process. In China, corruption is a serious offence and many found guilty are punished with long jail sentences, life imprisonment or face the guillotine. It may be harsh action compared to western standards, but somebody has to be a sacrificial lamb to show the public that the government is serious in punishing law breakers. Proverbs like 'spare the rod and spoil the child', and 'prevention is better than cure,' are coined by great thinkers to enlighten mankind about nipping problems in the bud before they become cancerous.

Is the Dalai Lama of Tibet a puppet of America?

This question is not meant to create a scandal or upset some readers. The information below is condensed from website and everyone is entitled to make his or her assessment on the reliability of the material available.

It was reported that the CIA orchestrated the Dalai Lama's exile into neighbouring India in 1959. The security, movements and welfare of the Tibetan leader and his entourage have always been controlled and financed by the CIA. Earlier rumours in 1959 that the Chinese planned to kidnap the holy one was typical American 'scare tactics' to spark off 'the battle of Lhasa' to create a civil war between loyal Tibetans against the ruling Red Army. The slanted journalism of controlled media was quick to mention that 83,000 people were killed in the uprising and the high casualties caused alarm to the world that branded China as a country that opposed human rights. But local estimates of the death toll came up to only 3,000.

Initially, India was reluctant to grant asylum to the Dalai Lama and his selected group of exiled Tibetan community for fear of offending its friendly neighbour. But the Americans broke the impasse and closed the deal when President Eisenhower proposed to allow 400 Indian engineers into America to enable them to learn about nuclear technology. In 1974, the first Indian A-bomb was made and given the cynical nickname of 'laughing Buddha.' Is this a strategic ploy to strengthen India and weaken China to balance power in Asia?

The story goes on to say that the March 2008 'peaceful demonstrations' in Lhasa by local monks were all part of a timely secret ploy to incite racial and religious hatred as China was on world stage when hosting the Olympic Games in August, 2008. Certain Tibetan lamas and youths were bribed to perform destructive acts by attacking Han (Chinese) and Hui (Muslims) to stir up a riot. Controlled media reporting of deaths were highly exaggerated to smear the image of China as human rights violators that oppressed peaceful religious Tibetans. The underlying truth points to the fact that America looks at China as the next major threat for world domination if its progress goes unchecked.

In 2007, China has taken the initiative to be a serious investor with many African and Latin American countries with multi-billion projects in exchange of technologies and resources for mutual benefit. The West appeared to have missed the boat for not taking the lead earlier. China's growing economic wealth and labour power were serious threats to American security and its dwindling economy. It would be detrimental to American interest in Asia if the many countries there create a Common Market tied to China and weaken American presence and control in that region.

The Dalai Lama has always been the 'secret weapon' of the CIA to break up the many factions in China like the way they dismantled the USSR by creating wars, coups and political unrest in order to slow down the might of a tiger for selfish reasons. The Chinese handled the 2008 uprising very calmly and did its best to quell the problems with little bloodshed and unconcerned about derogative reports from the media. Probably they have learned their lessons from history that confrontation with the *real* culprits is not the solution to a better world; it is more *rewarding* to promote a positive unifying agenda in their relations with other countries. *Retaliation* or seeking 'pre-emptive strike' when in conflict, is ancient war strategy of an arrogant and weak leader with little concern on the carnage of war that brings only sufferings on both fronts. The new leadership believes that wars are *barbaric* and a waste of resources not conducive to a better world.

In 2007, the jovial-looking Dalai Lama visited America and was presented the Congressional Gold Medal by President Bush, the highest civilian award given by Congress. The Tibetan leader was quick to praise Bush as a great leader and peacemaker in fighting human rights for the world. He smilingly called America 'the champion of democracy and freedom,' in front of a large group of international journalists and TV cameramen but those flattering words somehow did not go well with Bush as he had difficulty trying to fake a smile!

How do modern Chinese see America today?

When I was holidaying in China recently, I decided not to climb the Great Wall of China and instead, had a chat with my tour guide David and the lady bus driver Sue in a quiet tea-house enjoying the local tea and munching peanuts. 'The ruthless CIA has been *funding* and stoking the *Free Tibet* fires since the 1950s and causing violence and unnecessary deaths by enlisting trouble makers to inflame civil unrest and disorder with seditious ranting to run down our country,' says David when questioned about the rumblings about Tibet and China. 'The Americans are like children playing a dangerous game to *incite* hatred: they are fond of publishing twisted, biased news of China and *shamelessly* fabricate events and photos that are not real and never happened. We have seen pictures of *dead men walking again* as soldiers and policemen! I am not sure whether they are stupid or think we are. American diplomacy is now a joke in China and the locals prefer to call it *American hypocrisy*. They simply want to crush our loyalty, patriotism, happy new way of life and turn us against our government. Why are they so devious,' or words to that effect, an angry David grunted.

"They meddle in our country's internal affairs to give the impression to other nations that Americans are only trying to liberate the poor Chinese still living in the dark ages without human rights and work like slaves for the government. The only freedom they really want is freedom to *serve them and destroy our progress.* Their ploy is simply to force China to become part of the US camp like Japan, Korea, Vietnam and Thailand where they can dictate terms to change and weaken our political system, not so much to free the people but to collapse our government so that they can boss us around', bus driver Sue chimes in.

During one of my tours in Beijing, I managed to befriend a pretty lady called San who owns a boutique shop with the latest fashion in women's wear. 'Ha ha ha! American propaganda is now a laughing matter', San tried to cover her mouth with her hand when asked about her reaction about the negative reports about China in the American media. 'When we have more than a billion people, they said we were destroying the planet. When our government introduced the one-child policy, America condemned us for abusing human rights. When we expand our industries, they called us polluters. When we buy oil, they are quick to call it exploitation and genocide. When *they* go to war for oil, they call it liberation. When we loan them money, they blame us for their national debts. They have nothing good to say about our progress other than telling lies. I wish they leave us alone. I want the world to be united with one dream as this blue earth is big enough for all of us'; a smiling San said something to that effect in Mandarin mixed with broken English.

Peace is Change

> *I've said more than once,*
> *we make peace with enemies,*
> *sometimes with bitter enemies.*

Yitzhak Rabin

Is there a basic approach to prevent war or an impending crisis?

An ancient philosophy says that many of the world's problems can be resolved if we don't look for differences or divisions with one another but focus instead, on places of agreement or opportunities to share. The wise and honest will understand that they have to discard arrogance and haste and it is not humiliating to have dialogue *first* with fiery oppositions and find out what they want. You cannot simply *shut them up* and then rationalise for your actions. War and crisis are man-made: peace is dependent on how sincere your intention is to prevent conflict. The Iraq and Afghan wars immediately come to mind. The world has changed since 9/11 as mentioned by President Bush. But change doesn't mean more aggression on weak countries that can be bullied or manipulated. A true leader can show his greatness as a peacemaker when he is more concerned with mercy and compassion for others. The basis of strong leadership is all about integrity and love.

What are some issues the poor nations may be receptive to end war?

Most business people are aware that contract agreement with clients is easier signed when there are equal benefits for both parties to provide a win-win situation. Understanding the *needs* of each party is paramount in any peaceful settlement. Providing compensation with either money or exchange of services or both should be part of the agenda. For example: A country like Sudan or Utopia may need more food for their starving infants, clean drinking water and medicine to combat diseases, schools and hospitals to upgrade their lives, new roads, etc. The poor nations are probably more than happy to kow-tow to anyone or nation to relieve their sufferings in exchange for natural resources such as oil or minerals as they do not have the know-how to extract them or are aware of their worth in the international market. Exchange of technologies and labour for mutual benefit rarely fails when job strategy is carefully work out to ensure the poor can be self sufficient over the long term. Nation building is all about rasing the standard of living of the poor through economic development and achieve unity through education—and the hell with the usual *complex* political issues that are mainly excuses to delay assistance to the needy! The many requests of the poor are very basic needs of survival and genuine humanitarian efforts are not impossible dreams when *'where there's a will, there's a way.'*

Is money the stumbling block for world peace?

Money is secondary as the world is united especially during time of emergency when problems are life threatening. This can be witnessed in the 2004 Boxing Day tsunami in Indonesia where huge contributions from all over the world were poured in to help the needy that prompted former UN leader, Kofi Annan to say: 'The past days have been among the darkest in our lifetime. But they have also allowed us to see a new kind of *light*. We have seen the world coming together.' Unfortunately, it is now four years after the disaster and the funds are still not fully and fairly distributed because millions of dollars are being stolen by corrupt officials and overseas agencies. It was reported that food and medical supplies were being diverted from dirt-poor communities and sold on the black market at inflated prices. Corrupt officials had no conscience and openly bought new cars and homes while the needy were left to starve!

What about the billions spent on space projects? Our planet is only a speck of dust in the universe and human knowledge or science in space travel is only at its infancy stage and little will be derived from such exploration until a 'super fuel' is discovered to propel shuttles to travel as fast as light in outer space. Are we ready to live in Mars, Mercury or Pluto when we are still struggling to find out more about how our own planet operates coupled with the thousands of problems yet to be resolved on earth? Are all the space projects strictly power symbols and waste of taxpayers money? Are we jumping the gun or are we all *'son of a gun'?* Some world leaders should stop their quests in unproductive projects and get *real* to clean up their own backyard. America is in deep financial crisis yet its on-going space exploration and new shuttles with the occasional mid-air explosions, are hogging the headlines as if such costly project would save America because astronauts were able to bring home some red dirt from Mars! Meanwhile, the Chinese have quietly conducted their deepest manned undersea craft named 'Jialong',(after a mythical sea dragon) designed to reach a maximum depth of 7000m to exploit the vast resources of the ocean floor. As expected, the latest milestone for China's deep-sea achievement received only a two-line report in page 10 of most English newspapers. The man on the street should be able to work out the stupendous cost differences and the *practicality* of space and deep-sea projects to benefit mankind.

World peace is all about *true intent* and not cover-ups to stage a war. A respectable village or township can be built in any part of the world when war in Iraq, Afghanistan, Israel or any place is cut short or abandoned. This objective is only attainable when peaceful negotiations to end a war are *top priority* on the card. The senseless and huge expenditure in waging wars are not only unnecessary, but exact *replays* of ancient holy wars like the 'crusades' which tear people of different religion and culture further apart. Resources and manpower can be better used when channelled into nation building like reconstruction of war-torn places or providing poverty stricken places with basic infrastructure and teaching them survival projects like farming or marine fishing to kick-start a new beginning.

Are there examples for leaders to learn that peace can be attained without bloodshed?

Mahatma Gandhi of India, a humble and 'half-naked' devout Hindu, is probably the most famous person in history as a freedom fighter for democracy. He was a jailed political prisoner that led India's long walk to independence from the British Empire in 1930 without shedding a drop of blood. His passionate commitment of non-violence and willingness to accept punishment were his strengths. Nelson Mandella of Africa also showed the world that apartheid can be abolished through peaceful means and gave his people fresh hope of a better life.

Black American Martin Luther King Jr., is well known for his words, *'I have a dream.'* He started the Negro revolution in Birmingham in the 1960s fighting for equality for his people through long marches, street demonstrations, speeches and psalm singing in prisons. He was jailed 14 times but never gave up his belief in non-violence and truth to attain his goal. His unique theme of 'one voice, one vision,' have moved millions—both black and white—and made him The Man of the Year' in 1963 by Time magazine.

What about the charismatic Mikhail Gorbachev? The former Russian leader of the 1980s with the famous birthmark on his forehead was instrumental for breaking up of the Berlin Wall. The long cold war between East and West Berlin became one again when the wall crumbled into souvenirs peacefully without a single gunshot being fired in front of the eyes of the world. Gorbachev was not only a skilful mediator, but a brave man who was prepared to risk his life and showed the world that a bloodless revolution is possible. He became a patron for change and peace. More importantly, he did it without the usual political greed and conspiratorial intent.

What are some of the reasons that contributed to the collapse of the American economy?

When the US economy freezes, the whole world will feel the chill. Political analysts are quick to point out that the American leadership has a deep rooted arrogance in showing their might and power. Its leaders are 'obsessed' with military dominance and prepared to go overboard with huge defence budgets including space projects while its banking systems, housing industry and other domestic issues like Medicare are falling apart. *Basic* good government principles are ignored leaving little room for national growth. Its domestic policies appeared to be geared for only the rich and the middle class are the biggest losers. It should be clear that if a country is incapable of coming up with sound government policy *at home* for nation building, it is doubtful that decisions on foreign maters such as war, can be any better.

It was bad 'house-keeping' when 2008 statistics have shown that the nation's richest are *striking lottery everyday*—the top 0.1 % now earn more money than the bottom 50% of Americans and the top 1% are wealthier than the bottom 90%. Unproductive projects and unworkable policies should be changed or eliminated to ensure a fairer distribution of wealth across the board. Perpetuating the status quo of a failed policy is not only a waste of taxpayers' money but can also backfire and bring the country to its knees. Americans—entrepreneurs, corporations and showbiz moguls—must cut back excessive remunerations: many executives are in the million-dollar club and some senior executives earn more that Obama and *all* his staff put together in the White House! High earners are not well known to save up for a rainy day and likely to live it up or become greedy and reckless trying to double up their fortunes. When the stock or property markets point south, they go mad and likely to lose their integrity to recoup their losses giving rise to more economic woes!

Imagine, soccer player David Beckham from England is paid a staggering $300 million for a 3-year contract to play soccer in America. Has he got bionic legs or typical American extravaganza to grab the spotlight? What about Hollywood movie stars that command $20 million per movie? It was reported that actor Charlie Sheen made $1.8 million for each episode in the serial, 'Two And A Half Man', and he spent his lot on drugs, alcohol, women and rehab centres. Money spent has to be justified and 'pretty faces' don't qualify other than setting a trend of indulgence and waste. Who has the guts to rein in big spenders and risked being found in a river floating with face down? As an Australian I am proud to say that sports authorities down here impose *salary caps* for sports personalities to ensure a sense of *balance* in remunerations for professionals in other fields. Aussie rugby league superstars like

Benji Marshall, Billy Slater and Johnathan Thurston earn about $1.5 million for a 3-year contract and some seniors are complaining that these 'razzle dazzlers' of the field are overpaid because they are only in their twenties and likely to blow their fortunes away!

It is the filthy rich that are responsible for bringing the world to the brink of collapse and a new breed of tough taskmasters are needed in looking at *restoration* and not *deterioration* of morals and healthy living for human survival in the long term. It seems that there are two sets of rules for rich and poor: the rich are untouchables because money 'talks' and they behave like irresponsible citizens that have no code of honour. They only know how to grab as much as they can and don't expect thieves to have honour. If world leaders do not restore integrity, honour and trust as previously expounded by messengers of God and great leaders of the past, our world will be no better than the animal kingdom where 'dogs eat dogs'!

Former American presidential candidate, Michael Dudakis said that his country was *'waging the dumbest war'* in Iraq. The high death toll and squandering vast amount of money through arrogance and negligence can never be worth it. It cost the nation an unbelievable sum of a billion dollars a day to maintain its troops around the world and imagine how many lives can be saved or how much can be done with that kind of money! The American national debt amounted to a record high of $12 trillion in 2008 and world treasurers are shaking their heads wondering how the country can get out of this hole without going through deep recession. The Federal Reserve Bank chairman Ben Bernanke, has ran out of ideas how to boost the economy and suggested to Congress to *print* more money to save America! The tired-looking Bernanke may have found a temporary cure for current financial crisis and appears happy to put the country on long term pains. To put it simply: the Americans are spending and living beyond their means.

Why is America the only country in the world to have about 50 military bases strategically located in all parts of the world? Its foreign policies kept the world guessing whether they are the planet's best peace-keepers or otherwise. The world is beginning to see that the Bush administration sets missions for the military where it is incapable of performing.

Can the military or defence forces of superpowers be revamped for nation building?

Soldiers need not have to be armed from head to foot and hopefully they soon become relics of a bygone era. Young American military officers have wised up and are causing concerns to its government for quitting very early in their careers as defenders of their country. The modern generation realised that it is senseless to kill another human being like an animal or play 'robots' to their leaders with ignoble intentions. The new millennium needs people with peaceful approach to win harmony and unite the world. It is obviously a tall order but options are very limited other than a pure heart of true intent.

The armed forces is one of the best places for the young to learn about discipline, respect and physical fitness. But the military needs remodelling because of changing time to attract good and educated people who value self-expression to attain a meaningful life. Enrolling into the army, air force or navy should *not* be focused entirely on national security. *New* emphasis for change on humanitarian efforts in nation building should also be considered. The 'Peace Corps' needs revitalising and perhaps establishing a separate 'humanitarian college' is another option for specialisation.

Poor countries need medicine, nurses and doctors, police and soldiers, town planners and engineers, farmers and horticulturists, miners and business people, counsellors and linguists, and many other humanitarian needs. Productive work would greatly increase when an English, French or Japanese person is able to speak fluent Congolese to trainee farmers in outback Congo! The diversities of special training similar to a university become more enticing for both young men and women looking forward to a military career. An old military slogan, 'Join the army and see the world,' should be revived to attract 'humanitarian soldiers' who find it more satisfying to *serve* than to kill.

Is joint-venture business a solution to help poor nations?

This is a very workable strategy if professionally handled by NATO, UN or any powerful world body like World Vision. I am sure joint-venture business is already on-going in many places but the level of commitments by participating countries is questionable as many well intended projects failed to achieve its objectives because of lack of urgency, supervision and oversight. For example: The commander of UNIMID (an arm of UN) in war-torn Dhafur in Africa was desperately in need of helicopters to expedite basic food and medical supplies to the starving people in the outback inaccessible by road. His request was not met by UN because member countries preferred to have their cargo planes and helicopters be kept inactive instead of loaning them for a worthy cause!

Almost every country has its own natural resources like minerals and produce can be cultivated which may include cotton, corn, sugar cane or fruit trees and even unusual flowers. If rich nations are prepared to provide the expertise to develop the resources of third world countries through joint-venture; the road map for peace is in the offing as employment is the short-cut to eliminate terrorism and sufferings. It could be mining for gold or tin ore, setting up a canning factory for juices, a timber factory to build houses, dairy farm, planting rice or even a nursery not only for children but also for plants and flowers. Countries like China, India and even a place like Vietnam, can show the world that every type of business *is possible* when cheap labour is available.

An enterprising Australian company that specialised in breeding the popular *barramundi* fish in tanks, is doing a roaring business exporting the fish to America. Spawning in tanks can be accelerated with new science. Other concepts along similar line are definitely worth considering to kick-start economic development for the poor. Who knows, struggling countries like Sudan, Rwanda or even East Timor can revolutionise marine fishing such as oysters or crabs and become a big exporter of quality seafood to rich nations. The new generation is beginning to focus on healthy eating lifestyles and white meat is winning popularity against the benefits of red meat. But who is going to take the initiative and draw up a formal plan like breeding oysters for example, for a selected group (strictly for experiment and research) in poor areas and show the world that it can be done to reverse the fortunes of the starving? If the UN is prepared to provide security and funding, I am quite sure there will be volunteers who are prepared to do their bit for a worthy cause and happy to experiment and help out in such a project for the sake of peace over the long term. But like most suggestions, there is no urgency or *passionate commitment* by UN or NATO to expedite such projects other than patches of work here and there as if dragging their feet without true leadership. Complaints are mounting that employees from government funded organizations are generally complacent and ineffective in meeting datelines. Some concerned parties feel that certain humanitarian projects should be contracted to private companies that are buoyed by strong commitment to complete a project ahead of schedule motivated mainly by savings and profits.

Ken Foo

Commercial greed

> *Politicians are the same all over.*
> *They promise to build bridges*
> *even when there are no rivers.*

> *Nitkita Khrushchev*

Why are fuel prices skyrocketing all the time?

Some call it 'sweet revenge' for oil barons in the Arab world. The power of oil is a potent weapon of the Middle East today because it controls about 70% of world demands and advanced nations depend on this seemingly inexhaustible treasure. The world would stand still without oil—we have to walk to work, cross rivers and climb hills and mountains to reach our destinations!

The West has been critical on some small Muslim kingdoms and considered them as weak, not progressive or disunited. But the Arabs speak with one voice today and when they decide to raise the price of oil or turn down the tap, Western nations pay up like being held as hostages. The problem is further compounded by the fact that the processing of crude oil into petroleum is mainly controlled by the Organisation of Petroleum Exporting Countries (OPEC) comprising of resource-rich nations, notably Saudi Arabia. America is only a minor player in OPEC but acts like a key player by trying to control the activities of OPEC for financial reasons. Giant US corporations like Exxon, Shell, Esso or Caltex are well known for making sure that *record* multi-billion dollars earnings are achieved year after year with little regard for weaker countries or even its own suffering middle class community struggling to keep pace with the escalating cost of fuel.

Are there alternatives to combat the rising cost of fuel?

Scientists are seriously looking into alternatives to slow down the heavy reliance of fuel for two basic reasons: (1) rising purchasing cost (2) fossil fuel is not environment friendly. Research on transport and machineries powered by electricity, solar, clean coal fuel including extracts from crops like sugar cane, corns, potatoes and others for conversion to ethanol which is only about 50% of the price of petrol. Brazil has taken the lead to refine ethanol to a high quality and the world should learn a thing or two from this 'not so powerful' nation. The demand for ethanol is round the corner and the American petroleum giants may have plenty to say about this competitive product that may affect their multi-billion industry but good luck to them as long as there are savings for us!

The race is on for car manufacturers to develop the first mass-produced and *affordable* petrol-free cars for anxious consumers. In 2008, the CEO of Toyota Australia, Mr. Max Yasuda reported that without solving the environmental problems created by automobiles, the car industry has no future. Electric vehicles are currently on trial in Japan but the cost is way beyond the means of the average driver and new technology is still on the drawing board. The ideal solution to replace petrol is electricity or water mixed with chemicals as these natural resources will never run dry in the four corners of the world! But who's the next Einstein to do the research?

How can we fight against big companies that are hurting our pockets?

Every business is after our hard earned money and one of the biggest culprits is the banks; it's all about greed and exploitation of innocent clients to enable the board of directors to grow fatter and feather their nests. In Australia when the Reserve Bank raises interest rate by half percent, the four major banks would up the same rate for their clients the *next day*. When the RB lowers the rate by half percent, the banks would take about a *month* to adjust the benefits to clients with the lame excuse of extra administrative work. They have no respect for customers and treat them like simpletons or dopes! When you give business to the bank by taking up a mortgage loan, the bank *charges* an establishment fee. When you have fallen into bad time and wishes to cancel the loan because you can't afford to service the loan anymore, the bank slaps you with an exit fee. Imagine, if you forgot to pay off a $1 owing from a credit card statement, you can end up with owing of $100 after three months as there is a $30 monthly charge for late payment plus administrative costs. Complain about an oversight? 'Pay up or see you in court', the lender says. Big fish loves to eat the small fish; banks and most commercial enterprises love to slug us because we rarely fight back. Can you blame some unhappy customers when they accused the gutless government for being in bed with bankers?

Goods of necessities like bread, milk, veggies and meat must be controlled to prevent monopoly. A progressive government is expected to do its best by encouraging and *assisting* farmers with marketing strategies how best to promote their produce to benefit consumers at reasonable prices. More often than not, greedy *middlemen* like Woolworth or Coles are allowed to 'exploit and bully' simple farmers with ridiculous trading terms mainly to fatten senior executives of big businesses. The big boys can afford to hire 'smooth talking lawyers' and convinced farmers that selling cheap is good and just short of saying that 'you are our bankers and slaves'! It is heart-breaking to see suffering farmers during hard times where they have to flatten their orchards and dairy farms with bulldozers, shooting dead all their sheep when there is a drought or selling off their properties to *foreigners* for a song because of an uncaring and short-sighted government well known for lip service. Politicians prefer to party and dance with the wealthy with little regard to long-term national growth. Foreign investors are snapping up large tracts of the best farm land in many parts of Australia and farmers are showing concern and insisting on a public register to determine who is living next door and *where* the food is going. The embattled farmers are worried about future food security but is the federal government listening? The pride and joy of Australia: namely locally owned vineyards, mining properties and breweries are also disappearing fast. There will come a time when Australians have to pay *rent* to foreigners who own a chunk of land in their backyard!

Many of us are dazzled by huge spending or takeovers and billion-dollar profits of corporations because they grab the headlines. Not many of us are aware that small and medium-sized enterprises (SMEs) generate the bulk of employment. In Australia 50% of the workforce comes from SMEs but some owners are treated like second class citizens especially from banks that demand struggling owners to put up the family home or business premises as collateral before loans are approved. It has become a risky affair to start up a business as failure in a new venture could have drastic effects on family members. Stringent rules on loans have put SMEs in a distinct disadvantage to *compete* with corporations that are evaluated on business plans and future estimated earnings including share holdings of other companies. Personal wealth like the waterfront home and yacht owned by directors are not taken into account and corporate shareholders are likely to survive despite of bad times or recession. Monopoly of goods and services by corporations must be gradually dismantled because it doesn't increase productivity other than higher profits through higher prices to benefit greedy middlemen. This can best be done through government's intervention in *nurturing* small businesses as 'some good, sustainable advice goes a long way in a small business trying to find its feet,' says Mark Bouris, an expert financial adviser.

Its time to stand up to the bullies and show them that human consciousness as a *group* can change the world. Remember Ghandi and Martin Luther King's *one voice, one vision?* Our strength and security lie in the *collective* and united we stand. Boycott products that you think are unfairly priced; don't buy them. Protest in group of hundreds or thousands but oppose with *dignity* and not like angry animals waiting to be killed. Protest calmly in big numbers without violence as an eye for an eye tactic only makes the world blind.

When you are unhappy with a *particular* petroleum company noted for profiteering, go to another petrol station to fill up your car even though it may be a longer drive. Tell your neighbours and friends to follow suit and you can be assured that if there are enough people to stage a boycott, the company will yield to people's power. Take the same initiative with giant supermarkets; when they consistently over-charged, shop in another place with better price and service. The meat and veggies will rot within a week if everyone is united to take action against the profiteers. When we show our toughness and teach them a lesson, justice will soon prevail.

It is true that big corporations are 'untouchables' and their decisions are like law?

You think the banks are powerful? If there are 1000 of us demonstrating in front of the bank, the board of directors or the chairman of the bank will not have the guts to come out to speak to us. Those people wearing suit and tie are only *paper tigers* used to scaring us because their experience taught them that we are a selfish and disunited lot! Its time to prove them wrong; protest or *withdraw* your savings from the bank and your demands will be met as the directors can't afford to lose their cushy jobs and be denied of a 'golden handshake' when they retire. Ordinary people can do extra ordinary things when given the opportunity to function effectively as a group. When there's determination and passion for justice, there's no *boundaries* for success. Don't ever forget that the real strength of a nation is not the government or the entrepreneurs, but the *common people.* If you are serious in fighting for fair play, start by identifying your Ghandis and Luthers and be ready for battle against an unjust society. Remember, if you don't *stand* for something, you'll *fall* for everything and end up a 'yes-person'.

Global consumers can cripple any international corporation like sports giant *Nike* or prestigious watch maker *Rolex* when we are united. We can give the products the flick when companies exploit us through over-charging especially when their products are made in third world countries like India or Thailand and quality is below expectation. Any negative write-up in the media or via internet can be the end of the company when everyone stops buying. We'll be showered with *'freebies'* from greedy hotels, airlines, casinos, real estate agencies and restaurants when we fight for justice collectively with one voice, one vision.

What can the government do to curb the growing power of big organisations?

For starters, cut back the size of certain corporations to prevent monopoly and excesses like ridiculous eight-figure salary for top executives. For example: the biggest food chain stores in Australia are Woolworth and Coles but both organisations also have large subsidiary companies that control similar food chains including other consumers products like hardware, liquor, whitegoods and a string of other goods. When prices go up regularly, who's going to stop them when they already have a stranglehold for most goods in the market? Likewise, there should be restrictions to reduce the activities and size of financial institutions. They should be confined to lending and holding deposits like days of old and not allowed to make risky and complex investments like the Wall St *spending sprees* with little accountabilities that created financial chaos and hardship for the common people. Banks need competition to prevent them from slugging the public. Perhaps it is not mad to suggest that government owned Post Offices should be restructured by introducing basic banking facilities to prop up dwindling turnover as the easy excess of e-mail, internet, etc. have taken away a big chunk of postal services. This is a feasible project as the premises are already there and centrally located. It is only an extension of business to generate growth and employment and not 'close shop' over the long term. The public needs alternatives to keep greedy commercial banks honest. But which government is brave enough to overhaul the banking system or have the courage to downsize existing corporations and risk losing the next election?

Did any prophet predict the 2008 financial collapses of the world?

Yes, I find it very intriguing in one of Nostradamus' predictions for the 21st century:

> *The imitation of gold and silver inflate*
> *And after the crime are thrown in the lake*
> *It is discovered that all is exhausted by debt*
> *And all scripts and bonds wiped out.*

Bear in mind that Nostradamus made his prediction in the 16th century and did not have the convenience of a modern day dictionary explaining to him what was a stock exchange market or the many investments available today. He foresaw the 2008 Wall St crash in America and the domino effects on global economies. The key word of his prediction is *crime*—a cover-up by leaders to throw all blames into the lake! This is probably a more realistic version of end time: the end of a once powerful Western empire and the passing of the baton to another nation or group of nations to lead again.

Is the American stimulus package to save giant corporations a good thing?

It is my opinion that the stimulus package is just a spending orgy for everyone to dig in for more despite of poor performance.

Those responsible for corporate greed and excesses should not be 'rewarded' but *punished* instead. Sometimes the legal system gives the impression that it caters only for the rich. For example: When a petty thief got caught for stealing a loaf of bread to feed his family because he was broke, more likely than not, he is thrown into jail. But when a senior corporate executive manipulates the stock market, tell lies and bankrupt many investors and causing widespread unemployment for personal gains, he gets away with it because he has friends from 'higher up.' If it was in China or in a small country like Singapore, this *hotshot* would probably be facing the firing squad as a national disgrace because such *'fast buck mentality'* is a short cut to destabilize the economy. Who is the bigger offender that could bring down the country? The petty thief with dirty clothes or the executive who wears only branded suit, owns a private jet and a mate of a senator or judge? Many ordinary Americans feel let-down when some judges are gutless to nail the *guilty rich* giving rise to speculations about bribery and corruptions at the very top.

Our world—the West especially—will soon be heading to deep treacherous waters if stringent laws are not imposed to restrain corporate leaders and crooked politicians from 'looting' ordinary people coupled with the mentality that a white-collar crime is less offensive than a blue-collar crime. When we put some greedy and irresponsible fat cats behind bars or insist they work for free until the business trend is reversed, it is not a harsh move but necessary action to show others that 'crime does not pay.' Many underperforming CEOs got away with a slap on the wrist and some have the audacity to grant themselves with 'golden parachutes' or fat bonuses upon retirement despite being bailed out by taxpayers! It's similar to a bank robber being 'rewarded' for robbing the bank. Justice is really at its pits when you hear of executives from failed corporations like Wall St, General Motors, Goldman Sachs and financial institutions laughing their way to the bank and picking their teeth while taxpayers pay for the feast.

It is understandable for the Bush/Obama administrations to be concerned with unemployment, hardship for struggling families and the domino effect on properties and business in general. But empathy is causing the country a lot of trouble especially when funds are not evenly distributed. The stimulus package is directed mainly to big businesses that do not deserve to be bailed out when badly managed. Worst still, there was little accountability initially where the money had gone and it was reported that billions of dollars have been taken out of the country!

The Australian stimulus package has a better approach when the Rudd government gives money directly to *individuals* who are low income earners or pensioners instead of bailing out ailing companies. Basic household expenditures have been propped up and both consumers and retailers are kept afloat with the stimulus. The property and share markets did not take a bashing like most advanced nations in 2008-2009 and Australia appears resilient to the global financial downturn.

The world is a stage

For evil to flourish, all that is needed is for good people to do nothing.

Edmund Burke

Everyone knows that unity is strength but how many people earnestly strive to achieve this goal other than giving out hot air? The annual UN general assembly is like a playground for some vile and dangerous leaders to parade their fantasies and spew their hatred as speakers are given freedom of expression. We also hear of G20, OPEC, EU and many high sounding summits attended by world leaders of big and small nations but wars, terrorism and staggering poverty are still raging like wild fire around the world. More often than not, little is resolved in many *'talkfest'* conferences and probably at best, a recommendation is passed that 'a glass of water' be thrown at the forest fire to appease weak nations that are suffering or close to dying. The UN especially, needs restructuring to show more substance in leadership.

It is well known now that *some* powerful nations are not serious in putting their heads together to resolve urgent crisis because they are part of the problem. Former president, Ronald Reagan, was right when he said, '*Government is not the solution to our problems. Government is the problem*'. Think again why are there so many powerful nations selling war planes, guns, missiles and military equipment to third world countries? Isn't it obvious that they are partly responsible for inciting war or threatening the security of others for selfish gains?

Sometimes certain American diplomatic missions are only for show to hide their secret motives. Take for instance: The Secretary of Defence, Robert Gates was on a peace mission to Asia hoping to win support from allies to curb nuclear power expansion of North Korea. While in Singapore en route to Beijing, news broke out that Taiwan had bought *$60 billion* worth of fighter jet planes and other arms from America. When Beijing managed to confirm such a sale, a message was sent to Gates in Singapore that he was not welcome in Beijing and a red face Gates had to cut short his trip. Was China tough on Gates or simply not prepared to entertain a *war-horse in sheep's clothing*? It was also disclosed that Saudi Arabia had agreed to purchase another multi-billion arms deal from America but the transaction is on hold subject to approval from Congress; probably due to wide media criticism on the previous deal with Taiwan.

Firepower

The American government especially, relies heavily on its multi-billion dollar armament exports (obsolete stuff of course) to boost its economy and any slowdown or closure on the manufacture of milliary hardware would have a negative impact on the country's wealth coupled with the fact that unemployment rate would soar to record high. In order to sustain the arms industry, one of the ploys is to create small wars amongst weak nations as a way out to get rid of old stocks and, at the same time, help manufacturers to introduce new lines like 'bunker buster missiles,' to smoke out Osama bin Laden and blow him up to bits!

American hypocrisy on playing the good guys or portraying itself as the best peace-keeper on the planet has been exposed. The invasion of Iraq is a fine example of a bully that had its own military time-table and prepared to bulldoze its way to win over the support of other nations at all cost! The American economy is in turmoil and our planet is in peril at time of writing. An innovative and tenacious new leader is needed to 'purify America' to restore balance again. Change from fear-based policies is not only the way out to redeem the integrity and flagging image of America but also requires the unfolding for a new world order, a much needed catalyst to unite Americans and the world.

Cue from nature

The success and survival of unity or team-work can be illustrated in many forms and nature is always there as our informal universal teacher. One fine day when I was trying to gather more material on this subject, a TV documentary by National Geographic caught my attention. It was a real scene from the animal kingdom which I found it to be very enlightening.

A hungry lion was stalking a strayed deer. When within striking distance of its prey, the lion took a mighty leap and a crunching bite on the neck and the deer was history within a minute. Nearby, a pack of ten hyenas was also hunting for food. Their sharp noses were able to sniff out the smell of fresh blood and they followed the scent. When they saw the lion feasting on the deer, the hyenas immediately worked out an attacking strategy despite of their smaller size. They circled the lion and nipped at the deer whenever possible and then quickly retreated to make the lion scurried madly from one spot to another to protect its meal. The king of beast could not attack but had to watch its back and managed to give only an angry roar as the cunning hyenas distracted the lion by coming from all directions. The 'tease and roar' scenario went on for half an hour and the lion was getting tired and the fierce roar turned into a tame growl of distress; its hind legs and tail started to bleed from constant nipping from behind by the hyenas. The dejected lion realised it was fighting a losing battle and gave up its dinner and ran away to hunt another day.

Unity wins again and this common theme rarely fails in most situations. Perhaps its nature's way of telling us that the security of the weak (hyenas) lies in the *critical mass* or work as a group with focused intent. The lion may be big and strong but sheer numbers can swing the pendulum of power or control. From this example, nature is also giving another message that whether strong or weak, no one will go hungry *if* we are prepared to share our food or wealth. Human survival is all about team-work and sharing: a good leader knows it but no one is brave enough to say it and do it. For sufferings and evil to flourish, all that is needed is for good people to *do nothing*.

Nation building

> *Give a man a fish a day, he will not get hungry.*
> *Teach him how to fish, he will never get hungry.*

Confucius

The above simple words by *Confucius* are filled with wisdom because they make good sense. When you are genuinely keen to give a helping hand to a needy person, make sure that person can stand on his or her feet without any further assistance. The same spirit applies to rich nations that are sincere in helping suffering countries. The standard practice from UN or NATO to assist the poor is to provide food, medicine or other immediate needs to keep them alive. Most of the humanitarian efforts are only *temporary* and won't go away. It's like giving medical treatment to a patient suffering from malaria while children are not vaccinated and mosquitoes are still breeding and flying everywhere.

China has taken the initiative to change its foreign and investments policies by setting up joint-venture businesses with many African and Latin American countries. It was reported in 2008 that China profited US$56 billion but gave back the Africans $US51 billion. This was a win-win situation for both nations, especially to the Africans who have never seen so much money before. This is what nation building is all about: have a *long term plan* with *mutual benefits* and making sure the poor are also involved. It is less effective when a rich nation writes a cheque of ten million dollars to a poor nation and doesn't know where the money goes.

The West has given the tag to China as the latest *superpower;* but does it qualify as one? A Canadian businessman, Mr Shing, who is a seasoned traveller to many parts of China would disagree. He said the workforce in city areas are only *starting* to climb to middle class while the country's massive rural population is still widespread with poverty. His business partner in Shanghai, Mr Leong, added that China still needs lots of catching up: sending a satellite to the moon or having nuclear weapons doesn't mean automatic qualification to superpower status when half the population is still hungry. Although China is the biggest manufacturing nation in the world today, many of its goods are produced in *sweat shops* where workers are lowly paid and working conditions are not ideal compared to the West. The Chinese leadership has little interest in the arms race and policy makers are focused mainly in resolving domestic problems like providing jobs to its huge population and ensuring they have a roof over their heads. Nation building begins with charity at home.

Is the success story of China attributed to *firepower* or *butter* first? The answer is clear.

See the difference between the American and the Chinese governments? National growth to China means improving the quality of life for its people through peaceful trading with the view of expanding the manufacturing industry at home to sustain the workforce. On the other hand, America continues to scare the world by beefing up its military might and leaders show little concern when many of its domestic manufacturing plants are under receivership or forced to shut down. Is it good economics to buy too much from abroad because it is cheaper or make your own to protect local industries and employment? Some may argue that cheaper goods will slow down *inflation* which makes sense but where do you draw the line when about 70% of goods sold in shopping centres come from Asian countries? Take Japan for example: the Japanese can buy quality rice from Thailand or Burma but prefer to support local farmers even though they have to pay more than double against imports. The rational is quite simple: If rice is your staple food, why depend on foreigners to supply them? 'Cheap' may not be good all the time; self-reliance, loyalty and ensuring the survival of an old industry can be sound economics too and the Japanese are happy to 'sacrifice' for the sake of long term national interests. Another fine example is the automobile industry: you can see only a handful of imported cars like BMW, Mercedes or Ford cars in Tokyo but Toyota, Honda or Nissan are usually the most popular cars all over the world. Some may argue that it's unfair that they buy so much while the Japanese buy so little in return. The Japanese have a quick answer: 'We have no problems buying from you if your price is on par or cheaper that ours', or something to that effect. Another analogy is that: why pay three times the price for a plate of spaghetti in a restaurant when you can cook better at home.

Western corporations have a tendency to reap huge profits on exports while their counterparts in the East are only after volume and happy with lower margins to keep production going. A glaring example is the mining industry in Australia: the mining sector is virtually controlled by Asian demands especially from China and India. Local steel companies like Bluescope is down-sizing all the time because it is cheaper to send the tin ore to China and buy it back as steel because it *cannot* compete with Asian countries well known not only for cheap labour but also *established policy* in keeping margins low to *sustain* the workforce on the long term. Perhaps the West can learn from the East that modest lifestyles, self-discipline and lower expectations on immediate growth are some of the answers to stabilize the economy. I was told that many senior executives in China and Japan travel by train or bus to work and live humbly; something considered as *'weird'* by their counterparts in the West who own waterfront homes, chauffeured limousines and yachts.

It makes sense now why America owes China $US500 billion in 2008 and burdened with a national deficit of more than a trillion dollars in the same year. Americans love to buy from abroad for *short term* profits and convenience at the expense of long term unemployment that is likely to accelerate foreign borrowings at the same time. But who is going to provide a loan when you have a dwindling economy with nothing much to show that you can service the loan? It is very sad to see a great country hitting rock bottom where even fresh graduates are beginning to wonder whether their leaders read basic economics anymore.

Poachers to protectors

The captioned topic is condensed from an article in Reader's Digest written by John Dyson about survival in Africa in real life. I hope the story would motivate some genuine leaders to get serious and do their bit to cure the wounds and pains of the world.

Cosimo was the head man of 60 families in a village called Masoka in northern Zimbabwe. They relied mainly on growing corn and poaching for food. But the locals faced constant danger of being gored to death by rampaging elephants and buffaloes on top of having their corn fields destroyed. Wildlife belonged to the government and hunting the animals for food or protection is against the law. For the struggling villagers to survive, the animals were dangerous pests as well as sources of food. How can man and animal co-exist as National parks were simply not enough to halt the dwindling loss of nature's habitat for wildlife?

One fine day in 1986, Marshall Murphree—a university researcher who had a passion and a *plan*—for helping African wildlife arrived in Masoka. 'I see you live in a wealthy land,' Marshall said to Cosimo. You have no cattle but I saw the dung of buffalo and elephant. There is a way to make these animals ten times more valuable than cattle. You can manage your wildlife as livestock,' explained Marshall.

The idea was hatched by a small group of ecologists in 1975. They persuaded what was then the Rhodesian government to let private farmers use wildlife on their land as if the animals were their own. Doubters warned that farmers would shoot and kill every animal on sight to make a quick buck, but the opposite happened. Animal numbers soared as the majority of farmers went into the wildlife business. Compared to cattle, big-game hunting and *tourism* brought in up to four times more profit per hectare. Trophy hunters pay licence fees for every animal they shoot coupled with the fact that barren wasteland is turned to dense and luscious vegetation by locals to attract both animals and tourists. The next step was to draw up some regulations and control to protect wildlife and transfer the idea to the seven million people living on the vast areas of communal land which lead to the formation of a committee called the 'Communal Areas Management Programme For Indigenous Resources or CAMPFIRE for short.

Marshall realised that CAMPFIRE could also give villagers a chance to break free of government dependency and run their own affairs with common sense if given the incentive to do so. Marshall vowed that the project would avoid the pitfalls of many foreign-aid schemes that had failed because they were imposed from the *outside*. The success of CAMPFIRE arose from the energy and ingenuity of the people themselves. At the village in Mosaka, Cosimo says: 'The animals are setting us free. We are guarding and harvesting them like farmers in America. We have full bellies now. We are developing our village by *our own efforts* and we are rich—we have more animals than ever before.'

The above example is just one of the many projects the rich can help the poor if they are earnest about nation building. Helping those in abject poverty are not impossible dreams as 'where there's a will, there's a way.' Projects like farming, fishing, weaving, honey collecting and other income earning activities connected to the natural vegetation and resources of the area are all food for thought as labour is always cheap in poverty-stricken places. Life can be more meaningful when the hungry are taught to be more productive and self-sufficient.

Who's going to pay for all these survival projects? If some of the nations currently at war are prepared to lay down their arms for *one* month and call a truce, there should be more than enough savings to finance realistic projects including free barbecues and beer money thrown in for the labour force!

Is Obama the one?

We did not come here to fear the future, but shape them.

Barrack Obama

Are we expected to see a new breed of leadership in changing time?

It makes sense when US foreign policy expert and author Fareed Zakaria, in his book, *The Post-American World,* identified three power shifts in the last 500 years. First was the rise of the West. Next came the Americans. We are now living through the third: 'It could be called the rise of the rest,' he said.

The newly elected 2008 American president, Barrack Obama, has a simple slogan: 'Change we need', as the keynote in his election campaign. He wants Americans to change the 'Old Guard' politics of the Clintons and the Bushes—the politics of special interest groups, of lobbyists, of arrogance, corruption and secret agendas. Obama was practically unknown as an African-American black senator in Illinois before becoming a presidential candidate. Some who came across the name 'Obama' for the first time, thought it was the title of a new movie or someone related to Osama! His non-aggressive approach of change and hope emphasising that charity begins at home, is a breath of fresh air that resonated with many Americans. His rare presence of boyish charm, humility, warmth and casualness blend very well not only with Americans but also the world.

Is Obama the forerunner for world peace?

For starters, Obama's middle name 'Hussein', is a good omen to the Muslim world. Present sensitive spots are focused in Muslim countries like Iraq, Iran, Israel and Afghanistan including Pakistan. It is more likely that Muslim leaders will hear him out to discuss, negotiate and resolve sensitive issues at the round table. Someone says, 'He isn't just black; he's an Afro-Asian-Latin European from heritage of his grandparents.' That means he's also a global citizen and perhaps the much needed global leader to bring peace to our turbulent world. Within a year as President, Obama has proven to be a good salesman who speaks with conviction and without the usual arrogance and haste compared to his predecessor. His name is music to the ears for many as American arrogance and supremacy have taken a back seat because Obama appears to be one of those rare breeds who is prepared to *listen* first before he takes action. However, he has his knockers too; mostly conservative white Americans who are not used to having a black man as their leader. His opposition and those in the shadows (likely the more powerful ones) will use every trick in the book to discredit and run him down.

Obama has inherited a 'white house full of worms' from his predecessor and the task ahead of him is a hard, long road to show his mettle to win back his people and the world. But so far, Obama has his legions of supporters as his policies for change are not only very practical and inspiring for many, but spoken by a man of passion as if on a mission to fulfil his beliefs of uniting the 'haves and the have not' of the world.

Obama's new politics of co-operation, common sense, common purpose and shared sacrifices have an almost *messianic appeal* that deeply touched people with aspirations for change to something better. *Perhaps* the man from Kenya is the forerunner to make the world a better place and put an end to dirty politics of the Bush administration. For now, we can only wish him well as he will be measured by the quality of his work ahead of him.

Action speaks louder than words. What about Obama?

President Obama has taken the initiative to phase out US troops in Iraq by 2010 saying it's not their war. As for Afghanistan, he has taken action by despatching his top military chief, Admiral Mike Mullen and expert negotiator Richard Holbrooke, on a diplomatic and *economic development* mission that focus on protecting the public and building civil order. It is a refreshing change to see US highest military personnel Mullen mingling with Afghan farmers and giving them *free* wheat seeds instead of running them down with tanks! It's all about the soft touch now in nation building and *not* how to win a war. Perhaps 'losing a war' can be just as triumphant when both parties are prepared to treat each as *equal* and work out new strategy of atonement to prevent further hardship on both fronts. A genuine peacemaker understands that when we divide ourselves, we can't resolve problems. Obama has also taken steps to close down Guantamo Bay. So far, he appears serious in ending the Israel and Palestine problems and also made a tour to many Muslim countries shaking hands with 'feared enemies' like Mahmoud Ahmadinejad of Iran, Chavez of Venezuela and others to start afresh again without prejudice or malice.

World peace cannot be resolved overnight, but at least some positive efforts are made and Obama is reluctant to condemn any nation as 'rogue countries' or stumbling block to attain peace until such nations are given a chance to voice their grievances. His humility is infectious to other genuine leaders and many are optimistic that world harmony is close at hand when negotiations are focused on places of agreement and opportunities to share instead of sounding out differences not conducive to peace. But like any new leader, charity begins at home and he needs to fix the financial crisis at home first before he gets any support from his people on foreign matters.

Humour

The best medicine

A black man returned to his tribe in the mountains after living in the city for 20 years. An old man came out from a tent and waved.

'Papa, I nearly couldn't recognise you with your long beard!' The young man said.

'Welcome home, my smart boy. You have grown tall and lean like me. By the way, have you caught the elusive bandit yet?' the father asked.

'Nay pa, he's always hiding. If I find him, I'll kill him with my bare hands,'
The son replied.

'Don't give up and don't trust anyone.' the father said. Unable to hide the smirk on his face, the old man quickly hugged his son tightly and added, 'Watch your back Obama. You never know when he will appear and stick a knife in you!' the elusive Osama said to his son.

Chapter 7

THE NEW AGE

New broom sweeps clean.

Proverb

What is meant by a 'New Age'?

It is the consensus of astronomers that each astrological age last for about 2000 years and we have left the *Piscean* age and are entering *Aquarius* since 1990. A new age obviously implies change but the need for change comes from within the individual and *not* from governments or religious groups who impose their doctrines and code of conduct on us. It is widely accepted that a new age works in the *opposite* direction from the previous one where rules and regulations take a backseat as self-expression becomes the order of the day. We are now experiencing a consciousness shift where we become more self-reliance on how we should live based on *our* beliefs and values and not something dictated by political or religious masters. We are blessed with a new healing energy that will make us focus on *solutions and co-operation* and not *delusions and competition,* the common theme of the Pisces' period. Sanity takes over from now and we will work toward a win-win situation for all to make the planet a better world.

Why is a new age necessary?

Planet earth was like a rotten old car orbiting in space without an *overhaul* and likely to 'stop or crash' if some *bad parts* (old energy responsible for greed and power) were not replaced. Since the new millennium, the shift of the planet's *magnetic grid alignment* has altered the vibration rate of earth. It is worth repeating that the 'health' of our planet is determined by the quality of its vibration connected to magnetic energy. The effects of the new alignment are very noticeable with fierce changes in weather pattern like hurricanes, storms, drought and unexpected tsunamis and earthquakes. These events, coupled with *tribal wars* in the Middle East, are inevitable and should be looked upon as a *transition or cleansing* period before we can experience a better world. Our planet needs to be repaired, washed, and *balanced* so that it can go '*vroom, vroom*' again and not '*clink clang*' like an old car about to be turned to scrap metal!

The new vibration or *healing* energy is expected to stimulate and enhance our *mental and spiritual* growth giving rise to more evolutionary changes. We become more independent in decision-making by *bonding* with our higher self. However, in order to capitalise on this power, there must be *positive intent* on our part to ensure that our action or decision is for the betterment of mankind. When we work with love, our power will increase and nothing will harm us because we are partnering with our spiritual self—the piece of God. If our thoughts or actions are connected to greed or hate like the old energy, ascension becomes a slow process and many will be left behind.

Is there a connection between religion and the new age?

If you walk into a modern book shop today you are likely to find a section called '*The New Age,*' littered with books on self-discipline, meditations, feng shui, spirit guides, life after death, energy balancing, self-healing and almost any subject from A to Z regarding mind, body and soul. What about the sudden mushrooming of *angels' shops?*

The Aquarius age is not about the latest cult formed by 'weirdos' nor is a new religion. It has no system or doctrine but simply a *new world philosophy* that centres on *the inner power* of every human being so that life is not wasted. It focuses on a belief that all of us have a purpose in life and possess hidden power previously unknown to us. It is a period of awakening to honour ourselves and our feelings and maintain *self esteem* and not to short-change ourselves. Tolerant of others is also one of the main themes in the new age as everyone is born *spiritually equal:* the more reason we should love our neighbour as much as we love ourselves. The beauty of the new age is perfect freedom: there's no membership to any group, vows to take, regular subscriptions or clothing style to follow other than trusting ourselves to manifest blessings for our existence.

Aquarius is steering away from religion to ensure it doesn't interfere with knowledge. This doesn't mean that religion is bad or of little use. It simply means that we need to change our outlook to keep pace with changing time as more and more universal truths are revealed over the decades by not only modern prophets but also scientists and doctors with new discoveries that are for the betterment of the world. Check out the advances made in medicine, transport, education and particularly global communications networks that bring mankind closer together since the past fifty years. Such dramatic changes are part of the divine plan to enable mankind to leap forward and religious beliefs have to change too for better understanding of this special age. It's all about *balancing;* if we are rooted to outdated beliefs and tradition, we will not progress and be left behind.

How are some Middle Eastern countries faring?

It is common knowledge that there are also ruthless leaders who use religion as a front to amass as much wealth as possible for themselves and families and democracy is dead as seen in many Middle Eastern countries like Libya, Egypt, Yemen or Tunisia. The rulers are only interested in clinging on to power forever if they can help it. In 2010, Gaddafi of Libya has ruled with an iron fist after 40 years and those against him are either in jail or simply 'disappeared.' Mubarak of Egypt is still there after 30 years and the 'religious man' took the country for a ride and amassed an estimated wealth worth $40 billion. Perhaps he wants to be *mummified* and take his riches to the next world like ancient pharaohs!

Reforms to improve the quality of life for their people are moving at snail speed to meet the fast changing pattern of modern society. Most people have TV and internet now and able to compare themselves with progressive nations. The young especially, are better educated today and likely to revolt when they continue to walk the streets without proper jobs fuelled also by limited recreational and social activities to spice up their lives. Religious constraints have gone too far when women are treated like second class citizens with no voting rights or allow to drive a car and finding a decent job is like winning a special award. Many women are still wearing traditional black dresses and allowed to show only their eyes in public just in case they get knock-over! The uprising in Tiananmen Square in China is a case in point for all to learn that freedom of expression is the short cut to national harmony and prosperity. Religious leaders must buckle up to change with time and get serious in nation building as the young are not only getting restless but feeling *worthless* and unable to contain their silence anymore.

Is the new age telling us about the latest 'revelation' in spirituality?

Actually no; in fact the new age is taking us back in time to ancient India to uncover the early roots of spirituality. The oldest holy Hindu Scripture '*Vedas*,' commonly known as the '*Breath of God*,' teaches the Hindus to achieve union with *Brahman* or God. The Vedas said:

'*The aspirant who is seeking God must free himself from selfish attachments to people, money and possessions. When his mind sheds every selfish desire, he becomes free from the duality of pleasure and pain and rules his senses. No more is he capable of ill will. No more is he the subject of elation, for his senses comes to rest with the Self.*'

The new age rekindles the basic truth of human existence by restoring balance between the material and spiritual worlds. We are now entering the Aquarius age—the *flowering* of self-realisation of our duality and fulfilling the essence of this book regarding the purpose of human existence.

What are the basic differences between Piscean and Aquarius ages?

The old Piscean age saw the emergence of religions like Christianity, Islam and their many 'off-shoots'. Religion embracing a universal God was the fundamental belief for all but greed and power became the order of the day leaving behind a disunited world that can do more damage than good if allowed to continue. It is the prediction that the power of the church and other religious institutions will crumble during the Aquarius age as it is no longer necessary for them to act as a spiritual intermediary. The consciousness shift has provided everyone the power to understand more about the spiritual side in them. It is a period of healing for body, mind and soul. It will not be surprising that some readers have already taken the initiative as flag-bearers of today's quiet revolution of walking closer to God *once again.*

It is obvious that the Piscean period focused on materialism that triggered wars and hardship. Aquarius works the opposite way of Piscean where self-expression is paramount to happiness instead of relying on political or religious leaders for directions. Aquarius is the age of unity; humans will learn to find 'alternatives' to live in peace and harmony and 'red, yellow, black and white,' will come to their senses that they are *all one* with common goals.

What is the meaning of 'Rainbow Warriors'?

The prophets of the Hopi Indians in America are very well respected because they have foreseen the world wars, inventions of motor cars, airplanes, atomic bombs and predicted that the children of white men would live in *communal societies.* The Hopi shamans called the new generation the '*Rainbow Warriors,*' the blending of the various races to heal and restore the balance of nature in order to make the world whole again. They say that the greatest fear amongst the many cultures is that such communal living would destroy their traditions and identity. This is an *unfounded fear* and some nations today are unaware that *they* are the cause of their own miseries by creating hatred and fighting wars to protect their heritage. Take a good look at the on-going senseless war between Israel and Palestine. The keynote of the coming age is all about brotherhood—the spirit of sharing and creating harmony to find our common ground. The Hopi elders truly have rare insight and wisdom; they emphasised that *separate* countries and people are doomed for destruction as global survival is all about being *one*—the same philosophy of Sai Baba who mentioned that 'the only caste is humanity.' The various religions of the world then are no good thing in fostering peace or uniting mankind as one. For the sake of peaceful existence, it's time religions take a backseat in the world stage and both political and religious leaders should stop emphasising differences and instead, look for places of agreement and change 'a bruised earth' to a better world.

What is the Age of Redemption?

What's more, Aquarius is also the Age of Redemption. This means that the change to a new consciousness will free us from the bondage of karma. If we choose to return, we will be the rainbow warriors with only *one vision*: to heal and unite the world. Remember the 'Indigo' kids who enter the world with no karmic debt to repay?

Is there any similar prediction regarding the future of earth other than reading the stars and from prophets?

Strangely, yes. Many survivors of clinical death were able to witness or recall the coming of the new age and remarkably, they all share the same prophetic visions! Reinee Pasrow, a 17 years old has this to say on her death-bed:

'The vision of the future I received during my near-death experience was one of tremendous upheaval in the world as a result of our general ignorance of the true reality. Mankind, I was told, was being consumed by the cancers of arrogance, materialism, racism, chauvinism and separatist thinking. I saw sense turning to nonsense, and calamity, in the end, turning to providence.

At the end of this general period of transition, mankind was to be 'born anew,' with a new sense of his place in the universe. The birth process, however, as in all the kingdoms, was exquisitely painful. Mankind would emerge humbled yet educated, peaceful, and, at last, unified.'

Pasarow's quote is extracted from the book, *The Prophetic Revelations of Paul Solomon* by W. Alexander Wheeler.

What is the symbol and message of Aquarius?

The sign of Aquarius has always been depicted by a person pouring out water from a jar. Keen observers are quick to interpret that the pouring out of stale water represents the old energy or consciousness. Fresh water has to be replaced to give way to a new consciousness or new beginning. Changing contaminated water to fresh water is like enabling diseased fishes to breathe well and swim freely again. It will take a very brave person to refute the symbol as *'coincidental,'* in relation to the new age.

Is it going to be a smooth changeover from Piscean to Aquarius Age?

Aquarius is the age of ideals; of groups coming together and sharing common goals. All these are possible now because of positive changes in our mind. But intelligence alone is not an ideal quality and can be dangerous if wrongly used. Intelligence must be blended with *love* to attain the Christ quality of *love-wisdom* for universal balancing to fight any negative force. Author Sai Grafio, in his book, *Mysteries: Ancient and Modern,* explained that man must face the 'dweller on the threshold' before he can unfold the true soul culture. Mankind is now poised in evolution to fight the 'battle of Armageddon of the mind.' It is an internal war of the mind where one side resisting change, the other forcing it on.

It must be remembered that as long as we are living in the realm of duality in planet earth, co-existing with the anti-Christ forces is still a part of our reality. They will continue to thwart us with temptations to make us sense bound again and will try to convince us that everything can be explained in a materialistic, scientific fashion. The main motive of the dark forces is to make sure the many cultures are disunited and do not come together as one and chaos become the order of the day.

It is repeated many times in this book that humans will always be imperfect beings until we return to the spiritual realm. Our mental development and reasoning power will move forward but it is still *our choice* whether to walk closer to God or be victims of the negative forces. We are *'gods in the making,'* says Sai Grafio, and evolution is a crossroad whereby we must use our new knowledge *wisely* as moral decency is greater now than ever before.

The dark forces

> *Men are forced to fight and die for their country*
> *while the king feasts with the fairest in the country.*

S.F. Khean

What do you mean by' anti-Christs'?

According to the Bible, Jesus says:

> *Beware of false prophets who come to you in sheep's clothing*
> *but inwardly are ravenous wolves.*
> *You will know them by their fruits.*

Jesus had warned the world about the appearance of false messiahs 2000 years ago and people of that time did not really understand what that was all about. That warning was more for our generation where it has come to a stage when we have problems trying to identify the saints from the smiling assassins as they are all smooth talkers and great actors trying to win us over! 'You will know them by their fruits,' or wait and see whether they are good only in lip service or can actually *deliver* their promises, as Jesus said.

The word 'Christ' means *the true messenger of the living God* and does not necessarily apply only to Jesus of Nazareth as many

Christians tend to believe. If there's a second coming, it could be another Christ unknown to us. The anti-Christ forces are our greatest enemies who are all out to blind us with *only* materialistic concepts such as power, greed and immoral living. They want us to enjoy life to the fullest so that universal truth that there is life after death or we are 'gods in the making' becomes only a faint memory or a forgotten issue.

False masters and anti-Christs are in our midst today and they bring only evil to destabilise human existence and enable them to control our world for selfish reasons. They will create disharmony, hatred, wars, economic strife and immorality to prevent us from knowing that we are all spiritual beings on a mission. Remember our lessons on planetary healing? They want us to be zombies and enslave us or wipe us out to gain full control of the planet.

Who are the dark forces?

The dark forces, also known as the *black brotherhood*, is a secret group of very powerful and high ranking officials residing mainly in America and Europe. They will oppose the appearance of any Christ who preaches universal truth and eternal life as such teachings would resonate with our souls making us more determine to fight back and jeopardise their dark agenda. They are fond of using *'puppets'* to further their cause and we should be very weary of some political and religious leaders including high profile businessmen who may be used as pawns by the dark group that supported them in leadership positions. The world should also be weary of some well advertised investment opportunities from *new* organisations that promise quick returns. Many are scams to *bankrupt* you and later *recruit* you (because you are broke and desperate) for sinister work that is likely to create disharmony within the various groups. Many high fliers are merely watchdogs for an unsuspecting group who control their activities in order to *control* us—the common people.

Can the evil forces manipulate and play tricks to our minds?

The dark forces under the guise of law-abiding citizens are a cunning lot fully aware of the consciousness shift for mankind. As a desperate attempt to slow down our enlightenment, they have resorted to *deception* instead of fear by acting like benefactors with good intent or kindness to gain our trust. Be very cautious with *'ravenous wolves in sheep's clothing'* that cannot deliver. It is not surprising to hear that *ET channelling* on various subjects is on the rise to deceive and confuse humanity to chase for *higher* gods from other planets so that they become dreamers and unproductive people. Remember wandering and attaching spirits? They too can also *mimic* higher gods to make you *worship and pray* more in order to increase their hold on you. Many good people have unwittingly fallen prey to such hideous traps and *unaware* that they are actually aiding the cause of the bad guys.

Be reminded again that we are imperfect beings and false prophets and flawed leaders are everywhere to confuse and brainwash us. Don't accept everything new as *real* to enhance your spiritual power or be led by 'false masters' that you are the forerunners to a better world. The teachings of *any* Christ are meant for the masses whether rich or poor and *not* a select few. It is never too late to live humbly and stop chasing rainbows when you are *already* a spark of God. Learn the simple rules in life and trust your intuition to attain enlightenment.

Prophecy and Channelling

A god who allowed us to prove his existence would be an idol.

Dietrich Bonhoeffer

Can some old prophesies be explained differently?

Everyone is entitled to his or her belief system and interpretations of signs and visions can vary with the passing of time. According to great thinkers like Sai Grafio and spiritual healer Bill Anderson, many sources, especially *Revelation* from the Bible, have given too much emphasis on *fear based* predictions like destructive upheavals between the battle of *angels with the beast*, nuclear wars, terrorism and natural disasters of the physical world as the culmination to 'end time.' Perhaps the author of Revelation took his 'vision' too literally. Figuratively, 'angels' could mean the higher self and the 'beast' is the outer world or the conscious mind bound by the craving senses. Also, the 'second coming' is unlikely to be the appearance of another Christ but an experience where all can share as it represents a *renewal* of spiritual values and brotherly love.

Remember the holy Hindu scripture of the Vedas regarding the flowering of *self-realisation* and union with Brahman? The main thrust of the new age is not so much about changes in outer world events but a battle with our *inner self* to attain wholeness. There is no doubt that with the new healing energy, winning the battle is within the grasp of everyone. As our minds become clearer, problems will be resolved rationally to ensure we are part of the *solution* and not the trouble-makers. Wisdom will be acquired over time by not emphasising differences in our interaction with others and, instead, look for opportunities to share. Don't forget that new generations like the 'Indigo' and Crystals' are also here to help us do the healing on all levels—from new holistic healing for individuals, advanced technology and restoring balance for our bruised earth.

Has the Bible provided any insight about 'end time'?

The Old Testament mentioned that a Hebrew called Daniel who lived in Babylon around 600 BC, was the most respected seer in the king's court as he was able to interpret complex dreams accurately and had the gift to communicate with 'angels' that passed on messages to him on future events. His visions and dreams were spot on regarding the outcome of many wars and the fate of his king, people and country. But when he tried to *calculate* end time from a bizarre and spooky vision (too long and complicated to expand for this section) where the dead were resurrected and join forces with the angels and do battle with the living wicked, his prophecy did not come true.

In the book *Revelation,* written near the end of the first century AD, the message and events of judgement day or end time are almost identical to Daniel's failed prophecy. Is Revelation rehashed information from *'The Book of Daniel'*? Could it be the work of an unknown author and not the vision of John, the apostle as claimed? Biblical records have shown that John spent his final years as a prisoner where he was banished to an island called Patmos off the Agean Sea. He was thrown into the mines for hard labour. If Revelation was written by John, he would be *more* than 100 years old then. Moreover, John was only a common fisherman: where did he learn to write? John's easy access to pen, ink, paper, table, chair and lamp while being a prisoner who lived in a *cave* are very questionable. 'Revelation,' in my opinion, is not something from God to punish mankind—He is a loving God and not a fearful one threatening our demise—but the beliefs and writings of an angry man; probably a monk or cleric who witnessed the atrocities of the Romans that sent Christians to the arena to feed the lions. The author was likely to be in a rage and thought he knew best and stuffed it up repeating the dream of failed prophesy by Daniel.

Many seers and shamans from ancient time to the present have attempted to pin-point the date of end time but no one is likely to succeed. The failure is part of Holy Scripture to remind all lesser men to heed the warning of Jesus Christ:

'Of that day or that hour no one knows, not even the angels in heaven, nor the Son, but only the Father.' (Mark 13:32)

Many sources mentioned that year 2012 is end time. Please explain.

This is the prediction made by the ancient Mayan priests of Central America that the world will end in December 2012. The Mayans are well respected for their prophecies based on mathematical calculations of world events and their belief that history repeats itself. But as explained earlier, end time is not *doomsday*; the Mayan shaman might have seen the decay of a civilisation coming to its end but fell short to *follow through* that it was actually the start of another era with a *new time frame* or consciousness shift. Shamans, high priests or gurus are only humans; they see only what they *want to see*. Does end time—only four years from time of writing—mean that none of us will be left standing because of another great flood or the sun will stop shining? Many punters will be given very long odds that it will *not* happen. The funny side—who's going to collect when it happens?

What is the new timeline after 2012? According to *Kryon*, since the tilt of the magnetic grid of our planet in 1990, the new Aquarian ray will stimulate our body clock—or *aging process* in our DNA—to *slow down* and enable all of us to *live longer* as part of a reward for our efforts in planetary healing. This is awesome news and everyone should say a prayer of thanks for such *magical* gift! To complement our longevity, doctors are now able to rejuvenate certain vital body parts to relieve sufferings that are all in tune with the divine plan. Heart-bypass surgery can be done in most hospitals today and even spinal problems like damaged vertebrae can be replaced with artificial ones. What about the numerous detoxification recipes, digestive cleansers, vitamin pills, herbal and organic foods including breathing exercises to promote good health?

However, living longer is only applicable to those who take proactive and preventative action rather than react when ill-health is upon them. Many will miss out if they persist in abusing their bodies through over-indulgence or unprepared to change bad habits that are not conducive to healthy living. Change can be difficult for some because stubborn people do not believe in *sacrifice:* they simply cannot give up something they enjoy (like taking drugs, gambling, etc) in *exchange* for something they are unsure of its benefits such as drinking more water instead of guzzling a gallon of beer a day! What about the rich who love fatty food like suckling pig or thick untrimmed steak and dinner is not complete without rich desserts topped with many layers of cream. A great night also means that all the good food must be washed down with a few glasses of fine brandy or wine so that we can belch loudly. More often than not, the truth only comes to light for stubborn people when they have a heart attack or rotting away in a retirement home. Don't flaunt your wealth; eat and drink in moderation. The divine can only provide you with the tools to prolong your life; if you ignore and don't heed good advice, who's to blame? Remember it takes two hands to make a clap.

Where do we stand after 2012?

Many sources such as historians, authors and particularly the media are fond of distorting the reality of a prediction for the sake of grabbing the headlines to arouse curiosity and instil *fear.* I read in a magazine that a movie would soon be made about the *rumblings* of 2012 to enable film producers to cash in on end time! It is worth repeating that the year 2012 is the *beginning* of earth's ascension to a higher consciousness and everyone should be bursting with joy as it is the most glorious day in our earth history. The age of darkness will *soon* disappear and we will strive for harmonious living with more love enthroned in our hearts instead of acting like cats and dogs of old time! The new era is about *co-operation* and not *competition.* However, do not expect changes to happen overnight. Remember, 'Rome wasn't built in a day.'

Are there other claims to confirm our longevity?

It is also timely to mention that Kyron is not the first to mention of humans living longer as recent medical research has proven that it is not only possible, but almost a *certainty*. Since the cloning of 'Dolly' the sheep in 1996, major breakthroughs in biology have been discovered. The most intriguing find is the anti-aging puzzle found in *telomeres*, a clock that lies within every human cell containing DNA that keeps track of our age by counting the number of times the cells divides and copies itself. Scientists and researchers are optimistic that it will be a *matter of time*, perhaps another 15 years, that the required knowledge to unwind the clock backwards will be uncovered. Who knows, in the near future, maintaining a strong heart and getting rid of wrinkles and foggy eyes can be as easy as swallowing an aspirin!

Are we expected to know all the changes or workings of the new age?

Since the beginning of time, humans have always marvelled at the perfect harmony of nature and its survival. Over the ages, every religion pays homage to God as there is always a divine plan for humans to survive and progress. Remember during the middle ages when explorers like *Marco Polo* and *Christopher Columbus* found new worlds that evolved a period of cultural enrichment of languages, customs, food, philosophies and the rise of technology? Human evolution is inevitable over time—many of us are already computer literates and mobile phone owners and no longer have to use 'smoke signal' to communicate like ancient time. But the *working dynamics and timing* of evolutionary changes are not meant for us to know. We live in a planet where Mother Nature does not disclose her *secrets* readily and allow *unevolved* humans to *control* the unseen forces. The *timeless perfection* of nature is simply beyond the understanding of humans including scientists and those who *claimed* to be spiritual gurus!

Can we trust all the things we hear from channelling about changes?

There is steady demand for new age books since the new millennium and many authors try to capitalise on the 'gold rush' by giving *their* versions on the working dynamics of the new age or *rehashed* some old information. Some even have the audacity to claim they are *channels* for certain ascended masters and their books are sometimes treated like 'gospel truth.' Learn to be more analytical in what you read because every profession has its charlatans. Some authors and so called 'psychics' are laughing their way to the bank as *'heavenly matters'* cannot be *disproved* in the law courts nor can they be verified through mathematical calculation, in the laboratory or computer. This scenario is similar to the enduring and fascinating tale of *Atlantis* where it is said to have slipped beneath the dark waters of the sea, just beyond the grasp of scientific proof.

It must be emphasised that channelling provides only good tidings or *data* strictly for *reference* and nothing more than that. Channelling is different from predictions made by Nostradamus or fortune-tellers because it does not *predict* the future or *give advice:* it cannot tell us about political issues like who is going to win the next election nor is it able to predict the rise and fall of the stock markets or recommend a particular type of person we should marry for everlasting bliss! This is mainly because all entities of higher intelligence are expected to abide by the *universal code of non-intervention* of lower or evolving planets *unless* it is necessary. Is such a concept different from our society?

Remember guardian angels or spiritual guides? Our soul mates *cannot* do favours for us all the time because we are required to 'spar with the devil' for lessons and test our *free will* before we are able to find enlightenment. Similarly, even when we have 'big dreams' in full colour, it is not always easy to decipher the subtle message; otherwise all of us would hit the sack early and hope to dream of the next set of lotto winning numbers or the next winning horse in the Melbourne Cup!

Don't treat 'channellers' as *gurus*, they are not. In most cases, it is the blind leading the blind: channellers are well known for bringing in the strange and bizarre with fraudulent claims—all intriguing and holding interest, however briefly—mainly to confuse us. Many love *'to play god'* but are they really qualified or simply *think* they are? There is some following for certain new age books because many are attracted to colourful language, new ideas and not to mention about pictures of *'godly gurus'* (especially in 'oracle cards') that looked like film stars or great warriors instead of blotches of energy! Who has seen the *faces* of the many 'gods'? It is a human weakness that many get carried away by attractive images which prompted reputed German author and pastor Bonhoeffer to say that a god who allowed us to prove its existence can only be an idol. In the real world, humans—including psychics and false masters—cannot even predict the timing of a tsunami or earthquake that could have devastating effect on human lives because such *forces of nature* work silently and strike *unexpectedly*. What about the many blunders made by modern day weather bureau whether it's going to be rain or shine for *tomorrow*?

Why do certain people get carried away with some new age books?

We are very vulnerable beings burdened with cravings and emotions. Our imagination can run like wild fire and be *consumed* by it when we fail to *embrace reality*. Some who experienced *'hell and back'* would understand that truth can kill or be very painful. But reality can keep them alive. Books that are fictional are easy to compile when the author is imaginative. The subject matter can be based on anything that does not require any qualifying or *proof* as long as it holds interest and stir the mind like a good movie or any *paid* seminar or workshop. But true spiritual books are hard to come by as spiritual masters are few and far apart and they are a humble breed that does not rely on writing books to survive or need any publicity. Science-fiction movies and books are pure escapism mainly to *relax* your mind and not be consumed by them and dreaming your life away. Books and movies like *Star Wars and Harry Potter* are examples of very talented writers' fantasies that can affect dreamers from realism and *entertainment:* the hatching ground for those who think that they are *star people.* Don't get carried away and fall into the trap that you are of a special breed from a noble planet that can save the world; leave that to God. Our main task on earth is simply to conquer ourselves by living righteously to repay karmic debt.

Early signs of Change

Imagine all the people living life in peace.
You may say I'm a dreamer, but I'm not the only one.
I hope someday you'll join us and the world will be as one . . .
A brotherhood of man
Imagine all the people sharing all the world . . .

Lyrics from 'Imagine'

Some songwriters are so gifted that they composed verses as if they come directly from the heart. My eyes went blurry typing the above words because the lyrics of *'Imagine'* touched me in unexpected ways as though reaching a cord of the soul where legends live. How true, the verses are filled with wisdom where even the insect kingdom is aware of this very basic survivor's formula of unity. What about most of us?

What are some of the positives changes since the new millennium?

Have you noticed the quantum leap we have taken in both science and technology the last 20 years? Look at the tremendous progress made in communication; we have the internet, website and mobile phones to reach the four corners of the earth. World events can be shared and viewed through the comforts of home TV. We even have GPS to make sure motorists are able to reach their destinations in the shortest time. The reality of today is truly the magic of yesterday. Modern science and technology are paving the way to connect mankind together for better understanding and co-operation.

Are there other modern sciences that can change our lives?

It will not be far away when high-tech fertility centres will correct problems for mothers who cannot conceive and childbirth will no longer be a 'painful experience' for some. It is not surprising now that parents in California can have 'designer baby' when they can pick the gender of their baby from a *sex selection menu* including even the *personality* of the child though this highly controversial embryo sex-screening procedure is banned in most parts of the world. New technology will change the way we live.

Do humans have many strands of DNA?

Strangely, it has been reported that there are 12 strands of DNA in our matrix and scientists have discovered only 2 strands so far because they are chemical and visible under the microscope. The remaining *'invisible'* strands are basically spiritual and need awakening or waiting to be stimulated before they can be discovered. A lot of it has to do with cosmic energy and its magnetic effect on our bodies and the arrival of the Aquarian ray appears to be the catalyst to promote spiritual growth. It will take time to collate science and spiritual truths but our scientists and medical experts are getting there. Does the DNA information mean that we are presently using only about 16% of our intelligence? Is our knowledge or intelligence being controlled by some unseen forces? I am anxiously looking forward for my *third* strand of DNA to surface but will it be this lifetime?

Can we have some examples on the changing pattern of human greed?

'Come here quickly!' My good wife Keng was very excited when she shouted at me while I was cleaning the fish tank. She was watching Oprah's talkback show and something extraordinary was happening there. The queen of live shows gave a *brand new car* to all her audience that day and there were about 200 of them! Such generosity was not only staggering but also touched our hearts deeply. It was one of those rare moments when you spontaneously shared the joy of others as if your inner self had suddenly come alive. The natural and easy flow of tears from the shocked audience was also infectious as our eyes got cloudy too, but it was a good feeling. Oprah, her producer and the car manufacturer might have struck up a deal but that's immaterial; it's the mere thought of trying to add some sunshine to improve the lives of others that really counts.

On that same week, a current affairs program showed a billionaire gave away a whole block of waterfront apartments to a group of selected elderly people so that they can live through their twilight years in style and comfort! Is this guy for real or is he *Rama or Jesus* in disguise? Such an act of kindness and generosity is truly awesome and unlikely to happen even in our wildest dreams! All these are happening in the year 2004 and I am sure there will be more surprises in store for the world because the message is starting to trickle down to the very rich that money and power *cannot buy a slice of heaven!*

Will sports be a growing trend for the young?

Look at the sudden surge in sports by the young today. Tiger Woods has shown the world that it is cool to play golf as a teenager and his legions of fans and sponsors are growing everyday. Leggy teenager Michelle Wie is out-driving some top male golfers and a big drawcard everywhere she goes. Tennis is another growing sport and charismatic Roger Federer and Rafael Nadal have proven to sports personalities that it is not necessary to throw tantrums in court to be a champion. Do you know that Russian tennis players have more representatives in most major tournaments today while the Korean women will be topping the list in golf soon? I thought the normally shy Korean ladies are only good in the kitchen and looking after children and it never cross my mind that they can be potential golf champions. All these new happenings are changing times of the world where freedom of expression is on the card for all to show their talents. It is a sobering thought and sometimes hard to quantify how those countless *young guns* who excel in sports are richer than their Presidents or the highest paid brain surgeon!

Can world leaders learn something from sports?

A university degree may give you a kick-start in life but there's no guarantee that you can be a millionaire or even a happy person. Sports are just another example to show that success in life is all about self effort, dedication and discipline. Singing, cooking, fashion designing and hundreds of other activities can make you comfortable in life too. Everyone is given a fair go to make good in the new age irrespective of backgrounds. Rich nations like America, France or Australia have the best training facilities for their athletes capable of becoming champions in swimming, gymnastic, equestrian and ring events like boxing or judo. But when it comes to endurance events like the marathon, African runners are usually the favourites to win despite the lack of training facilities because endurance is part of their survival. This is all part of universal balancing that money cannot buy everything.

Sports have shown us that the world can be united as one—whether it's the Olympic Games or soccer World Cup—every winner or nation is given the same accolade. National anthems are played and *respected* whether winners are black, brown or white because religion is *tabooed* in the sporting arena. This is a wake-up call to our leaders that the world can come together as one *provided* all activities are conducted openly, fairly and without any form of discrimination or cover-ups. Are you ready for *ping pong?*

Will there be changes in entertainment to promote healthy living?

Do you realise that even our movies and TV programs are getting more wholesome? Some of the movies we used to watch are verging on the point of pornography as if the main theme is selling sex. Women fashion shows are no better; many are not elegant and women are constantly exploited to dress scantily and 'display' as much flesh as possible. *Decency* has got the better of many designers and entertainers to leave something for the imagination!

Of late, very *chaste* projects are starting to roll again with global mainstream audience. Look at 'World Idol' and spin offs, home renovations, quiz shows, wild life, home and gardens, master chefs and dancing series are sweeping the small screen while violent and crime movies with the senseless *'bang, bang' and 'kill, kill'* themes are slowly taking a back seat. Latest investigative serials on TV such as *'CSI' and 'Law And Order'* programmes have strong following because the storylines are realistic and people like to be entertained and be *educated* at the same time. Our minds are transforming to give reality issues a better reception all over the world because people are beginning to question the purpose of their existence and where they fit in to make the planet a better place to live. *'No money, no talk,'* is fading as the ultimate aim in life. Is our new love energy working?

What's going to be the 'new religion?'

Sai Baba, the great one from India and revered around the globe today, says:

The lotus on the lake is far, far away from the sun; but the distance is no bar for the dawn of love; the lotus blooms as soon as the sun peeps over the horizon.

Sai Baba reminds the world that the 'only religion that unites is *love;* the only caste is *humanity.*' If that's still not good enough for some, I would like to recommend septics to join a very fast growing new religion: its 'karaoke'—the favourite entertainment package for most today. Learn to sing a few songs and the world will be a happier place. When you let your hair down and participate in a happy environment, you learn to be free; it will grow on you because joy begets joy just like love. Learn to be young again and don't be afraid to let go and sing: be as free as the wind like innocent children and give yourself a good time and enjoy a good laugh. Shakespeare says, '*If music is the fruit of love, play on,*' and why not?

Some of the material in this chapter is partly condensed from *Fortune Telling,* by author Bill Anderson who runs the successful *Pilgrim Centre* in Gloucester, England. Bill is also very well known as a spiritual healer who teaches many self-help courses in mind and body to relieve stress.

Humour

The best medicine

A spaceship landed near the city and a piggy-looking Martian walked to the city and entered a pub. He saw a man drinking at the bar, sat next to him and said, 'Hello, I am Yuli from Mars.' 'Oh yeah?' said the drunk, 'My name is Jesus from heaven, and for Christ sake, take that stupid mask off. This is a pub not a place for a fancy dress party!'

Chapter 8

THE LAST SAY . . .

And now the end is near,
And so I face the final curtain.
My friend, I'll say it clear,
I'll state my case of which I'm certain . . .

Lyrics from 'My Way'

The previous chapter, *The New Age,* was completed before the American election in September 2008 and I thought that was the final chapter for this book. The next thing I wanted to do was to find a good publishing agent. But I was at a complete loss how to find an agent or a publisher initially and decided to take my time by going for a holiday in Hong Kong and a few places in China which I have always wanted to visit. My manuscript was gathering dust on the shelf for more than a year as I had other interests in mind after my vacation. Perhaps it was meant to be that way to give me a breather and add a thing or two before putting the book to print. I only continue writing again after I got a 'slap' on the head in a dream one night reminding me of some unfinished business.

I like to remind readers that as stated from my introductory message of this book, what have been written so far in previous chapters are basically expansion on the teachings and opinions from great thinkers, authors, past and present prophets including sages whom I have great respect. Their messages have become part of my inspiration in life but need not necessarily be the truth as there is no yardstick to measure *'truth'* on many issues. I am now prompted to add another chapter partly to summarise what I have written and more importantly, my *personal truth* and views to round up my last say.

Realities of Life

> *The journey of a thousand miles*
> *begins with one step.*
> *The road to enlightenment*
> *begins with each moment.*

Taoism

There are numerous blockbuster books written on successful living and there are also many seminars conducted to help us enjoy life to the fullest. Some books and seminars are really great stuff and admittedly they are hard to gun down. I have decided to say my piece differently by focusing on old teachings patiently expounded by past sages and great thinkers regarding the basic concepts of happiness. I believe that *basic truths* echo the very basis of human existence that many people tend to forget. We need to *reconnect with simple truths* to attain our freedom to act by shunning attachments.

In our modern era of frenzied activities where there is little time to think, survival no longer means having a roof over your head and the promise of three decent meals a day. Having a good life in the modern age means a wardrobe stacked with designers' clothes, a collection of 'plastic cards,' scrambling for the top job, a great home, flashy car and *'what you can do, I can do better'*! Certain aspirations to achieve real happiness are beginning to look like chasing rainbows: they are unrealistic and bordering on the ridiculous. Many people are simply trying too hard and motivated only with an unquenchable thirst for greed and pleasure! It's time to go back to basics and '*Stop. Revive. Survive*'—an Australian slogan for tired drivers to go slow and rest.

Facts of Life

Buddhism preaches that there are five '*mission impossible*' that no-one is able to accomplish in this world:

1   To stop growing old.
2   To prevent sickness.
3   To prevent death.
4   To deny extinction when there is extinction
5   To deny exhaustion.

These are simple facts of life and neither magic, the latest medicines or reputed *shamans* can help you. But those who understand enlightenment accept them as part of life because they are aware that these are *unavoidable*. Life and death is inseparable like a rotating wheel. Death calls on all of us; the worrying part is *when?*

There are four basic truths in this world:

1   All living beings rise from ignorance.

2   All objects of desire are temporary, uncertain and the cause of suffering.

3   All existing things are also temporary, uncertain and the cause of suffering.

4 The words 'ego' and 'mine' are created by man mainly for self gratification.

Human nature is also not difficult to understand. There are three kinds of people in the world. The first are those who are like letters carved in rock; they easily give way to anger and retain their angry thoughts for a long time. The second are those who are like letters written in sand; they give way to anger also, but their angry thoughts quickly pass away. The third are those who are like letters written in running water; they do not retain their passing thoughts; they let abuse and uncomfortable gossip pass unnoticed; their minds are always pure and undisturbed.

It is well known that *'anger'* is found in all of us; the difference is how well each of us can contain it. Some can blow up at the slightest irritation while others have more tolerance and understanding by holding their peace. There is always a solution to finesse our character and the wisdom of Buddha is very meaningful when he said: *'Anger will never disappear so long as there are thoughts of resentment in the mind. Anger will disappear just as soon as thoughts of resentment are forgotten.'*

Desire, Passion and Lust

Stealing is prevented when we don't value treasures.
Confusion is prevented when we don't see desirable things.

Lao Tzu

Human desires are endless. It is like the thirst of a man who drinks salt water: he gets no satisfaction and his thirst is only increased. So it is with a man who seeks to gratify his desires; he only gains increased dissatisfaction and his woes are multiplied. Desires always leave behind unrest and irritation that can never be allayed. When the gratification of his desires is thwarted, there will be rumblings of threat and fear on loved ones and friends.

Desires arise from the five senses; the many forms the eyes see; the sounds the ears hear; the fragrance the nose smells; the pleasant tastes attract the tongue; things that are agreeable to the sense of touch. From these five doors of desire comes the body's love of comfort.

People love their *egoistic* comfort, which is a love of fame and praise. But fame and praise are like incense that consumes itself and soon disappears. If people chase after honours and public acclaim and leave the way of truth, they are in serious danger and will soon have cause for regret.

Money is *not* the root of all evil. If you work smart and earn it righteously, you are entitled to abundance. It is the *love* of it that makes most men tumbled and crumbled. A man who chases after fame and wealth and love affairs is like a child who licks honey from the blade of a knife. While he tastes the sweetness of honey, he has to risk hurting his tongue. He is like a man who carries a torch against a strong wind; the flame will surely burn his hands and face.

Of all the worldly passions, lust is the most intense. Other worldly passions seem to follow in its train. Lust seems to provide the soil in which other passions flourish. It is like a demon that eats up all the good deeds of the world. Lust is a viper hiding in a flower garden; it poisons those who come in search of only beauty.

Times of luxury do not last long, but pass away very quickly; nothing in this world can be enjoyed forever. Therefore, people should cast away, while they are young and healthy, all their greed and attachments to worldly affairs, and should seek earnestly to live righteously. There can be no lasting reliance or happiness apart from the search of your true existence on earth. Our lesson in this life is mainly to '*conquer ourselves before we can become great warriors.*' But there is no *instant* recipe for someone to change dramatically overnight. Perhaps the following *evergreen* quotation from Taoism can expedite change. If you are able to commit it to memory, this ancient wisdom may become a turning point in your life.

In life, don't look for divisions,
But notice, instead, the places of agreement.
Don't emphasize differences, instead look for
opportunities to share.
Don't pay undue attention to your failures
but honour your successes, no matter how small.

Journey of Life

The wheel of life keeps turning,
One day up, the next day down.
By not holding on to the good times
We are better able to deal with the bad times.

Taoism

True love never runs smooth; so is the journey of life because we are imperfect beings. Good and bad is found in all of us but in different measures. Our good fortune may be 'one day up, the next day down,' to enable us to experience pain and joy including a valuable lesson that the many ups and downs are like passing clouds that are *not* permanent. However, when we come to *understand* about the spiritual side in us, our approach in life from *thereon* will be more balanced as greed, attachments or blind passion are no longer top priorities. We become more conscious that life can be more meaningful when we learn to *serve* rather than simply living it up. With that positive frame of mind, we tend to be more cautious with our words and actions that are likely to make us more tolerant with people. When we have a deeper understanding of ourselves and others, humility becomes part of our nature. In times of crisis, hardship and difficult periods are easier to endure especially when we are aware that they all part of life cycle for us to *grow* from them.

In essence, our existence is all about being open to learning, making mistakes, confronting our fears, learning and a *willingness* to leap into the unknown.

Our earthly lessons are connected to planetary healing and the purification of our soul. Repaying karmic debts may not be possible in one lifetime but cutting it short is definitely possible as karma is all about correcting past mistakes and not compounding them. Our worst enemy is *ourselves* and we have to stoop to conquer ourselves. Do not let history repeats itself and this is why employees all over the world are taught that sound judgement is the result of experience. In reality, our existence is a *sacred* journey for us to understand our duality of being a human and a spiritual entity. On top of that, learn to understand that there is also a wonderful mystical law of nature that the three things we crave most in life—happiness, freedom and peace of mind—can always be attained by *giving* them to others. It should be clear that the world can only be one when *love* for all is the ultimate aim for our survival.

It is good to highlight again that *we* are all *authors* of our own destiny. Our destiny is written by us, not for us. However, once we are born a *memory censor* is implanted on our mind and we will be groping in the dark to work out our contract or mission. To make our lessons even tougher, we are given *free will* which can make or break us depending on our lifestyle.

In truth, to live a harmonious and balanced life takes a level of commitment that is not easily found in the ordinary person. It is *not* something you can learn in a weekend workshop, reading a book or watching a video. Teachers can certainly help but it is really one's own *self-cultivation* that will produce the light to illuminate our life. It is taught in Taoism that the most balanced person is not always recognised for what he is; when you look at him, you will not see anything outstanding about him. It's all about *humility* and the ability to follow the flow. It is to our best interest that we don't judge others unless we want to be judged! But take heart, we can give ourselves a pat on the back as there is *no greater* gift to God than the human who sacrifices higher dimensional existence by 'walking the quicksand' and trading punches with the 'devil' of low vibrational earth simply for lessons!

Successful Living

> *Fear less, hope more;*
> *whinge less, breathe more;*
> *talk less, say more;*
> *hate less, love more;*
> *and all good things are yours.*

Swedish proverb

Savour Moments of Peace

Realistically, happiness is *not* a permanent condition contrary to what most psychologists and other so-called 'experts' are drumming to our ears. They flood the marketplace with advice that when we are *not* on top of the world, there's a problem with either our physical or mental health or both. More often than not, our daily experience is something more ordinary; a mixture of *'unsolved problems, ambiguous victories and vague defeats—with few moments of clear peace,'* an accurate assessment from a lesser known person who is still in touch with reality.

Happiness is like a visitor; it comes and goes—but we can make sure we savour it when it appears. For instance: you are not a habitual gambler but won a few hundred dollars at the slot machine while entertaining clients at a club. You have a mood swing and not only shouted beers immediately but also insisted on buying dinner to celebrate the unexpected windfall. What about the exciting time when you had your first date with someone you really like or when passing an exam with flying colours? There is little truth regarding the *pursuit* of happiness but the discovery of joy is real.

It is our nature to brood more and laugh less because our expectations are either too high or *unrealistic*. A woman can be sad and miserable for days after a lovers' tiff or losing her favourite lipstick. But if she makes the effort to recall mostly the good times with the lover or how stunning she looked with the lipstick, there will be good energy in her and it is *very* possible that the difficult period can turn into a healing process. Misery is the creation of the sentimental and emotional; the strong and practical seek healthier options to allay disappointments and treat life as a challenge to move on.

Savour the wonderful spurts of happiness or peace descending upon us unexpectedly at times. It could be some happy feeling watching a group of playful birds pecking away at the lawn, a loved one cooking our favourite dish, someone complimenting our beautiful garden, a grandchild giving us a loving hug or an unexpected call from an old friend. Michael, a golfing mate of mine says that happiness is when he has the longest drive in a golf game! Moments of happiness are countless and have little to do with karma. It's more about adopting the right attitude in the *present* to create our own world of happiness.

Success—East and West

What are the secret ingredients for happiness to enable us to enjoy life as if there is no tomorrow? The common aspirations today are: *be wealthy, get smart and look good*. It is a trend for the young to better themselves with higher learning for *higher* earnings and enhance their appearance at the same time as cosmetic surgery, special diets and exercise can do wonders these days! In a report by 'New Scientist Magazine' in America, researchers discovered that 'these three highly desirable goals were no guarantee to happiness.

In fact, they paled in comparison with the luck of *your genetic make-up* or *natural good looks, a wedding ring and close relationships with friends and family.*'

Just as '*beauty is in the eyes of the beholder,*' happiness or contentment varies considerably between cultures. To take a cue from 'Journal Of Happiness' by Professor Veenbhoven, it mentioned that in America, they found satisfaction comes from personal success, self expression, pride, self-esteem and a distinct sense of self. In Japan, happiness arises from fulfilling family expectations and meeting social responsibilities coupled with self-discipline and co-operation.

Veenbhoven says, '*In America it is perfectly appropriate to pursue your own happiness. In Japan you are more likely to find happiness by not directly pursuing it.*' Obviously different cultures have different values for success and happiness and the lesson here is not to judge others by your own standard. Sure, it's great to be rich and have many friends: but how you attain your wealth whether righteously or otherwise determines your character or respect from those who know.

There are heaps of books with different definitions of happiness in our modern time and perhaps the wisdom of Henry Drummond who lived in the 19th century sums it up well: 'In the pursuit of happiness half the world is on the wrong scent. They think it consists in having and getting, and in being served by others. Happiness is really found in *giving and serving* others.' It is more satisfying when you make others happy as a result of your efforts that are highly appreciated. It could be giving away your old car to a poor relative who needed transport badly instead of trading it for a new one. Mowing the lawn for a sick neighbour, baking a cake or simply giving some of your time to cheer up the sick person can be looked upon as doing God's work sometimes. True happiness then is *not* in mere possession like owning a big home or a priceless antique; it is in us—the satisfaction of having done something right where we can sleep with a clear conscience.

Growing Old Gracefully

> *Youth is a work of nature*
> *But living old is a work of art.*

> Dr. Bernard Jensen

An old timer once said that he's still chasing women, but can't remember why! The grey reveller is going through that last-fling period where he isn't dangerous to anything except his reputation. All the girls love this 'silver fox' for all he's worth—after he passes the *assets* test! What's the point of living to a ripe old age when you fumble and tumble all the time?

Strange things are happening today because science is so advanced that the rich are challenging the courts that they wished to be *frozen* instead of being buried or cremated when they die to perpetuate their legacy. If it was thirty years ago, some would roll on the floor laughing when someone wants to *'cheat death'* by becoming an *iceman!* But do you think this is a laughing matter in 2010? Since the cloning of *'Dolly, the Sheep,'* medical science is able to reverse the aging clock. New discoveries in maintaining certain organs for longer functioning coupled with new knowledge of our DNA are all conducive to longevity and many of us may be around longer than we think. Why be permanently dead when there's a chance you may be alive again in 10 years time? A new rejuvenating injection or wonder drug may help frozen organs like heart, liver or kidney to start ticking again or perhaps making you looking younger too. Remember the reality of today is the magic of yesterday? When you had a glorious life before and wished it to continue for another decade or more is not madness. Who knows, perhaps you wish to right some wrongs of your past or curious to see whether your children have squandered away their inheritance or double it. But does the law permit us to cheat death because we are too afraid to die? Will the world be happy to see that only the rich can live longer?

On the other hand, is living over 100 that important when you cannot remember the names of your grandchildren or what you had for dinner the previous night? Many would prefer to say 'ta ta' world, when they become a burden to loved ones. Unfortunately life is such that you cannot make an early exit according to your wishes; you can only choose how you are going to *survive* before your time is up because there are also lessons to be learned even at a ripe old age. It is good advice then *'to live as if there is no tomorrow. Learn as if you were to live forever.'* Sometimes it is very sad to see an elderly person throwing tantrums all the time unaware not only of the emotional and very often financial strains imposed on loved ones coupled with the fact that he or she took no part in planetary healing.

Life is precious; just living is not enough. One must have sunshine, freedom, and a little flower. An actor once said, 'Don't think of retiring from the world until the world will be sorry that you retire.' It makes good sense to retire in style when colleagues still look up to you. But a time will come when your memory starts to slip and the hand starts to shake when you write out a cheque. Retirees must be realistic and remember that *'once over the hill, you begin to pick up speed,'* despite of your vast business acumen over the years. Accept the fact that you have seen your best days and learn to hand over the ropes. The next step is to face reality and make the necessary *adjustment*s for a new phase of life to enable you to grow old gracefully.

There is no denying that genes play a crucial part in determining when we depart to 'our happy hunting ground.' However, latest research figures have indicated that more than 70% of longevity is derived from lifestyle factors. We are all aware of some basic rules such as regular exercise, proper diet, smoking less and drinking a little. But there is more to it if you want relatives and friends to attend your centenarian birthday. Let's run through some key ingredients of gaining respectability in our old age.

a) *Acceptance*

I still find it very puzzling when some women are reluctant or sensitive to reveal their age when they are already in their seventies. Why? Still thinking they are a thing of beauty and a girl forever? There's nothing to be shy about 'vintage' especially when it's an old one! I for one would be more than happy to tell the truth about my age when I am still able to enjoy a nice drop of wine and capable of cooking a decent meal for my family even though I may be 85! I am sure my children will be proud of me then.

We're all fearful of losing the power we possess during our youth, irrespective whether it's mental, financial, emotional or physical. 'Fear of losing our mental sharpness is huge,' says Dr Ross Walker, a renowned cardiologist. 'We're all going to suffer the consequences of ageing.'

'It's this fear that is partly to blame when people choose to have an affair by bedding a younger partner', Walker says, 'they are trying to cheat the ageing process, but only end up destroying their family.' Sure, ageing comes with a sense of loss but the experts say we need to accept this loss and learn to live with it. 'A friend of mine loved playing tennis his whole life,' says Walker. 'But as he aged his injuries increased and he couldn't play any more. He came to terms with that and started playing golf. He lost something he loved doing, accepted it, and then replaced it.'

Another woman lost her husband who was also her best friend, got over it and became indispensable to her young grandson who loves her dearly. She has never been happier; a grandson who not only adores her but depends on her for his successful upbringing. Learn to be flexible and live happily again from new experiences that can add sparkle to your life.

'Acceptance is the key. *Only* then can you make adjustments and look forward to new challenges rather than mourning the loss of old ones,' says Walker.

b) Say 'Sayonara' To Stress

I remember the song very well, 'Sayonara, Japanese goodbye.' It is almost unbelievable that some retirees simply cannot change their habits and reactions despite the biological happenings related to age. Take Anna for example: When her best friend Joe said that her grey hair is becoming noticeable, Anna gets very upset and spends valuable time and money to get the most expensive dye to cover up the obvious even though she is 75. Remarks like 'Your bums are dropping,' or 'your wrinkles are getting deeper,' are capable of killing her. Some psychologists say vanity kills, its beginning to make sense!

Stress is usually self-inflicted and fuelled by a stubborn attitude to change. Angry words like, 'I cannot change,' are from losers not prepared to venture into the unknown that is forever vibrant to move us forward. Remember that change is inescapable and we have no control over it other than to follow the flow? Learn to give more reins to flexibility in reasoning and the world will be more on your side than you previously thought. It is well known that humility and understanding are well known antidotes for stress. 'I was beaten in bowling and bought beers today only because I had a crook back and didn't sleep well last night,' or 'I hope the neighbour will move soon because her oriental cooking smell is giving me sinus trouble.' In any sport, somebody has to lose. Respect is untarnished when you accept defeat graciously. Control your whingeing and be more tolerant to neighbours and friends who may not be aware of your problems and not in arms against you.

It is hard to believe that some people can have their blood boiling on simple issues such as when the newspapers did not arrive on time, favourite TV program was cancelled, bus shows up five minutes late, the cat only eats half its food, the precious roses looking unhealthy, missing out on a grand sale or the toilet bowl is not flushing properly. Don't stress yourself out over trivial matters; think big and resolve problems as if life is all about sorting out things calmly. If grandpa starts to curse and swear over a burnt sausage, his grandchildren would probably remember him as the 'grumpy old bugger' instead of the 'wise old man'.

Be reasonable about the things you want. When we envy other people; what they are and what they have, tension builds up inside us. How unhappy we can make ourselves and how much joy we miss because we are obsessed with getting, and having, and being as good or better than others! How can we hope to be anything but unhappy when we live in a continuous state of competition with those around us?

Be done with it now and say goodbye to stress. It is not worth the havoc it plays with your blood pressure. Reduce that stress by counting your blessings and being thankful for what you are and what you have. Learn to let go of worrying thoughts. Try to replace them, if only for a minute or so, with some pleasant restful image like a grandchild giving you a loving hug, remembering the sweet fragrance of the roses or having a great time with good friends.

c) *Social Circle*

It is imperative that we have a sense of connection when we grow old. Life is sweet when surrounded by loved ones and good friends that are always there to support you. A sense of belonging is a vital ingredient to help you live longer and maintain good health at the same time.

When Lisa and hubby Chino finally retired after 30 years of hectic life in the city, they decided to switch to a quiet lifestyle by moving to the country. They enjoyed the change of environment the first two years but life was too quiet for comfort and having dinner for two most of the time becomes boring. Sure, they made new friends but they are not comrades in arms like in the city where you laugh at dirty jokes with close mates and even shed a tear or two together for a departed friend. Friendship is crucial for our survival and happiness. Certain people are like our 'soul mates,' without them life seems incomplete. Lisa and Chino admitted their mistake in moving to the country but quickly made up their minds to sell the country home and moved back to the city just to be closer to relatives, friends and Chino's golf club where all his mates hang out.

It's a perfect example of our need for social contact. 'When retirees move away they often become lonely, isolated from their family and social circle,' says Dr Walker. 'You must keep people around you who are important to your life. Cultivate and nurture relationships with people you love and don't take them for granted.'

d) *Be Passionate*

Staying slim is not sufficient to make you live longer, but if you add *maintaining mental fitness* to your agenda, you are on your way to becoming a centenarian. Learning new things actually encourages the growth of new brain cells and strengthens old ones at the same time. To keep the mind working and ticking away you must cultivate passion in your work or hobby. Having a purpose in life gives tremendous mileage towards growing old gracefully.

Passion comes in countless forms; it could be a special interest in gardening, lawn bowling, 'tai chi' exercise, cooking or baking cakes, knitting, antique collecting, wine tasting or playing bridge or *mahjong* with good friends just for laughs and keeping up with the latest gossips and winning and losing are secondary. Life can also be just as meaningful when you take time and interest to help something grow; it could be a club, a small business, a grandchild, animals or even birds and plants. Enjoying life to the fullest means having something to live for. When you don't feel like waking up early to greet the new day, it's time you reassess your situation and see whether you have any passion left or have simply become a straggler without much anticipation in life. To have a long life is really quite meaningless when you have no interest to make others happy but prefers to be a whinger or live like a vegetable waiting for others to care for you. For oldies who are not senile, there is fine distinction between self-pity and love and the lessons on karma is so profound because it teaches us to be *useful* at all ages and not being *useless*.

e) Humour and a Good Host

'*Every woman can keep a secret,*' there was a pause as uncle Chun took a sip of wine during dinner. With a twinkle in his eyes, he continued, '*provided she's given enough chloroform!*' You can never go wrong with any crowd when you have a good sense of humour.

Many parents who are now seniors are not only fun to be around but are also excellent cooks and remember their children's favourite food. It goes a long way making the effort in the kitchen to win over loved ones. They have your blood and it is perfectly okay to spoil them and make sure they love you more. Any party or gathering will work out well when you plan ahead and do your best to be a good host whether entertaining family or guests.

Try to picture yourself as the unifying force for the family by being alert to current and domestic affairs. Give the young a kick-start in life by *humbly* passing down the wisdom you have acquired over the years on work ethics and successful living so that they don't fall into the same trap like you did. Let the young look up to you as a pillar of wisdom and inspiration to move on. That means taking an interest in all the children's welfare and provides support and advice accordingly. Learn to enjoy the *little things* like making others happy or laugh; for one day you may look back and realize they were the big things. Somebody once said that to love and be loved is to feel the sun from both sides. Isn't that very healthy to have rosy cheeks? When seniors become knowledgeable and caring people whom others love to be with, a sense of joy and fulfilment is completed and 'going home' becomes less fearsome.

The Last Say . . .

> *The Taoists believe that it is humanity's refusal*
> *to regard itself as a part of a greater order*
> *that causes confusion, ignorance and sorrow.*

Deng Ming Dao

Sages have chanted down through the ages that the starry sky, majestic mountains, mighty oceans, the caressing breeze, the land and all the things in it including animals and human beings are all part of nature: *we are one.* There is *order in creation* and even our top brains accept that as the truth and for once, scientists dare not open their mouths to ask for proof as a mark of respect for the greatness of God. Nature's order is not about how you arrange your clothes neatly in the cupboards or how documents are systematically filed from A to Z. Those simple tasks are considered very basic and crude when you compare them to a bamboo plant that is perfectly obvious that the plant has order. Have you ever wondered about the order of the four seasons and the blooming of certain plants and flowers in each season? What about the greater order of the sun and rain that gives life to all things on earth? Such timeless perfection is not only simply beyond our intelligence but can be very humbling too.

Our Creator made us the most intelligent creatures walking on earth by giving us a wonderful mind. The human mind is undoubtedly our most important asset because all our beliefs, hope, inspiration, excitement and sense of goodness stem from it. In order to ensure that the mind is kept pure, it is said that during the golden age or beginning of time and space; angels and prophets were sent down from time to time to make sure humans become simple, humble and childlike by speaking their minds and telling the truth so that they can be as free as air and be part of nature. Words such as 'greed' and 'guilt' were non-existence during the golden age as humans were pure then. But what went wrong? A noted mythologist, Micea Eliade, has this to say: 'every civilization has its own idea of perfection from the beginning of things. The people live in peace and harmony because they believe in God. But when humans break away from God and fall victim to temptation and greed, they are on their own and have to fend for themselves without the saving grace of God.' This is the position today; our world is all fouled up with materialism because we rebelled against God and turn the world to confusion and sorrow. It always has been for thousands of years and it is not surprising that our constant thirst for power and material needs will fall short of the divine plan *again* (similar fate of legendary tale of Atlantis) and the demise of another scientific civilization may not be far away *if* we do not mend our ways. Where or what is our future?

It is my belief that the future—or the *unknown*—is exactly where we are headed. There is no such thing as predestination because *without* the many mysteries of nature, our world simply cannot survive because of human weaknesses. History has shown us that the various cultures are not honest and wise and incapable of shaping a peaceful world. The greatest moral failure in our world is that we don't abide by simple ancient wisdom that says: '*what you do not want to do to yourself, do not do to others.'* That profound principle for survival is like a message scribbled by God to mankind to live in peace through a clear conscience. But are our leaders abiding to that basic principle for world harmony or prefer to exploit and grab as much as possible from others? Look at our world today: the majority of humans are still a selfish lot that does not believe in sharing its knowledge or wealth for global balancing. The disparity of wealth among the many races are simply too glaring. Corrupt officials, false masters and countless crooked leaders in sheep's clothing are everywhere and it will be a Herculean task to put all of them behind bars. A vital ingredient for harmony in our planet is lacking in *most* of us—*love.*

Our modern science and technology have served us well so far but *when* can they resolve major problems like poverty and crimes; sickness and diseases; pollution of the environment or plundering of earth's resources? Can the experts prevent earthquakes and tsunamis or explain the relationship between human and the soul? Scientists don't even know the purpose of our existence or our earth's history and many are still clinging on to the *big bang theory* which is probably 'junk' science when compared to universal science. I can't help laughing when a comedian said scientists believed that humans were related to monkeys at one time. It was only when the modern toilet bowl was invented that God separated humans from monkeys because it could be messy when the tail got wet and smelly!

How long will it take for humans to realize that they are all a piece of God and only in opening themselves to *His influence* that their deepest destiny can be fulfilled? Are political leaders making critical decisions based on trust in God or faith in themselves or those supporting them with dark agendas? When can leaders of organised religions going to get serious and get out of their comfort zones and do some *real work* for a change like uniting the various cultures so that God can smile on them? The grace of God will always be on our side when we are in partnership or seek His influence to make a better world. God is a necessity that we can't live without as He is our Creator. When we lose faith in God, there is nothing more dreadful than *doubt*. Doubt separates people: it is a thorn that irritates and hurts; it is a sword that kills.

We have *spiritually transgressed* over the centuries and lost the battle of peaceful existence mainly because of greed and attachments. But the all-forgiving God—like a good parent—has not forsaken us despite the fact that we have been living like *misfits* in this big blue earth. Our Creator is patiently trying to reverse the trend by *strengthening* our spiritual and mental capacity with a consciousness shift. However, because we have been living *unrighteously* for so long, the change will be gradual similar to a new born child that requires time to develop awareness. But there is no guarantee that the world can attain *'oneness'* as *free will* is still a major part of our existence and God can only wait for the unfolding by watching from a distance. In a nutshell, the real future is *not* logically foreseeable because planet earth is only a speck of dust in the universe that needs a great amount of healing. At this stage, it can be safely assumed that humans will be around for a long time as our species have yet to reach the *top* of the evolutionary scale. We are still *far, far* from whole as depicted on the book cover where the modern man is still 'devilish by nature' and can be the smiling Buddha one day and Satan the next! The timing of our enlightenment or evolving to a higher dimension is in God's hand.

Humour

The best medicine

Brian, a retiring CEO, was given a stag party by his colleagues. After dinner and over a few drinks, his younger mates asked him to share some of his exploits with the opposite sex as Brian was a seasoned traveller and a flamboyant character.

'Why not,' he said. 'I have my fair share of the good times with many types of women during my travels. From my experience, women resemble the continents of the world. At the age of 15 to 18, they are like Africa, innocent and free like an unexplored land. From 19 to 25, they are like Asia, hot and exotic. When they come of age from 26 to 34, you are in America, money talks and there's plenty to see, but plenty of cover-ups too! From 35 to 45, you are in Europe, they may be running low on resources but there are still some interesting features. Once over 45, you are in Australia, everybody knows it's down there, but who cares!'

About the Author

Ken Foo was born in Malaysia and migrated to Australia in 1987 with his family (wife Keng and children Jason and Jasmine) to join his brother Brian in Sydney. But starting from scratch again was not as easy as anticipated. Ken was jumping from one sales job to another and prepared to accept any work that could help pay the mortgage. His dream of a good life in down under started to crumble during his early years in Sydney. Frustrated, VB beer became his 'best mate' where he would find solace to drown his sorrows and his vision of life became a big blur!

His life only started to change after a strange dream. He saw himself standing in a garden and witnessed a grey cloud of dust flew out from his body. The cloud suddenly turned into lively sparkling translucent stardust particles in various colours and started to form a rotating ring. The ring of light was spinning and dancing as if it was alive! 'The ring moves towards me and went back straight into my body with a gentle glow,' Ken said. When he woke up he felt great as if a burden taken off his chest. Strangely, he was 'pulled' to the garden and to his astonishment, for the first time in his life he realized that flowers, plants, shrubs including the grass were so beautiful. 'Everything about nature is so balanced,' he said.

According to Ken, tending the garden now is no longer a chore; it is the flowers and plants that are nurturing us.

Ken considers himself very lucky to be given spiritual healing. He believes that other than the physical self, there is *another entity* (ring of light or higher self) that can do wonders for us when the two are blended as *one* like team players in decision making. He said that writing *Befriend the Unknown* was the last thing that crossed his mind but his dreams and intuition kept reminding him to do it for years and the last word was always to 'speak your mind'. When asked: 'Is writing the book your mission?' He thought for a second and said: 'Maybe. Perhaps I get my kicks in exposing cover-ups in the past and present of flawed leaders mainly to caution people not to be too trusting and, at the same time, give the world a good laugh,' he smiled.